HOWARD ZINN

DAVIS D. JOYCE

HOWARD ZINN

A RADICAL AMERICAN VISION

FOREWORD BY NOAM CHOMSKY

Prometheus Books

59 John Glenn Drive
Amherst, New York 14228-2197

Published 2003 by Prometheus Books

Inquiries should be addressed to
Prometheus Books
59 John Glenn Drive
Amherst, New York 14228–2197
VOICE: 716–691–0133, ext. 207
FAX: 716–564–2711
WWW.PROMETHEUSBOOKS.COM

07 06 05 04 03   5 4 3 2 1

Library of Congress Cataloging-in-Publication Data

Joyce, Davis D., –
    Howard Zinn : a radical American vision / Davis D. Joyce.
        p. cm.
    Includes index.
    ISBN 1–59102–131–6 (alk. paper)
    1. Zinn, Howard, 1922– 2. Historians—United States—Biography. 3. Zinn,
Howard, 1922– —Political and social views. 4. United States—Historiography.
5. United States—Politics and government—Historiography. 5. United States—
Politics and government—Historiography. 6. United States—History—Book reviews.
I. Title.

E175.5.Z56J69 2003
973'.072'02—dc22

                                                                            2003016864

Printed in the United States of America on acid-free paper

In memory of

JOHN S. EZELL,

mentor

CONTENTS

Foreword
Noam Chomsky   9

Preface   15

Acknowledgments   21

The Life and Writings of Howard Zinn: A Brief Chronology   23

One.   Growing Up Class-Conscious, 1922–1956   27

Two.   The South and the Movement, 1956–1964   47

Three.   You Can't Be Neutral on a Moving Train, 1964–1973   81

Four.   You Can't Be Neutral on a Moving Train, 1973–1988   135

Five.   Failure to Quit, 1988–Present   185

Six.   Howard Zinn's Radical American Vision:
A Preliminary Assessment   231

Index   257

FOREWORD
NOAM CHOMSKY

T he country has changed a great deal since Howard Zinn boarded his "moving train" a half century ago. It has changed along very different trajectories. Some have been rich in achievement, often exhilarating, and full of promise for a better future. Others, in part in reaction to them, are ugly and ominous in their import. Which will prevail? It's hard to overestimate the significance of the question. It's hard to think of a better way to gain a clear understanding of what is at stake, and what can be done about it, than by reading, and pondering, the fascinating story of Howard Zinn's crucial and intimate participation at every point, in thought and action.

One trajectory is illuminated by warnings from prominent figures, in the leading establishment journal *Foreign Affairs*, that for much of the world—probably most of it—the United States is "becoming the rogue superpower," which they consider to be "the single greatest external threat to their societies" (Samuel Huntington, March/April 1999); "in the eyes of much of the world, in fact, the prime rogue state today is the United States" (Robert Jervis, then chair of the American Political Science Association, July/August 2001). That was well before the Bush administration announced a doctrine that sent many shudders around the world, including substantial sectors of the foreign policy elite at home: that the United States intends to rule the world by military force, the dimension in which it reigns supreme, and to rely on aggressive war (mislabeled "preemption") to bar any potential challenge to its domination. Many analysts warned at once that the "new imperial grand strategy" announced in September 2002 threatens to "leave the world more dangerous and divided—and the United States less secure" (John Ikenberry, *Foreign Affairs*, September/October 2002). One indication, revealed by public opinion research a few months later, was a sharp increase in fear of the United States around much of the world, and dislike or even loathing of its political leadership. Another was a reported increase in recruitment for al Qaeda–style terrorist organizations as a result of the Iraq invasion, and apparent acceleration of moves toward proliferation of weapons of mass destruction. These were widely predicted reactions to the aggressive unilateralism that was brazenly declared and violently implemented; the motivation might be revenge, or, more broadly, deterrence by the only means available to those who are targeted. Closely integrated with Bush administration global planning is the dedicated effort at home to accelerate the Reaganite program of dismantling the progressive legislation of the twentieth century, which grew out of the popular struggles of the conflicting trajectory.

Changes resulting from the activism of the past half century are indeed dramatic. The country has become far more civilized as a result. The driving force in the early years was the civil rights movement, spearheaded by the young people for whom Zinn was a mentor, and a participant in their courageous initiatives—the "new abolitionists" of SNCC, whose triumphs and travails he recorded memorably, in part from firsthand experience. Atlanta, where he began to teach in an African American women's college in 1956, underwent a remarkable transformation, as did the South in general, with effects throughout the country. Just to give one personal illustration, at about the time Zinn began his teaching career at Spelman College in Atlanta, I joined the faculty at MIT in Cambridge. Walking through the halls at the time, one saw neatly dressed white males. In the same halls today half the students are women, the undergraduate student body is fairly diverse, and formalities have been replaced by much easier interactions throughout the institution. As I write, the first woman and the first African American have been appointed to head departments of science and engineering. The experience is replicated throughout much of the country. There is a long way to go, but the accomplishments are real, and instructive.

In the 1960s there were only the bare beginnings of the women's and environmental movements, which became major forces in the following years, with far-reaching effects on the society and culture, and on prospects for decent survival. Attitudes toward the resort to violence have also been transformed. Forty years ago John F. Kennedy was able to attack South Vietnam, arousing little interest or concern. It is scarcely even remembered that in 1962, his government initiated the bombing of South Vietnam that demolished much of the country, along with chemical warfare to destroy crops and ground cover and programs to drive millions of villagers into what amounted to concentration camps, in which they would be "protected" from the indigenous guerrillas who, the administration knew, they were willingly supporting. Protest was virtually nonexistent. It did not reach a substantial scale until years later. By then, hundreds of thousands of U.S. troops had invaded the country, the war had spread to the rest of Indochina, and the consequences had become so horrendous that the leading Indochina specialist and military historian Bernard Fall—no dove—in *Last Reflections on a War* warned that "Vietnam as a cultural and historic entity . . . is threatened with extinction . . . [as] . . . the countryside literally dies under the blows of the largest military machine ever unleashed on an area of this size." He was referring to South Vietnam, always the main target; shortly after he penned this warning he was killed there, observing combat.

Opposition to the Vietnam War, much of it stimulated by the civil rights movement, was slow in coming, but finally became a considerable force. Throughout, Zinn was a constant, indefatigable, inspiring presence. His book on "the logic of withdrawal"—which appeared at the same time as Fall's grim warnings—provided the first careful, sustained argument for commitments that were just coming to animate sectors of the popular activist movements, and was an important stimulus for them. A year later, after the January 1968 Tet offensive, the Joint Chiefs of Staff were reluctant to respond to the president's request to send more troops to Vietnam because they were uncertain that "sufficient forces would still be available for civil disorder control" as protests mounted against the war, joining with other rising popular movements. The Department of Defense feared that further troop deployments might provoke "a domestic crisis of unprecedented proportions." By 1969, 70 percent of the population described the war as "fundamentally wrong and immoral," not "a mistake," departing sharply from the elite consensus; the figures have remained fairly stable to the present, even though they receive virtually no articulate support within the mainstream.

Influential radical nationalist ("neocon") commentators deplored "the sickly inhibitions against the use of military force" that were hobbling policymakers (Norman Podhoretz, *New York Times*, October 30, 1985). As it took office in 1981, the Reagan administration, in a triumphalist mood, assumed that the sickly inhibitions had faded, but quickly learned otherwise. Facing a serious threat to traditional centers of violence and repression in Central America, they attempted to follow the Kennedy model of South Vietnam. But they drew back in the face of an unanticipated public reaction, resorting instead to clandestine terror: "clandestine," in the sense that it could be more or less concealed from the American public.

But not completely concealed. Popular opposition to terrible Central American atrocities organized or supported by Washington was broad-based, more so on Main Street than in elite centers. It also opened new paths in the history of opposition to imperial violence. Many thousands of people, often from generally conservative social sectors, were not satisfied with educational efforts, protest, and resistance, but went to live with the victims, to offer help, and also, by their presence, to offer at least some limited protection against state and paramilitary terror. Few had ever contemplated living in a Vietnamese or Algerian village under brutal attack by their own state, just to take a few recent examples; nor had this been considered before. The international solidarity movements that developed from these roots have since spread to large parts of the world, compiling a very honorable record of courage and dedication. In the same years, popular movements concerned with the threat of possibly terminal nuclear war became a force that could no longer be ignored.

When Bush #1 took office in 1989, his administration was presented with an intelligence analysis advising that in conflicts with "much weaker enemies"—any imaginable case—the United States must "defeat them decisively and rapidly," or "political support" would erode. It was no longer the 1960s. Tolerance for aggression and terror had sharply declined among the general public. Forty years after Kennedy's war against South Vietnam was publicly launched, there were huge and unprecedented protests against a war even before it was officially announced, not delayed until many years later when the targeted country was "threatened with extinction."

By the 1990s, solidarity movements were taking new forms. In the United States, and throughout much of the industrial world, large-scale global justice movements were forming, and joined with mass-based popular movements in the South to work for new directions in global economic integration, shifting priorities from investor and corporate rights—the policies called "globalization" within the doctrinal system—to the needs of the general population for freedom, democracy, and equitable and sustainable development. These and related popular movements, bringing together many concerns of prime significance and drawing from many social sectors, began to gain some institutional form in the World Social Forum that has met annually in Brazil, by now with many regional offshoots and with participation rising steadily in scale, energy, and enthusiasm.

There is, of course, no single source for these complex and multifaceted historical processes. They grow from the sources that Howard Zinn has highlighted and brought to general awareness in his historical work, and contributed to so impressively in his life of engagement and dedication: in his words, "the countless small actions of unknown people" that lead to "those great moments" that enter the historical record—a record that will be profoundly misleading, and seriously disempowering, if torn from its roots. For the most part sources are not even easily detectable, except to direct participants in these countless actions, though some are: Spelman College, to mention one of the most significant.

There are people whose words have been highly influential, and others whose actions have been an inspiration to many. It is a rare achievement to have interwoven both of these strands in one's life, as Howard Zinn has done. His writings have changed the consciousness of a generation, and helped open new paths to understanding history and its crucial meaning for our lives. He has always been on call, everywhere, a marvel to observe. When action has been called for, one could always be confident that he would be in the front lines, an example and trustworthy guide.

It has been a wonderful privilege to have been able to join Howard on his "moving train" on many occasions over these years of challenge, inspiration, torment, and persistent concern over impending catastrophe. Like everyone who knows him, I, too, have been struck by his enduring optimism, which goes well beyond "optimism of the will" and challenges us also to question the "pessimism of the intellect" that complements it in the slogan that Antonio Gramsci made famous: "pessimism of the intellect, optimism of the will." Howard's life and work are a persistent reminder that our own subjective judgments of the likelihood of success in engaging human problems are of little interest, to ourselves or others. What matters is to take part, as best we can, in the small actions of unknown people that can stave off disaster and bring about a better world, to honor them for their achievements, to do what we can to ensure that these achievements are understood and carried forward. In brief, to follow the model provided for us by the subject of this welcome biography.

PREFACE

You would not have to know that his life has been too busy with causes he believes in for him to keep things neat—Howard Zinn's office gives that away by its appearance. When I visited him there in March 1997, the office he shares with two other professors emeriti at Boston University could be described as somewhat dilapidated and quite messy. Water, for example, was leaking from a heating radiator, soaking the carpet, and ruining boxes and sacks of books sitting around on the floor in a seemingly random pattern.

But more than the neatness or lack thereof, the signs of Zinn's busy, activist life are everywhere. On one wall is a poster with this anonymous quote:

> I swear to you
> I swear on my common woman's head
> The common woman is as common
> As a common loaf of bread . . .
>   and will rise.

Also on the wall is a poster-size copy of the front page of the February 23, 1970, edition of the Boston University *News*, according to Zinn, the student newspaper at that time. The main headline says simply "Strike!" There is an illustration of a fist upraised in the popular "power to the people" manner of the day, and specific demands include "release of jailed students and reinstatement of expelled students," "an end to the injunction against demonstrations," and "an end to proceedings against professors Zinn and Fleischman."

Additional visible items include posters for productions in England and Japan of Zinn's play about the anarchist Emma Goldman, a French art poster, a flyer for an evening of "Jazz Tap Dancing" in New York, and photographs of the prominent anti–Vietnam War Roman Catholic priest Daniel Berrigan being arrested and of Zinn himself being arrested at a protest against police brutality on campus at Boston University.

The appearance of Zinn's office seems to suggest that the words "radical" and "historian" often used to describe him are really in his case very closely linked. Indeed, perhaps it is more than a mere word game to suggest that they are somewhat closely related definitionally as well. See any good dictionary. To be radical is to get to the root of a matter; the word implies fundamental, or basic. And one of the root words for history is the Greek *historia*, to inquire. Is it too much to suggest that, in the context of the history of the United States, if one inquires, without limits, into the roots of our past, what one will find is exactly the radical tradition that Howard Zinn tends to write about, and to celebrate, in his historical works?

Howard Zinn's approach—in his writing, his speaking, his teaching— has always tended to provoke strong response, whether positive or negative. Few are able to know him, his work, his life, and feel neutral. In a file folder in his office labeled "Evaluation Fall 1981," two students in a row (though perhaps that was just a coincidence of filing) illustrated this with their remarks under the "additional comments" heading. One said: "The course is useless!!!" The other said: "Howard Zinn should be immortalized!"

It seems important here to confess: I have long been one of those who responded very positively to Zinn's work. I admire him. I have been influenced by his work. In 1967 I read his little book *Vietnam: The Logic of Withdrawal*. For me, as for so many others, it served as a catalyst for involvement in the anti–Vietnam War movement. In 1970, when *The Politics of History* came out, I read it and remember thinking that at last someone had systemized and illustrated history for me as I was beginning in my own floundering way to see it as a young assistant professor. *The Pol-*

itics of History seemed to be a *true* "gateway to history" for me and others of my generation in a way perhaps similar to what Allan Nevins's 1938 book by that title had been for an earlier generation. Then, in 1980, when *A People's History of the United States* was first published, I remember thinking that at last someone had written a textbook that made sense, that synthesized all the "New Left" history and events and personal experiences of the 1960s and after. So—and most confessional of all—when I read in a Budapest hotel room in 1995 from Zinn's 1994 memoir, *You Can't Be Neutral on a Moving Train: A Personal History of Our Times,* about his travel around the country after retirement on the lecture circuit, that wherever he went, "there was always a cluster of men and women who cared about the sick, the hungry, the victims of racism, the casualties of war, and who were doing *something*, however small, in the hope that the world would change"—"whether Dallas, Texas, or Ada, Oklahoma, or Shreveport, Louisiana, or New Orleans or San Diego or Philadelphia, or Presque Isle, Maine, or Bloomington, Indiana, or Olympia, Washington"[1]—when I read that, I was moved. For you see, I lived in Ada, Oklahoma, at the time, and I felt with some degree of confidence that Zinn intended to include me in that group of people. I had met him just a few years before when he came to Ada to lecture at my university. We had dinner together. We exchanged autographs in our latest books. I introduced him when he spoke that evening. All that constituted a major occasion for me, meeting and interrelating with a person whose life and work I so greatly admired, who had exercised, and continued to exercise, such an influence on me. Subsequently, he had kind words for one of my books, words which were used on the dust jacket.

Biography presents a unique set of problems for the writer. In the 1996 edition of *The Writer's Handbook*, there is an essay by David Robertson entitled "When a Biographer's Subject Is Less Than Perfect."[2] Aren't they all? And aren't all biographers as well?

Linda Simon writes in the same volume, in "Writing a Life," that "biographers admit that even when they are not actually conducting research or writing, their subject becomes a companion, someone they think about often. They begin to see events in their own lives through their subject's eyes; they reflect on their own experiences in light of what they learn about their subject." Biography, suggests Simon, invites introspection, and she finds this a good thing: "Personal introspection—thinking about why people behave as they do, about the forces that shape us and the way we affect other people—is good training for the biographer's work."[3]

But Gale E. Christianson suggests in still another essay, "Biographer at Work," that "identifying too closely with the subject violates the constraints essential to writing biography."[4] This has sometimes been termed "biographer's disease." Christianson is especially strong in her warning about writing the life of a living person. *"Caveat emptor!"* she warns:

> Since the life is not a finished thing, its telling will be superceded [*sic*] by future works based on a sounder perspective. Access to information may also be a problem, even if the subject is cooperative in the beginning. What is gladly given with one hand can be angrily snatched away by the other, especially if the subject's views and those of the biographer clash. With so many other wonderful subjects to choose from, why run the risk?[5]

Yet, despite all these facts and warnings—and despite the fact that, as of this writing, Howard Zinn is indeed alive and well—here it is, a biography of Howard Zinn! It is a biography that will focus primarily on his writings, true enough, and therefore perhaps even more a historiographical work, but it is a biography nonetheless. I experienced writing such a work about a historian, Edward Channing, many years ago.[6] But Channing had been long dead when I began my work, and I was able to approach him with a considerable amount of what we historians have always called "objectivity." Many would suggest, based merely on what I have already said, that I cannot be "objective" in a study of Howard Zinn. Well, I will differ with him on certain subjects, including prisons, the space program, and teaching methods/academic standards. And besides, one of the important things Zinn has taught us is that objectivity is, and has always been, problematic in historical writing.

For now, let's look at only one of the places where he said that. He was interviewed by Barbara Miner for a publication called *Rethinking Schools: An Urban Educational Journal*, a few years ago. Miner asked Zinn, "Is it possible for history to be objective?" He responded:

> Objectivity is neither possible nor desirable.
>
> It's not possible because all history is subjective, all history represents a point of view. History is always a selection from an infinite number of facts and everybody makes the selection differently, based on their values and what they think is important. Since it's not possible to be objective, you should be honest about that.
>
> Objectivity is not desirable because if we want to have an effect on the world, we need to emphasize those things which will make students more active citizens and more moral people.[7]

In short, perhaps the most we can do is to be honest, open, and up-front about our biases, and then proceed to write the best history we can. I have already tried to be honest, open, and up-front about my biases—or at least the ones of which I am aware. What follows is the best history (or biography) I can write. The focus, as stated, is on Zinn's writings. I attempt to summarize and evaluate each of his important works, and to place each in the context of his life and the time in which it was written. I also attempt a preliminary assessment of his work and its impact.

Why Howard Zinn's "radical American vision"? That is explored more thoroughly in the final chapter, but briefly: Zinn's views are radical because they seek to bring about fundamental change in the political/social/economic order, to get to the roots; they are American because they are deeply rooted in the ideals on which the United States of America was founded, as spelled out in the Declaration of Independence and elsewhere; and these views constitute a vision because they are not yet reality but hope. The story of Zinn's life and writings is the story of one person's effort to make the vision a reality.

DDJ—June 2003

NOTES

1. Howard Zinn, *You Can't Be Neutral on a Moving Train: A Personal History of Our Times* (Boston: Beacon Press, 1994), p. 203.

2. David Robertson, "When a Biographer's Subject Is Less Than Perfect," in *The Writer's Handbook*, ed. Sylvia K. Burack (Boston: The Writer, Inc., 1996), pp. 305–309.

3. Linda Simon, "Writing a Life," in *The Writer's Handbook*, p. 361.

4. Gale E. Christianson, "Biographer at Work," in *The Writer's Handbook*, p. 375.

5. Ibid., p. 377.

6. Davis D. Joyce, *Edward Channing and the Great Work* (The Hague: Nijhoff, 1974).

7. "An Interview with Howard Zinn: Why Students Should Study History," *Rethinking Schools: An Urban Educational Journal* 7, no. 2 (winter 1992–93): 8.

ACKNOWLEDGMENTS

First and foremost, I must acknowledge the support and assistance of my wife, best friend, and editor, Carole.

At East Central University, thanks are due to many people. The Research and Development Committee gave me a small grant to hire a student research assistant in the spring semester of 1997; even more important, they approved a reduced teaching load in the spring of 1998 so that I could complete the research on this volume and get started on the writing. The committee chair for the first grant was Dwight Myers; for the second, Judy Goforth Parker. My former department head, James R. Harris, cooperated fully with me on setting up a teaching schedule that maximized blocks of time for "working on Zinn." The student assistant I hired was Jamie Miller; during those months, she was a crucial and creative part of my research. Scott Barton, my department head until my retirement in May 2002, also served as colleague, friend, and computer advisor. Alvin O. Turner Jr., dean of the School of Humanities and Social Sciences (and fellow historian), and Duane C. Anderson, vice president for academic affairs (and fellow historian), were both also very supportive of my work. And Frank Shanklin, if you're reading this, you don't need to continue— you listened to me talk through the whole thing over coffee already. Thanks, buddy!

I wish also to thank Howard Zinn. He has been a most cooperative biographical subject, granting interviews, answering all queries by e-mail, giving me free access to all his papers, professional and personal—and never suggesting in any way that he might want to check on what I wrote prior to publication.

At the University of Oklahoma, while I was working on my Ph.D. many years ago, John S. Ezell proved himself the finest teacher I had known. Over the years, he was also remarkably supportive of my development, both professionally and personally. The dedication is a small and belated recognition of all this.

THE LIFE AND WRITINGS OF HOWARD ZINN
A BRIEF CHRONOLOGY

August 24, 1922 —born in New York City of poor Jewish immigrant parents

1943–1945 —Air Force bombardier

October 30, 1944–present —married to Roslyn Shechter (two children: daughter Myla and son Jeff)

1951 —B.A., New York University

1952 —M.A., Columbia University

1956–1963 —chair, Department of History, Spelman College; active in the civil rights movement

(1958) —Ph.D., Columbia University

(1959) —first book, *LaGuardia in Congress*

(1960–1961) —postdoctoral fellow in East Asian Studies, Harvard University;

(1961–1962) —director, Non-Western Studies, Atlanta University

1964–1988 —political science professor, Boston University (visiting professor, University of Paris, 1974, 1978, and 1984)

1964 —*The Southern Mystique* and *SNCC: The New Abolitionists*

1965 —*New Deal Thought* (ed.)

1967 —*Vietnam: The Logic of Withdrawal*; beginning of intense involvement in anti–Vietnam War movement

1968 —*Disobedience and Democracy: Nine Fallacies on Law and Order*

1970 —*The Politics of History*

1972 —*The Pentagon Papers: Critical Essays* (ed., with Noam Chomsky)

1973 —*Postwar America*

1974 —*Justice in Everyday Life* (ed.)

1980 —*A People's History of the United States*

1988 —retired

1988–present —active lecturer, especially on topics related to *A People's History of the United States*

1990 —*Declarations of Independence: Cross-Examining American Ideology*

1991 (and after) —active in movement against the Gulf War and subsequent sanctions against Iraq

1993 —*Failure to Quit: Reflections of an Optimistic Historian*

1994 —*You Can't Be Neutral on a Moving Train: A Personal History of Our Times*

1995 —Fulbright Distinguished Professor, University of Bologna

1997 —*The Zinn Reader: Writings on Disobedience and Democracy*

1999 —*The Future of History: Interviews with David Barsamian*

2001–present —active against the "war on terrorism" and war on Iraq

2001 —*Howard Zinn on History, Howard Zinn on War*, and *Three Strikes: Miners, Musicians, Salesgirls, and the Fighting Spirit of Labor's Last Century* (with Dana Frank and Robin D. G. Kelley)

2002 —*Terrorism and War*

ONE

GROWING UP
CLASS-CONSCIOUS
1922–1956

A t age eighty, Howard Zinn still has a twinkle in his eye. A twinkle of friendliness, accessibility, nonpretension. But a twinkle that can quickly become a fire when the peace and justice causes come up to which he has devoted his writings and much of his life.

Zinn is six feet, one inch tall, weighs 155 pounds, and has, in his own words, "once black now gray hair!"[1] He is always ready with a smile. Even those who differ strongly with his ideology find it hard to dislike him. "Everybody likes him," proclaimed one of the secretaries in the political science department at Boston University where, as a professor emeritus, he still maintains an office.

David Barsamian, the founder and director of Alternative Radio, has spoken of Zinn's ability to relax, even in front of a large audience, to make people "sense that they're with a friend. They're with somebody who is not lecturing them or lecturing to them but is talking with them."[2] Noted linguist and American foreign policy critic (also friend of Zinn) Noam Chomsky has expressed a similar view:

What has always been startling to me, and not a little embarrassing (to be honest), is Howard's astonishing ability to speak in exactly the right terms to any audience on any occasion, whether it is a rally at a demonstration, a seminar (maybe quite hostile, at least initially) at an academic policy–oriented graduate institution, an inner-city meeting, whatever. He has a magical ability to strike just the right tone, to get people thinking about matters that are important, to escape from stereotypes and question internalized assumptions, and to grasp the need for engagement, not just talk. With a sense of hopefulness, no matter how grim the objective circumstances. I've never seen anything like it.[3]

Howard Zinn was born in 1922—in a sense, and appropriately, at the beginning of "modern times" in the United States. The first commercial radio broadcast had taken place in 1920, as had the census, which revealed that, for the first time, more people lived in cities than on farms. *Time* magazine was founded the year after Zinn's birth. The 1920s also saw immigration restriction taking on a newly discriminatory tone, recession followed by prosperity (for some), rather floundering efforts at disarmament (while rejecting membership in the League of Nations), major scandals such as Teapot Dome, the height of the Ku Klux Klan, the Scopes "monkey trial," the first "talkie" at the movies, and Ford Motor Company's Model A.

Zinn's birth date was August 24; the place, New York City. Both his parents were European Jewish immigrants. "Eddie" Zinn was apparently from the Galician city of Lemberg, at one point part of the Austro-Hungarian Empire, Poland, and the Soviet Union, and now known as Lvov in Ukraine. It is fortunate that Zinn's family left when they did, for the Germans exterminated most of the city's Jewish population during World War II. "Jenny" Zinn came from another Jewish family, Rabinowitz, in the Siberian city of Irkutsk, on the shores of Lake Baikal near Mongolia. Zinn says it has been suggested many times that he "looks kind of Oriental," to which he responds, "Well, my mother came from near outer Mongolia." More seriously, he says, "I don't think there's any Mongolian in our background, but it was my private joke. So she was brought up in Irkutsk, and their family left and made their way eventually to the United States."[4] As did the Zinn family, obviously.

Zinn shares delightful stories about his name, and his Jewishness. People have frequently asked, he says, if Zinn is a shortened, American version of something. No, he responds:

I don't know that it's shortened from anything. And I have run into Zinns around here and there. Most of them are not Jewish. It's fundamentally a

German name, Zinn. And I have a choice thinking that it was German, spelled Z-i-n-n, that would be pronounced "sinn," and it would mean ten, or I have a choice of in German S-i-n-n, which would be pronounced "zinn," and would mean mine, which I prefer.[5]

Asked if his family had continued to be Jewish in terms of religious practice, Zinn replied no:

In fact, my parents themselves were not very. I mean they were sort of perfunctorily religious, in a way that probably most Jewish families were, so they sort of did things that were expected, sort of kept it kosher, and you go to a kosher butcher so the meat would be blessed or whatever, and you go to a synagogue on holidays, you know, you don't go every Saturday the way really religious Jews do. You fast on Yom Kippur, you get bar mitzvahed, which to me was just a very compulsory experience. And I went to Hebrew school for about a year to study Hebrew. Just enough to get me through the ceremony. Once I was bar mitzvahed, and I had done my religious duty, and my family needn't be ashamed of me anymore, . . . that was the end of my religiosity.[6]

Later, when Zinn and his wife had a son and daughter of their own, "they knew they were Jewish, they knew we were not religious. Occasionally my wife had a little more sentimental ties to that Jewish background than I did."[7]

Zinn has written movingly of his family and early life in one of his later books, a sort of memoir entitled *You Can't Be Neutral on a Moving Train: A Personal History of Our Times*—in a chapter significantly entitled "Growing Up Class-Conscious."

Poverty was clearly a prominent part of the Zinn family's life. Eddie worked in factories in New York, worked in many different jobs during the Depression (window cleaner, pushcart peddler, necktie salesman, WPA worker in Central Park), but settled into the job of waiter, at weddings and in restaurants; he also joined the Waiters Union. Zinn remembers working alongside his father for New Year's Eve parties and hating every moment of it, especially "the way the bosses treated the waiters, who were fed chicken wings just before they marched out to serve roast beef and filet mignon to the guests."[8] Zinn remembers his father fondly in many ways: "He was always physically affectionate to his four boys, and loved to laugh." But mostly he remembers:

All his life he worked hard for very little. I've always resented the smug statements of politicians, media commentators, corporate executives who talked of how, in America, if you worked hard you would become rich. The meaning of that was if you were poor it was because you hadn't worked hard enough. I knew this was a lie, about my father and millions of others, men and women who worked harder than anyone, harder than financiers and politicians, harder than *anybody* if you accept that when you work at an unpleasant job that makes it very hard work indeed.[9]

One thing he remembers about his mother is that she "worked and worked without getting paid at all."[10]

Jenny Zinn's life had indeed apparently always been hard. Her mother died when she was in her thirties, and her father deserted the family, leaving Jenny, a mere teenager, in charge of raising her three younger brothers and two younger sisters. She worked in factories until they grew up enough to find jobs. It was in one of those factories that she met Eddie's sister and, through her, Eddie himself. Howard Zinn says his parents' was "a passionate marriage all the way." Eddie had a fourth-grade education, while Jenny had made it through the seventh grade, but Zinn insists "her intelligence went far beyond that; she was the brains of the family. And the strength of the family."[11]

Strength was clearly needed. Jenny Zinn gave birth to five sons. The first died young of spinal meningitis. Howard was the second. He suffered from rickets, and was treated by a doctor who was also a family friend and thus charged very little, sometimes nothing. Zinn remembers moving around a great deal, "evading the landlord."[12] The family lived in a succession of tenements, usually with just three rooms. Some winters they were lucky—the building they were currently living in had central heating. Other winters they were caught living in a "cold-water flat," in which the only heat came from the coal cooking stove in the kitchen, where they also boiled the water for the washtub that did double duty as the family bathtub. If paying the rent was a challenge, so was paying the utility bills. Zinn remembers coming home from school and finding his mother knitting by candlelight because the electricity company had turned off the power due to nonpayment of the bill. He also remembers how excited he got when his father let him go along for a long walk through the city that culminated in the purchase of a secondhand radio. There was never a telephone. For a time, friends and neighbors would call a member of the family to the phone at a candy store down the block. Roaches were an ever-present reality. Despite it all, Zinn says, "I don't remember ever being hungry," obviously still amazed at his mother's being so "ingenious at making sure there was always food."[13]

Jenny was also somewhat ingenious at adapting the English language to her needs. She would talk with a friend about "very close veins" or "a pain in my crutch," look in the dairy store for "monster cheese," or say to her husband when he forgot something, "Eddie, try to remember, wreck your brains."[14]

Zinn says he and his three brothers—Bernie, Jerry, and Shelly—grew up together "sleeping two or three to a bed, in rooms dark and uninviting." So he spent a lot of time outside, in the streets or the schoolyard, playing handball, football, softball, stickball, or "taking boxing lessons from a guy in the neighborhood who had made the Golden Gloves and was our version of a celebrity."[15]

When he was in the house, he was reading: "From the time I was eight I was reading whatever books I could find." His first book, found in the streets with several pages missing, was Edgar Rice Burroughs's *Tarzan and the Jewels of Opar.* There were no books in the family home when Zinn was growing up. He seems sure his father never read a book, and remembers his mother reading mostly romance magazines. They did both read a newspaper, but knew little about politics "except that Franklin Roosevelt was a good man because he helped the poor."[16]

Eddie and Jenny may not have read much, but to their credit, they encouraged young Howard to do so. He tells a wonderful story about how they secured him a complete set of the works of Charles Dickens ("of whom they had never heard, of course") because they knew he loved to read. He was about ten years old when the *New York Post* offered the deal, in which coupons clipped from the paper plus only a few cents could get a Dickens volume each week. In that fashion, Zinn secured and read *David Copperfield, Oliver Twist, Great Expectations, Hard Times, A Tale of Two Cities,* and so on. He had no idea where Dickens fit into literary history, he says, but "what I did know was that he aroused in me tumultuous emotions. First, an anger at arbitrary power puffed up with wealth and kept in place by law. But most of all a profound compassion for the poor." Indeed, Zinn clearly still defends Dickens, talking about how "wise" he was "to make readers feel poverty and cruelty through the fate of children who had not reached the age where the righteous and comfortable classes could accuse them of being responsible for their own misery," and comparing his works favorably with today's "pallid, cramped novels about 'relationships.'"[17]

Poverty, the streets, odd jobs, family, the limited reading he was able to do—all these constituted major elements of Howard Zinn's informal education. For his formal education, he attended various public schools, since the family moved around so much. Indeed, he remembers going into sixth grade at a new school, carrying a folder that included a slip for every school he had attended to that point. Once, as he arose, all the slips fell out "and signaled to everybody around how many different schools I'd been in. I remember feeling terribly ashamed." Zinn was doing so well he skipped at least one grade on the way to Brooklyn's Thomas Jefferson High School. Important to his development there was the fact that the principal was a poet and encouraged a writer's program and club, which Zinn joined. In the meantime, he had taught himself to type on a typewriter his family had managed to purchase for him, and was typing (only for his own edification) reviews of everything he read. Because of financial problems at home, however, interestingly, Zinn became "totally alienated from school," and played hooky for weeks at a time, even managing to intercept letters from the school to his parents notifying them of what he was doing and devising "all kinds of schemes to evade the truant officer." But the officer finally caught him, and he went back to high school "with a vengeance" and got "really high grades."[18]

After graduating from Thomas Jefferson High, Zinn attended Brooklyn College briefly; as he said, "it was free." But his family's economic circumstances continued to be bad, he felt alienated, and he saw no reason at that point to go to college.[19]

In the meantime, he had had an experience that was a crucial one in his radicalization. He was about seventeen years of age; thus, it was about 1940, just after the beginning of World War II. He knew several young Communists. He argued with them about some things, including the Russian invasion of Finland. But he also agreed with them on a number of things—they were as "indignant as I was about the contrasts of wealth and poverty in America." He also admired them for their knowledge of politics, economics, what was happening in the world, and for their courage in the face of police hassles. "And besides, they were regular guys, good athletes." One evening he accepted their invitation to participate in a demonstration in Times Square. It was "orderly, nonviolent," focusing on "peace and justice and a dozen other causes of the day." Zinn and one of his friends decided to carry one of the banners. He shares no memory of what it said, but he does share a memory of what happened. Suddenly he heard sirens and screams, "and saw hundreds of policemen, mounted on horses and on foot, charging into the lines of marchers, smashing people with their clubs."[20]

"I was astonished, bewildered," Zinn remembers. "This was America, a country where, whatever its faults, people could speak, write, assemble, demonstrate without fear. It was in the Constitution, the Bill of Rights. We were a *democracy*." Nevertheless, someone smashed Zinn also. He remembers coming to with a painful lump on the side of his head, and:

> More important, there was a very painful thought in my head: the young Communists on the block were right! The state and its police were not neutral referees in a society of contending interests. They were on the side of the rich and powerful. Free speech? Try it and the police will be there with their horses, their clubs, their guns, to stop you.[21]

"From that moment on, I was no longer a liberal, a believer in the self-correcting character of American democracy," says Zinn. "I was a radical, believing that something fundamental was wrong in this country—not just the existence of poverty amidst great wealth, not just the horrible treatment of black people, but something rotten at the root." This revelation also suggested different methods: "The situation required not just a new president or new laws, but an uprooting of the old order, the introduction of a new kind of society—cooperative, peaceful, egalitarian."[22]

Zinn is willing to consider the possibility that his memory after so many years exaggerates the importance of that one experience. "But I think not. I have come to believe that our lives can be turned in a different direction, our minds adopt a different way of thinking, because of some significant though small event."[23]

Zinn suggests in his memoir, *You Can't Be Neutral on a Moving Train*, that the next few years following his Times Square experience might be called his "Communist years," but that raises an interesting question about his ideology, which is perhaps best dealt with here before continuing the story of his life.

August Meier and Elliott Rudwick, respected professional historians, have written: "In his teens Zinn moved to the left, . . . on the eve of World War II joined the Communist party," and functioned "as an active party member for almost a decade." Interesting. But Meier and Rudwick give no source for this statement. The paragraph they devote to Zinn ends by referring to his book on the Student Nonviolent Coordinating Committee (SNCC), and the footnote is to some of his early writings on the civil rights movement.[24] Peter Novick tells an even briefer version of the same story, but it turns out his only source is Meier and Rudwick.[25] What is going on here? Zinn himself, told about all this, responded: "I don't know where Meier and Rudwick got that information. . . . From the FBI? In any case, not true." Zinn knew Meier, he says, but certainly never told him that. "The accurate story is what I say in my memoir—that I hung out with young Communists for several years, while partly agreeing with them, partly disagreeing, admiring many of their commitments, then during World War II developing deep antipathy toward the Soviet Union."[26]

Asked further about his political philosophy, about what label or labels he would be comfortable applying to himself politically, Zinn responded, first, "Of course, labels are so misleading." Among the labels he proceeded to discuss as possibilities were Marxist, socialist, anarchist, radical, liberal, anticapitalist, and democratic socialist.[27]

He had already written, in *You Can't Be Neutral on a Moving Train*, of his early attraction to Marxism, upon first reading *The Communist Manifesto*, written, he noted, by Marx and Engels when they, too, were young radicals. "The history of all hitherto existing society is the history of class struggle," he quoted, then said he found that "undeniably true, verifiable in any reading of history." Marx and Engels's analysis of capitalism, he insisted, "made sense: capitalism's history of exploitation, its creation of extremes of wealth and poverty, even in the liberal 'democracy' of this country." And their socialist vision "was not one of dictatorship or bureaucracy but of a free society," with the "dictatorship of the proletariat" a transitional phase toward the goal of "a classless society of true democracy, true freedom." This would include a "rational, just economic system," in which everyone would have a short workday and freedom and time to do as they liked, whether writing poetry, being in nature, participating in sports, whatever, and nationalism would be "a thing of the past. People all over the world, of whatever race, of whatever continent, would live in peace and cooperation."[28]

As Zinn writes, or speaks, eloquently about these ideals, it is easy to see that they still have a great deal of appeal to him. However, he had quoted, in a 1988 essay in Z magazine, the famous saying supposedly once uttered by Marx himself: "Je ne suis pas un Marxiste"—"I am not a Marxist." (Still, it was also in that essay that Zinn insisted that Marx "had some very useful thoughts," and that "perhaps the most precious heritage of Marx's thought is his internationalism, his hostility to the national state, his insistence that ordinary people have no nation they must obey and give their lives for in war, that we are linked to one another across the globe as human beings.")[29] And in an interview, he said specifically, "I don't want to be labeled as a Marxist. Although, some of Marx's ideas I embrace heartily." His concern seemed to be not only that all such labels are misleading, but also that the Marxist label specifically in this country tends to associate one with the now-defunct Soviet Union. Zinn deserves quoting at some length as he considers some other labels:

> Socialist sounds good to me. If you remove from it the onus of those countries, dictatorships, that have called themselves socialistic. If you think of the socialism of Eugene Debs, Mother Jones, Emma Goldman. Anarchism appeals to me, if you remove from that the bomb-throwing stigma, a really tiny proportion of anarchists who threw bombs. And you think more of Tolstoy, Thoreau, and Kropotkin. So, socialist, anarchist, radical, I don't mind those labels so long as I can, "guilty with an explanation, your honor," as long as I can explain them.[30]

Perhaps surprisingly, he said he did not even mind liberal, but then added quickly, "though I'm very distrustful of liberal; it includes too many people with whom I don't want to politically associate." Certainly, he said, "I've always been anticapitalist. By that, I mean critical of capitalism." He followed that with a brief account of the material about growing up class-conscious, hanging out with young Communists, and so on, and concluded apparently with some degree of finality, "So, I guess I consider myself a democratic socialist." There exists, of course, an organization called Democratic Socialists of America. Reminded of that, Zinn said he thought he was a member, indeed that it might be the only organization he belonged to. "I'm very, very eclectic in my support of organizations," he continued. "I will give my money to and my name to organizations I think will do good things, even if I don't believe totally in everything they do."[31] This seems to suggest a distinctively pragmatic, independent kind of radicalism, not at all "pure" ideologically and not at all concerned about that.

All this, of course, Zinn had not worked out at age seventeen; indeed, in a healthy manner, it has obviously been a lifelong process. Perhaps it is always true that our ideology, political and otherwise, is shaped to a significant degree by our life experiences; certainly it is true with Zinn. Asked about his personal life and how it might have influenced his work, he responded, with obvious emotion:

> Growing up in a working-class family of Jewish immigrants (when I read Mike Gold's *Jews without Money* I thought: that's so true!) being skinny and having rickets and watching my mother raise four boys and take care of all our medical and biological needs . . . gave me the kind of class consciousness which affected my teaching and writing of history. Going to work in a shipyard at the age of eighteen, finding young radicals to work with in organizing the young shipyard workers, playing baseball in the

street and basketball in the shipyard tournaments, going into the Air
Force, seeing combat duty as a bombardier overseas and concluding that
war, even "the good war," solves no fundamental problems—all of that
profoundly influenced my work. Teaching and living in a black community in the Deep South, becoming involved in the southern civil rights
movement, brought history alive for me, made me want my writing to be
not "objective" but participatory. Becoming a husband and a father while
still in my twenties, having a wife who shared my values, my indignation
at racism, injustice, inequality, war—all of that encouraged me in what I
was doing.[32]

But the incident with the young Communists in Times Square was certainly a formative experience. Not long after, he took a civil service examination, did well, and got a job as an apprentice shipfitter in the Brooklyn
Navy Yard. The pay was $13.89 per week; he would give $10 of it to his
parents and use the remainder for himself. It was an "ugly, dirty, noisy, and
even dangerous job." Not surprisingly, Zinn was soon cooperating with
three other young radicals to organize an "apprentice association, a sort of
union of the young shipyard workers."[33] He held that job for about two and
a half years. Then another turning point—he enlisted in the Air Force.
(Actually, he enlisted in the Army Air Corps. Zinn, like almost everyone
else, commonly refers to "the Air Force," but the Air Force did not really
come into existence as a separate branch of the military service until 1947,
two years after the end of World War II.)

The story of his enlistment is remarkable. His friends were not in the
shipyard, but in the military. He considered them heroes. He was "imbued
with anti-fascism," and considered World War II at that time "a good war,
a just war." The "spirit of adventure" was also calling. So without telling
his parents, he decided to enlist in the Air Force. He arranged for the Air
Force to send him a notice so that it would look like he was being drafted,
but of course nobody got drafted into the Air Force. What he really did was
volunteer for induction. Still, he had to take a series of tests, physical and
mental. There were various model airplanes on the desk of the officer he
talked to—Zinn knew nothing about airplanes. He waited outside after it
was all over "in emotional turmoil, because I knew I was going to be
rejected, and I wanted more than anything to get in." He was right; they
came out and said "rejected." But he said he wanted to see the officer again,
by his own account a "nervy" thing to do. "I went in and gave him a speech
on how much the war meant to me, . . . why I wanted to be in the Air
Force." The officer "must have been bewildered," but "he listened and lis-

tened and it worked!"[34] Then, "to make absolutely sure, I asked the draft board clerk if I could mail the induction notice myself, and I dropped it in the mailbox just outside the office."[35]

Such enthusiasm for getting into the Air Force is especially ironic for one who was to become as consistently, passionately antiwar as Howard Zinn. Indeed, already by the end of World War II, his views had changed to the point that he wrote the words "Never Again" on an envelope of wartime mementos as he filed them away.[36] What came in between? First, four months of basic infantry training at Jefferson Barracks, Missouri. (One of his most memorable experiences there was seeing a squad of black soldiers taking a break and singing "Ain't Gonna Study War No More.") Then to an airfield near Burlington, Vermont, to learn to fly—a Piper Cub. Then to Nashville, Tennessee, for a battery of exams to determine whether he would become a pilot, a navigator, or a bombardier. The decision: bombardier, but with some navigation training to be included on his agenda as well. So it was off to preflight training in Santa Ana, California. Then six weeks at a gunnery school outside Las Vegas, Nevada. And finally, four months at Deming, New Mexico, "learning all about the famous hush-hush Norden bombsight—theory and practice. . . . I was good at it," Zinn recalls, "and graduated from bombing school with the gold bars of a second lieutenant on my shoulders and bombardier's wings pinned on my chest at graduation." It was now time for Zinn to enjoy his first furlough, eleven days at home before shipping overseas.[37]

Here the military story must be interrupted by a humorous, yet moving, story of romance. Howard Zinn was still working in the shipyards when he met Roslyn Shechter (sometimes spelled Schechter). A friend already in the service asked Zinn to deliver his Army insignia to her as a sign of his affection. "I, in one of the great acts of betrayal, I suppose, in my life," recalls Zinn—but then, perhaps rationalizing, "Well, my conscience didn't bother me, because she wasn't enamored of him anyway. But still, nothing would have happened between them, but I delivered the insignia, met her, we just had a few dates" before he left for his military training.[38] During those few dates, Howard and Roz were obviously attracted to each other, discovering that they had much in common. "She had long chestnut-blonde hair and blue eyes and the face of a Russian beauty," he recalls, "and we had lots to talk about." They were both readers: he was reading Marx and Engels at the time, and Upton Sinclair; she was reading Dostoevsky and Tolstoy. They "seemed to share the same outlook on the world, the war, fascism, socialism." One of their dates was a moonlight sail organized by his fellow workers. Zinn remembers it as "a star-filled, romantic evening." When the sailing was over, they did not want to go home. So they went bowling! He took her home about 4:00 A.M. Roslyn's father was not pleased, either about the hour or about her companion. "A twenty-year-old shipyard worker with outrageously radical political views was not his notion of a proper boyfriend for his princess of a daughter."[39]

After Howard left for training, he found himself lonely and thinking of Roslyn a great deal, so he struck up a correspondence with her that became more and more intense, more and more intimate. But in that correspondence, spread out over almost a year and a half, marriage never came up. The first night he was home for the furlough, it did. "Four days later, I in uniform, Roz in a skirt and sweater, our hastily assembled (and somewhat bewildered) parents and brothers and sisters in attendance, we were married." The date was October 30, 1944; the marriage has lasted more than fifty years. But it was not really an auspicious beginning. "A week of 'honeymoon' in a cheap hotel in Manhattan," writes Zinn, "and I left for Rapid City, South Dakota, to meet my air crew." The new bride was able to join the young airman for a while in this final stage of his training, before shipping overseas; this, recalls Zinn, was the "real honeymoon."[40]

Howard Zinn's time in the Air Force spanned the period from May 1943 to December 1945. Obviously, by the time he got to Europe, the war was winding down. On the voyage over, on board the *Queen Mary*, he had experiences that raised his consciousness about both racism and the class system. A mix-up in the usually segregated dining hall led to a white sergeant sitting uncomfortably next to a black man. "Lieutenant!" he yelled at Zinn, whose assignment was to "keep order" in the mess hall, "Get him out of here until I finish." Zinn was angered, and for the first time in his military career pulled rank. He shook his head and informed the sergeant, "If you don't want to finish your food, you can leave. What the hell is this war all about, Sergeant?" It was a long time till the next meal, notes Zinn in telling this story, so the sergeant stayed and ate. "I learned something from that little incident," Zinn says, "later reinforced in my years in the South: that most racists have something they care about *more* than racial segregation, and the problem is to locate what that is." The unique class system of the military also bothered him. His nine-man crew, who had become good friends, with "no saluting, no 'yessir and nosir,'" were separated on board. The five enlisted men even ate separately. To Zinn, "It was bizarre, with us sailing through submarine-infested waters on the way to a war."[41]

Despite these experiences, Zinn arrived at his assigned air base in East

Anglia, England, still gung ho about the war. Just as he had traded places with other bombardiers while in South Dakota to get on the short list for overseas duty, so here he argued vehemently with another bombardier about which one would get to go on a particular mission. The most important bombing mission Zinn participated in—for him, at least, if not for the course of the war—was at Royan, near Bordeaux, on the Atlantic coast of France. It was ten months after D-Day, just three weeks before Germany's final surrender. Zinn remembers that he and other members of the bombing crews looked at each other in a bit of confusion when informed that they would be dropping bombs on France at this point in the war, when our armies were already well into Germany. But he did not really question— the official explanation was that there were several thousand German soldiers near Royan, and the bombing raid would take them out. Not mentioned was that Royan had once before been bombed, and practically destroyed, during the war. And not much emphasized was the fact that the planes would be carrying, instead of their usual five-hundred-pound demolition bombs, thirty one-hundred-pound cannisters of "jellied gasoline" or "liquid fire." Zinn has written powerfully of his participation in this mission in an essay entitled "Hiroshima and Royan," juxtaposing his experience at Royan with that better-known bombing. The "liquid fire," he says, "was napalm, used [at Royan] for the first time in warfare."[42] "At our bombing altitudes," he writes, "we saw no people, heard no screams, saw no blood, no torn limbs." He remembered only "seeing the canisters light up like matches flaring one by one on the ground below. Up there in the sky," he concludes, "I was just 'doing my job'—the explanation throughout history of warriors committing atrocities."[43]

Just doing his job. It was only after the war that Zinn began to reflect critically on his wartime experiences, including Royan. He became so interested in Royan that he visited there some twenty years after the war was over, spending some time at the library he had once helped destroy, as a part of his research for the Hiroshima/Royan essay. "The evidence seems overwhelming," he wrote there, "that factors of pride, military ambition, glory, honor were powerful motives in producing an unnecessary military operation."[44] Even more powerful, and worth quoting at length, not only because of what it says about Royan but because it gets into some of Zinn's most basic, and most radical, views:

> More and more in our time, the mass production of massive evil requires
> an enormously complicated division of labor. No one is positively responsible for the horror that ensues. But everyone is negatively responsible,

because *anyone* can throw a wrench into the machinery. Not quite, of course—because only a few people have wrenches. The rest have only their hands and feet. That is, the power to interfere with the terrible progression is distributed unevenly, and therefore the sacrifice required varies, according to one's means. In that odd perversion of the natural which we call society (that is, nature seems to equip each species for its special needs) the greater one's capability for interference, the less urgent is the need to interfere.

It is the immediate victims—or tomorrow's—who have the greatest need, and the fewest wrenches. They must use their bodies (which may explain why rebellion is a rare phenomenon). This may suggest to those of us who have a bit more than our bare hands, and at least a small interest in stopping the machine, that we might play a peculiar role in breaking the social stalemate.

This may require resisting a false crusade—or refusing one or another expedition in a true one. But always, it means refusing to be transfixed by the actions of other people, the truths of other times. It means acting on what we feel and think, here, now, for human flesh and sense, against the abstractions of duty and obedience.[45]

But again, all that reflection came later. Zinn admits freely that "it would not have entered my mind to stand up in the briefing room that morning and ask, Why are we killing more people when the war is about to end?" Indeed, he recalls only one point during the war when any doubt at all entered his mind "about the absolute rightness of what we were doing." He had become friends with a gunner on another crew. They were both avid readers, both interested in politics. But he startled Zinn when he suggested, "This is not a war against fascism. It's a war for empire. England, the United States, the Soviet Union—they are all corrupt states, not morally concerned about Hitlerism, just wanting to run the world themselves. It's an imperialist war." Zinn asked him, if he felt that way, why was he in the war? "To talk to guys like you," was the response. Zinn recalls being impressed that his friend was risking his life in the war when his real goal was to wage a war of his own to persuade others of his point of view, but also recalls not being entirely convinced by what the friend said.[46] Still, Zinn never forgot it, and at the end of the war, even though he had become a second lieutenant and received an Air Medal and two battle stars, there were those words, "Never Again."

With the war over, Zinn wanted to resume his education. But it was to be a few years before he was able to do so. Roslyn, his still-new bride, got a job as a secretary. He went back to work in the shipyard for a while, but also "knocked around at various jobs," including waiter (like his father), ditchdigger, and brewery worker, collecting unemployment insurance between jobs. They tried living with her parents for a while, "which was not a great experience," so they were "very happy to get into this little basement apartment to escape from the in-laws."[47] Elsewhere he has described it as "a rat-infested basement apartment in Bedford-Stuyvesant." Still, "We were a young, happy married couple," he recalls. Then their first child—a daughter, Myla—was born. And at the age of twenty-seven, Roslyn pregnant with their second child—to be a son named Jeff—Howard began college, again, as a freshman at New York University. It was 1949, three years after he had gotten out of the Air Force. It soon became obvious that he was far more serious about being a student this time than when he was a teenager at Brooklyn College. Financially, the G.I. Bill of Rights helped a great deal. (Says Zinn: "Whenever I hear that the government *must not* get involved in helping people, that this must be left to 'private enterprise,' I think of the G.I. Bill and its marvelous nonbureaucratic efficiency.") Still, Roslyn worked part-time, and Howard worked full-time loading trucks from 4:00 P.M. to midnight, in addition to going to school. With all this assistance and effort, the family was able to move into a nicer place, a low-income housing project near the East River in downtown Manhattan, with "no rats, no cockroaches, a few trees and a playground downstairs, a park along the river."[48] He finished his bachelor's degree in 1951, taking only about two and a half years, thanks to overloads, summers, and some credit for courses he had taken while in the military.[49] Then it was straight on to graduate school at Columbia University.

At Columbia, Zinn majored in history and minored in economics at the M.A. level, then majored in history and minored in political science at the Ph.D. level. He studied under some of the great names in the profession at the time, including Henry Steele Commager, David Donald, Richard B. Morris, Jacques Barzun, William Leuchtenburg, and Richard Hofstadter. Asked who among those he was most influenced by, he admired most, he answered for influence, Hofstadter, and for admiration, Donald. The details reveal much about Zinn as well as those two professors. Zinn never took a course with Hofstadter, though Hofstadter did chair his dissertation defense, due to Leuchtenburg, the dissertation director, being in England at the time. But Zinn remembers hearing consistently that Hofstadter was not a particularly good teacher because he was so focused on his writing. It was his writing that impressed Zinn, his writing style and specifically his most famous book, *The American Political Tradition*. "Because I think it was written when Hofstadter was quite radical," explains Zinn. "It was a radical critique of the American political system in which basic principles undergirded both the Democrats and Republicans, both liberals and conservatives." These principles included "private property and free enterprise, nationalism and the capitalist spirit." To this day, Zinn concluded, he still recommends *The American Political Tradition*. Reminded that Hofstadter is frequently classified as a "consensus" historian (as opposed to conflict), and that consensus historians are frequently considered conservative, Zinn said he did not believe that fit Hofstadter at all, and added, "That's why I thought that the use of a consensus school was always sort of obfuscating. Because it lumps together people who were happy with a consensus, like [Daniel J.] Boorstin, and people who were dissatisfied with it"—obviously including Hofstadter. The admiration for David Donald was directly related to his teaching, specifically because "he had a passion for his teaching." Zinn remembered Donald "giving a lecture on the abolitionists with tears in his eyes," and concluded, "I was impressed by teachers who would allow themselves to be moved by things that they were talking about."[50] Obviously not standard fare among historians, but it was to become Zinn's style of teaching as well.

Zinn's Ph.D. minor in political science was to play an important role in his career. He is best known, in terms of academic position, as a professor of political science, not history, at Boston University from 1964 to 1988. The way that developed is interesting. Zinn strained his back in his job at the warehouse. He felt compelled to find other work, and was able to find part-time teaching at both Upsala College, in nearby East Orange, New Jersey, and Brooklyn College. He took courses in constitutional law, for example, as a part of his minor, and Upsala needed government taught more than history. As Zinn put it, "They just gave me whatever courses, you know how it is, very often, the administrators don't even care if you know anything about the courses." The dean who interviewed him, he said, seemed "absolutely not interested" in his specific fields; he "just wanted to know my hours, etc."[51] So he began to teach political science, courses in American government, whatever. The trend was to continue in his first full-time teaching position at Spelman College, and, obviously, throughout his career in the political science department at Boston.

Zinn's M.A. thesis was on the Colorado coal strike of 1913–1914; the essence of it can be found in the chapter "The Ludlow Massacre," in *The Politics of History*. His Ph.D. dissertation was on the congressional career of Fiorello LaGuardia; it was to become, in revised form, his first book,

LaGuardia in Congress, in 1959. But before he published that book, indeed before he actually received the Ph.D. from Columbia, Zinn was to secure his first full-time job as a professor.

"I did not seek out a 'Negro college,' in the year 1956, because of an urge to do good," recalls Zinn. "I was just looking for a job." The placement bureau at Columbia contacted him to see if he was interested in an interview with the president of Spelman College, who was visiting New York. At the end of the interview, Zinn was offered the job as chairman of the four-member history and social science department. He was offered a salary of $4,000 a year, but courageously insisted on $4,500 since he had a wife and two children. "True, it was a tiny department, and scoffers might say being its chairman was like being the headwaiter in a two-waiter restaurant," Zinn wrote in his memoir. "But in my situation it was very welcome. I would still be poor, but prestigious." Though he had not sought out a teaching job in a black setting, many of his experiences had made him receptive to it, including his reading of such works as Upton Sinclair's *The Jungle*, John Steinbeck's *The Grapes of Wrath*, and Richard Wright's *Native Son*; seeing black men excluded from labor unions and being given the toughest jobs; and witnessing segregation in the military. He had come to see racial oppression and class oppression as intertwined. Also, in the low-income housing project in which he and his family had lived, friends and neighbors included African Americans along with Irish, Italians, and Puerto Ricans.[52]

So, in August 1956, the Zinn family—Howard, Roslyn, Myla (age nine), and Jeff (age six)—packed themselves and their belongings into a Chevrolet (age ten), and headed south to Atlanta, Georgia. Zinn remembers poignantly his father, Eddie, clearly upset about the family moving so far away, but saying nothing, except "Good luck. Take care of yourself." It was to be the last time they would see him alive.[53] Almost forty years later, reflecting back on that point in his life, Zinn wrote:

> That was my world for the first thirty-three years of my life—the world of unemployment and bad employment, of me and my wife leaving our two- and three-year-olds in the care of others while we went to school or to work, living most of that time in cramped and unpleasant places, hesitating to call the doctor when the children were sick because we couldn't afford to pay him, finally taking the children to hospital clinics where interns could take care of them. This is the way a large part of the population lives, even in this, the richest country in the world. And when, armed with the proper degrees, I began to move out of that world,

becoming a college professor, I never forgot that. I never stopped being class-conscious.[54]

NOTES

1. Howard Zinn, e-mail message to the author, October 7, 2002.

2. Howard Zinn, *The Future of History: Interviews with David Barsamian* (Monroe, Maine: Common Courage Press, 1999), p. 147.

3. Noam Chomsky, e-mail message to the author, July 29, 2000.

4. The primary source for the material in this paragraph is: Howard Zinn, interview, Boston, Mass., March 13, 1997. (Tape recording and transcript of this interview are in the possession of the author.)

5. Ibid.

6. Ibid.

7. Ibid.

8. Howard Zinn, *You Can't Be Neutral on a Moving Train: A Personal History of Our Times* (Boston: Beacon Press, 1994), pp. 164–65.

9. Ibid., p. 165.

10. Ibid., p. 166.

11. Ibid.

12. Zinn, interview, March 13, 1997.

13. Zinn, *You Can't Be Neutral on a Moving Train*, p. 167.

14. Ibid., p. 168.

15. Ibid.

16. Ibid.

17. Ibid., pp. 168–69.

18. Zinn, interview, March 13, 1997.

19. Ibid.

20. Zinn, *You Can't Be Neutral on a Moving Train*, pp. 171–72.

21. Ibid., p. 173.

22. Ibid.

23. Ibid.

24. August Meier and Elliott Rudwick, *Black History and the Historical Profession, 1915–1980* (Urbana: University of Illinois Press, 1986), pp. 164–65.

25. Peter Novick, *That Noble Dream: The "Objectivity Question" and the American Historical Profession* (Cambridge: Cambridge University Press, 1988), p. 419.

26. Howard Zinn, e-mail message to the author, April 4, 1998.

27. Howard Zinn, interview, Boston, Mass., March 14, 1997. (Tape recording and transcript of this interview are in the possession of the author.)

28. Zinn, *You Can't Be Neutral on a Moving Train*, p. 175.

29. Howard Zinn, *Failure to Quit: Reflections of an Optimistic Historian* (Monroe, Maine: Common Courage Press, 1993), pp. 146, 149. The essay actually appears in *Failure to Quit* under the title "Je Ne Suis Pas un Marxiste," but had appeared in *Z* as "Nothing Human Is Alien to Me."

30. Zinn, interview, March 14, 1997.

31. Ibid.

32. Howard Zinn, e-mail message to the author, October 17, 2002.

33. Ibid.

34. Ibid.

35. Zinn, *You Can't Be Neutral on a Moving Train*, p. 87.

36. Ibid., p. 95.

37. Ibid., pp. 88–89.

38. Zinn, interview, March 14, 1997.

39. Zinn, *You Can't Be Neutral on a Moving Train*, p. 89.

40. Ibid., pp. 90–91.

41. Ibid., pp. 91–92.

42. Howard Zinn, *The Politics of History* (Boston: Beacon Press, 1970), p. 262.

43. Zinn, *You Can't Be Neutral on a Moving Train*, p. 94.

44. Zinn, *The Politics of History*, p. 269.

45. Ibid., pp. 273–74.

46. Zinn, *You Can't Be Neutral on a Moving Train*, pp. 94–95.

47. Zinn, interview, March 13, 1997.

48. Zinn, *You Can't Be Neutral on a Moving Train*, p. 179.

49. Zinn, interview, March 14, 1997.

50. Ibid.

51. Ibid.

52. Zinn, *You Can't Be Neutral on a Moving Train*, pp. 15–17.

53. Ibid., p. 166.

54. Ibid., p. 180.

TWO
THE SOUTH
AND THE MOVEMENT
1956–1964

In 1956, when Howard Zinn and his family moved from New York to Atlanta for him to begin his teaching career at Spelman College, a school for African American women, the country was supposedly tranquil, affluent, and all that. But there was, of course, much more. Internationally, the Cold War was raging—1956 was the year of the Suez crisis. At home, Elvis Presley, especially with his appearance on television, had begun to popularize rock-'n'-roll music, which was to have profound impact on the youth culture in America in the coming years. More relevant, the Montgomery bus boycott had already occurred, marking the initial rise to prominence of Martin Luther King Jr. and the civil rights movement. Even before that, in 1954, the Supreme Court, in *Brown* v. *Board of Education of Topeka*, had started the country on the long, hard road toward integration. But we should let Zinn himself describe some of the climate of the times, and how it affected him and his move south. The country in that period, he says, was "very much in the grip of the Cold War, at home and abroad." Dwight D. Eisenhower as president essentially took no stand on the *Brown* decision, and Adlai Stevenson, his opponent for the second time in 1956, was also "very cautious on civil rights matters, reflecting the traditional Democratic Party alliance with the white South." It was only the political need for black voters, Zinn insisted, surely accurately, which "led the Republicans to push through a Civil Rights Act in 1957, weak as it was."[1]

Beginning to relate the climate of opinion to his own situation, Zinn noted that "McCarthyism was plaguing colleges and universities throughout the country . . . and it may well be that black colleges were a kind of refuge (although I did not consciously seek out Spelman for that reason!) for white radicals." After all, black colleges needed teachers with both good educational credentials and the motivation to come into the black community, "and so radical whites (me, Staughton Lynd, others) were especially welcome, and since our radicalism was expressed mostly in our views on race relations, well, that fitted in with the black community quite well."[2]

Before he got too deeply involved with what was happening in the civil rights movement, however, Zinn had to complete his Ph.D. He wrote the dissertation during the first two years of his teaching. Those who have experienced the fine art of balancing family, writing, and teaching (especially when all course preparations are by definition new) will understand what a difficult period that must have been. In Zinn's case, it was even more complicated, since he spent the summers of 1957 and 1958 in Denver, Colorado, on a Ford Foundation grant to study the uses of television documentary in presenting history. Still, he persevered, and received his Ph.D. from Columbia in 1958. His adviser, William E. Leuchtenburg, obviously thought highly of his work, a study of Fiorello LaGuardia's congressional career; he submitted it to the Beveridge Award competition of the American Historical Association. It finished second, the reward for which was publication, by Cornell University Press, in 1959.

Leuchtenburg describes his relationship with Zinn as "altogether cordial," though he admits they have seen very little of each other over the years and attributes this in part to their "different political outlooks." Zinn, he says, "is regarded as a leader of the New Left, and that is not my orientation." However, their outlook on LaGuardia, he recalls, did not differ substantially. And Leuchtenburg obviously looks back with pride on his student's work, saying, "He holds a special place for me because he was my very first student to receive the Ph.D. And his dissertation won Honorable Mention for the AHA's Beveridge prize." If that sounds to anyone like "Also Ran," insists Leuchtenburg, "in fact, the award means that the judges voted it the second best dissertation written in the U.S. that year." Describing the dissertation process, Leuchtenburg remembers being "very impressed by the quality of the chapters" Zinn sent him—"first rate"—and also by "the speed at which he got them to me, especially remarkable since he had a teaching load at Spelman that was very heavy." (Interestingly, though on a somewhat different note, Leuchtenburg takes credit for bringing Zinn together with Staughton Lynd, "who had audited my lecture course at Harvard, with regard to Lynd's teaching at Spelman.")[3]

The dissertation, under the title *LaGuardia in Congress*, became Zinn's first book; it was his last one to be essentially a standard historical monograph. And even in it, there are signs of the direction Zinn's work would take subsequently.

First, the story of how Zinn selected LaGuardia as a topic for his dissertation deserves telling. He was first interested in writing about "Big Bill" Haywood, having already become very attracted to labor history in general and the IWW (International Workers of the World, nicknamed Wobblies) in particular. But he discovered that the Department of Justice, which had acquired Haywood's papers, had burned them sometime during the 1920s! Then he decided to pick "some civil liberties issue (it was around 1952, height of the Cold War abroad and at home)." But when he talked to Prof. Henry Steele Commager about that, Commager, to Zinn's "surprise and disappointment," told him to "stay away from a civil liberties issue—the atmosphere is not conducive for that, pick a safer, easier topic for your dissertation, then when you get your degree you can write on whatever you like." So, stymied for the time being on the topic selection process, wandering around lower Manhattan one day, Zinn passed by a decrepit old building marked "Municipal Archives." He walked in, up the stairs, into a huge warehouse-type room. A woman sat at a desk, the only piece of furniture in the room, which was otherwise filled with hundreds of filing cabinets spread messily all around the room. Zinn asked, "What do you have here?" The woman replied that LaGuardia's widow had just left the LaGuardia papers! Most of the cabinets were filled with materials from LaGuardia's mayoral career. A smaller number of filing cabinets over in a corner, Zinn learned, related to his congressional career. Zinn admitted, "I didn't even know he had a congressional career." But he started looking through the materials, and became excited. "LaGuardia, though colorful and progressive as a mayor, still seemed very much of the Establishment. But in Congress he was obviously a rebel, a radical." Zinn decided he had found his topic. Leuchtenburg, his adviser, agreed, but informed him that another historian, Arthur Mann, was at work on a "life and times of LaGuardia." They felt, however, that if Zinn worked only on the congressional career of LaGuardia, there would be no real conflict.[4]

Fiorello LaGuardia, of course, is best known as the tempestuous mayor of New York City during the years of Franklin D. Roosevelt's New Deal. But Zinn insists, in *LaGuardia in Congress*, that those years matched his mayoral years in drama and perhaps surpassed them in lasting achievement. LaGuardia served in the House of Representatives from 1917 to 1933, except for brief breaks to serve in World War I and as president of the New York City Board of Aldermen (1920–1921). During those years—"the decade of Harding, Coolidge, and Hoover, of scandal and revelry and unbounded prosperity. Or so it seemed until 1929"—LaGuardia "conducted his own bustling side show for reform." Zinn acknowledges that he "attracted only a small audience," and that he was not a "big wheel" on Capitol Hill, but also insists that he was an important transitional figure: "LaGuardia, it appears, was an important link between two periods of reform, picking up the progressive football upon entering Congress in early 1917 and finally handing it over to Roosevelt in early 1933." Most of the small number of congressional progressives during the 1920s came from the prairie and mountain states, but LaGuardia represented a slum district in East Harlem, a district with Italians, Jews, Puerto Ricans, and other national groups living in firetraps while "statesmen, under white-domed palaces, thanked God for the blessings of prosperity."[5] LaGuardia and his fellow progressives, Zinn insisted, represented "the conscience of the twenties":

> As Democrats and Republicans cavorted like rehearsed wrestlers in the center of the political ring, LaGuardia stalked the front rows and bellowed for real action. While Ku Klux Klan membership reached the millions and Congress tried to legislate the nation toward racial "purity," LaGuardia demanded that immigration bars be let down to Italians, Jews, and others. When self-styled patriots sought to make the Caribbean an American lake, LaGuardia called for the removal of marines from Nicaragua. Above the clatter of ticker-tape machines sounding their jubilant message, LaGuardia tried to tell the nation about striking miners in Pennsylvania.[6]

Is there not a tone of admiration for LaGuardia and his progressivism even in these remarks from Zinn's preface?

The preface also reveals several other things that should be noted. Zinn thanked Professors Leuchtenburg and Hofstadter of Columbia University for their assistance. His thank-yous—as well as his footnotes and bibliography— also reveal that he did extensive research in the LaGuardia papers in the Municipal Archives of New York City; some research is evident in the FDR papers at Hyde Park and the Manuscripts Division of the Library of Congress. Zinn also interviewed Marie Fischer LaGuardia, LaGuardia's widow. Finally, Zinn began a practice which was to continue throughout his career by thanking his wife, Roslyn. And he also added "a word of thanks to the students of Spelman College and my friends in the Atlanta University System for making life interesting for me between sessions at the typewriter."[7] (More later about that interesting life.)

On March 5, 1917, the day LaGuardia first arrived to take up his duties in the House chamber, he walked down the aisle until he found an empty seat—in the front row. By taking that seat, he had violated House protocol, the beginning, notes Zinn, of LaGuardia's "long career as a political upstart." His first bill showed his support for World War I—or at least for those who would fight it. It asked imprisonment in time of peace and the death penalty during war for anyone selling inferior food, clothing, ammunition, or arms to the Army or Navy. LaGuardia was doubtless remembering the death of his father, and many others, from spoiled beef provided to troops during the Spanish-American War. The bill was referred to the appropriate committee, where it died—the fate of many of LaGuardia's efforts. He specifically supported U.S. entry into the war, but opposed the Espionage Act; he was, notes Zinn, always "quick to bridle at intimations that the foreign-born were less patriotic than native Americans." And while he supported the war, he was certainly at odds with the Wilson administration at times: "While Wilson was making grandiose statements about the political democracy at stake in the war, LaGuardia maintained that the justification for the war must come in the present as well as in the future and in terms of economic as well as political democracy." Indeed, the failure of the war to produce these deep changes led to LaGuardia's—and many others'—later disillusionment with it. After the war, LaGuardia and other progressives, including Robert La Follette and George Norris, began to close ranks; Zinn refers to them as "the unpopular little band which began hammering against the stone wall of postwar reaction." They protested against profiteering, denounced special privilege, and defended the exercise of free speech. LaGuardia even gained positive response from minorities when he spoke up for Jews by protesting the anti-Semitic outbreaks across Europe after the war, and for African Americans when he insisted that the American Legion should be open to all who served in the war, without discrimination.[8]

Within a few months, during his time as president of the Board of Aldermen, LaGuardia's daughter died of spinal meningitis and his wife of tuberculosis. He took a ten-day rest in Cuba, but impressively, says Zinn:

"When he returned, his sorrow was buried deep inside him, his voice was as powerful as ever, and an inner engine, strengthened perhaps by his torment, drove him once again at top speed." As his aldermanic term ended, for example, in December 1921, he issued a farewell statement in which he said, "New York is the richest city in the world. But until every child is fed and every home has air and light and every man and woman a chance for happiness, it is not the city it ought to be." Back in Congress, he took up the progressive cause again, and explained well that it "is not the result of the ambitions of any one man, nor is it a movement artificially created. The Progressive movement is simply the inevitable result of economic and political conditions throughout the country."[9] The much-vaunted prosperity was clearly hollow and partial.

In view of his work for peace, free speech, the rights of the poor, and the rights of minorities, it is not surprising that when a list was compiled in the mid-1920s, at the height of the "Red Scare" phenomenon, of those Americans who had most often been attacked by the "100 percent Americans," Fiorello LaGuardia occupied a conspicuous place. He was also a harbinger of FDR's later "Good Neighbor" policy in Latin America, and played a crucial role, along with George Norris in the Senate, in preparing the way for the Tennessee Valley Authority. Throughout the 1920s, says Zinn, LaGuardia spent most of his time battling against the high cost of food and rent, for the rights of strikers, for a redistribution of wealth through taxation, "and in general for government aid to that part of the population which was bypassed in the national rush toward better living." Zinn concludes: "In the course of these conflicts the plastic of his social and economic philosophy hardened, took more definite form, and, in the era of greatest triumph for laissez faire, pointed unhesitantly and challengingly toward the concept of the welfare state."[10]

Not surprisingly also, LaGuardia was not always comfortable in the Republican Party. Sometimes he was a Progressive; always he was progressive. He did not shy away from the label "radical," noting that some "radical changes" were indeed needed. There is no mention of him complaining when a House colleague seemed to place him in the socialist camp. Certainly with the crash of the stock market and the beginning of the Great Depression, LaGuardia's rhetoric became more radical. He talked, in a major speech on December 21, 1931, of the need for "fundamental and sweeping measures," saying mere "palliatives will not do; a major operation is necessary." He called for government relief, a public works program, and a national system of unemployment insurance. When all these early signs of the New Deal were attacked by colleagues as unconstitutional, LaGuardia replied impatiently, "If the Constitution stands in the way, well, the Constitution will simply have to get out of the way."[11]

LaGuardia's approach to the problems of the day led him into sharp conflict with Herbert Hoover. "Personally," he said, "I am sick and tired of hearing this patronizing, smug expression of help given in millions of dollars to powerful corporations 'percolating' or 'dripping down' to the individual." He was bitter about Hoover's veto of the Wagner bill in 1932, and pointed to the barren stretch of land opposite the Capitol called Anacostia Flats where some twenty thousand veterans were encamped, living reminders of the work still to be done. After Hoover ordered out the troops to drive off the veterans and their families, and said proudly, "A challenge to the authority of the United States Government has been met swiftly and firmly," LaGuardia wired him: "Soup is cheaper than tear bombs and bread better than bullets in maintaining law and order in these times of depression, unemployment, and hunger."[12]

By this time, Zinn notes, LaGuardia had become "the leading spirit and master organizer of the progressive bloc in the House of Representatives." He led a battle against a sales tax, and won. He led a battle for an anti-injunction bill, and won. All that was needed for this "dynamic, depression-based progressivism" to become the New Deal, insists Zinn, was the catchy title and attachment to a major party. As the depression deepened, nativist ideas were strengthened in some quarters, and LaGuardia again led the crusade against them. The *Denver Post* recognized his leadership of the movement against immigration restriction when it editorialized bitterly, "It goes against the grain of real Americans to have anybody by the name of LaGuardia telling the American people how to run their government." LaGuardia, suggested the *Post*, should go back where his ancestors came from. "New York has been a cesspool into which immigrant trash has been dumped for so long that it can scarcely be considered American any more." Foreign affairs did not seem terribly important to people struggling for the basics of food, clothing, and shelter, but when they intruded, LaGuardia spoke out on behalf of "his favorite ideas: peace, disarmament, and removing the profits from war."[13]

Zinn's last chapter in *LaGuardia in Congress*, before he attempted an overall appraisal of LaGuardia's congressional career, is ironically entitled "Political Defeat and Moral Victory, 1932–1933." And it is true: "After his win in the 1930 election, LaGuardia did not imagine that he would wage only one more congressional campaign or that his defeat in 1932 would usher in an era of victory for all the proposals he had been making throughout the decade."[14] In his final appraisal of LaGuardia, Zinn emphasizes that he was "a vital link between the Progressive and New Deal eras." But he also insists that ideologically LaGuardia went even beyond the New Deal. Unlike many of his fellow progressives, he was never an isolationist; he backed the League of Nations and various peace and disarmament conferences. Though he apparently never read Marx and was not a member of any organized socialist movement, "when his congressional colleagues accused LaGuardia of being a socialist, they were close to the truth." And he did show, says Zinn, "a certain pride in being considered a radical."[15] One begins to sense that Zinn is identifying with LaGuardia here, and to sense the direction of some of his subsequent work. This is especially manifest in his conclusion to the book:

> If, out of all this, there is one quality which may be singled out as crucial, it is perhaps that LaGuardia combined a profound sense of social responsibility with an irrepressible individualism. He was a rebel, but not a nihilist, a man who smashed wildly through party and organizational walls, but only to follow his principles wherever they led. In a time of conformity and irresponsibility, when so many minds are imprisoned by rigid loyalties and so many others luxuriating in the freedom of indecision, the recollection of LaGuardia's untamed but conscience-stricken spirit seems a precious gift to those in our generation who will receive it.[16]

Still, Zinn's work on LaGuardia was close enough to the mainstream of the historical profession as of 1959 to secure some very good reviews—and, not to be forgotten, it won an award from the establishment American Historical Association. The reviewer for the *Saturday Review* said that Zinn had "meticulously reviewed" LaGuardia's congressional years, and produced "an admirable book, lively, objective, nostalgic." And the reviewer for the *American Political Science Review* quoted Zinn's conclusion (see above) and suggested this might account for the high level of interest in LaGuardia at the time—a musical comedy entitled "Fiorello" was running on Broadway, and several books had been published. Zinn's was referred to as "exceedingly well written," "highly readable," and "well documented."[17]

One of those other books on LaGuardia, however, presented an interesting situation affecting the reception of Zinn's. Several publications, including the *Bookmark*, the *Nation*, the *Political Science Quarterly*, and, interestingly, the *American Historical Review* (published by the American Historical Association, which had awarded Zinn's volume second place for the Beveridge Award), reviewed Zinn's book jointly with Arthur Mann's *LaGuardia: A Fighter against His Times, 1882–1933.*[18] It was, of course, the volume Leuchtenburg had warned Zinn about when he was considering LaGuardia for his dissertation topic. And Zinn's book usually suffered by comparison with Mann's.

Fred J. Cook wrote the review of Mann and Zinn for the *Nation*. Suggesting that "history seems to be repeating itself," Cook quotes Mann on the 1920s and suggests the words could apply equally well to the 1950s: "America was indeed run by boobs, bigots, idiots, and hypocrites. The only recourse for a man who really cared was dissent, exposure, and ridicule." Thus, LaGuardia. But when Cook compares Zinn's book on LaGuardia with Mann's, he clearly prefers Mann's. Zinn's book, focusing almost entirely on the record of issues and debates, seems to Cook "one-dimensional." While Zinn's *LaGuardia in Congress* is just as well researched as Mann's *LaGuardia*, "it lacks the bounce and the flavor of The Little Flower [LaGuardia's nickname], something that Mr. Mann conveys so well."[19]

Wallace S. Sayre, a political scientist at Columbia where Zinn had initially produced his volume on LaGuardia (though in history), reviewed Zinn—and Mann—in the pages of the *Political Science Quarterly*. Once again, the reviewer liked Mann's work better than Zinn's. Mann had produced "one of the best political biographies of the decade," Sayre insisted. And he was not terribly impressed with Zinn's claim that LaGuardia was "the herald of a new kind of progressivism," not only preparing the way for Roosevelt's New Deal but moving beyond it. "These are larger claims than Arthur Mann makes for LaGuardia; and, while Mr. Zinn presents his case persuasively, the more modest judgment is the more convincing."[20]

The *American Historical Review* selected the distinguished historian of the Populist era John D. Hicks, of the University of California at Berkeley, to review Zinn's first publication effort. He liked it, and emphasized the contribution it made toward understanding LaGuardia as "a significant link in the Progressive chain." Interestingly, and perhaps in contrast to Sayre's judgment, Hicks considered Zinn's book "a trifle more restrained and professorish [than Mann's], as becomes a prize-winning AHA product." Still, he said, it was "sprightly and reads easily." Both Mann and Zinn had clearly done "indefatigable research," especially in the LaGuardia papers.[21]

Zinn's word of thanks, in the preface to *LaGuardia in Congress,* to his Spelman College students "for making life interesting" is an important one, and helps transition to his next major focus in his writing, and his life: the South and the civil rights movement.

Zinn remembers vividly (and beautifully) that when he and his family arrived in Atlanta in 1956, it was a hot and rainy night. "We were in a different world, a thousand miles from home, a universe removed from the sidewalks of New York," he puts it in his memoir. "Here was a city thick with foliage, fragrant with magnolias and honeysuckle. The air was sweeter and heavier. The people were blacker and whiter; through the raindrops on the windows they appeared as ghosts gliding through the darkness."[22]

The next two years Zinn acknowledges to have been "a time of difficult transition from one culture to another, North to South, white to black." The family found out that landlords in white neighborhoods in Atlanta were none too anxious to rent to them when they found out Zinn was teaching in a "nigra college." So they found a small house in a white working-class neighborhood in Decatur, at the eastern edge of Atlanta. There, he remembers, neighbors tended to be quite friendly even after they found out where he was teaching. Indeed, after six months or so, the Zinns even dared to invite black friends to their house, and no one in the neighborhood said a word. "It was a relatively quiet time in the South," Zinn recalls, "between the Montgomery bus boycott and the 1960 sit-ins, but all sorts of things were simmering beneath the surface, ready to explode."[23] The same was true at Spelman. "I soon learned that beneath my students' politeness and decorum there was a lifetime of suppressed indignation." So it did not take Zinn long to get involved. "I knew that it was wrong for me, a white teacher, to lead the way," he says. "But I was open to anything my students wanted to do, refusing to accept the idea that a teacher should confine his teaching to the classroom when so much was at stake outside it."[24] That approach to teaching/involvement would prevail throughout Zinn's career.

Just a few months into his Spelman tenure, Zinn and a group of his students decided to visit a session of the Georgia state legislature. Apparently they had planned no action, just a learning experience watching the legislature go about its business. But when they saw the small section marked "colored" at the side of the visitors' gallery, which of course they should have expected, something clicked. The students conferred and decided to ignore the signs and sit in the main section, which was quite empty. The members of the Georgia House were debating a bill on fishing rights, but when they saw the black students sitting in the white gallery, panic erupted. The Speaker of the House "seemed to be having an apoplectic fit." He took control of the microphone and shouted something like, "You nigras get over to where you belong! We got segregation in the state of Georgia." Other members of the legislature were shouting up at the group as well.

Police appeared. "Students were not yet ready, in those years before the South rose up en masse, to be arrested," recounts Zinn. "We decided to move out into the hall and then come back into the 'colored' section, me included." Then things changed. Or, as Zinn puts it, "What followed was one of those strange scenes that the paradoxes of the racist, courteous South often produced." A guard came up to Zinn, perceiving him to be in charge of the group, "apparently not able to decide if I was 'white' or 'colored,'" and inquired where they were from. Zinn told him. A moment later, the Speaker again took the microphone, but this time said, "The members of the Georgia state legislature would like to extend a warm welcome to the visiting delegation from Spelman College."[25]

Next, Zinn and his students—specifically the Social Science Club, of which he was the faculty sponsor—decided to intentionally take on a project involving social change. A student suggested trying to break down the segregation of Atlanta's public libraries. And they did it! Zinn tells the story well, and then concludes: "I have told about the modest campaign to desegregate Atlanta's libraries because the history of social movements often confines itself to the large events, the pivotal moments." He is correct, of course. Typically, surveys of the history of the civil rights movement limit themselves to the Supreme Court decision in the *Brown* case, the Montgomery bus boycott, the march on Washington, the Civil Rights Act of 1964, the Voting Rights Act of 1965, and so on. "Missing from such histories are the countless small actions of unknown people that led up to those great moments," insists Zinn. "When we understand this, we can see that the tiniest acts of protest in which we engage may become the invisible roots of social change."[26] That emerges as a central point in Howard Zinn's philosophy.

It was out of this background, the South and the civil rights movement, that Zinn's next two books emerged. *The Southern Mystique* and *SNCC: The New Abolitionists* were both published in 1964.

Actually, Zinn had written an article entitled "The Southern Mystique" for the winter 1963–64 issue of the magazine the *American Scholar*. Angus Cameron, an editor with the publishing company of Alfred A. Knopf, apparently read it, liked it, and asked Zinn to develop it into a book.[27] The result was *The Southern Mystique*, published, as noted, in 1964. It was Zinn's second book; it was by no means a standard historical work. Rather it was an interpretive essay on the South and its history and culture. Interestingly, Zinn did not even mention it when asked about his books that he was proudest of—but neither did he mention it with some of his books he had serious reservations about.[28] Perhaps it is not central to understanding his work as a historian. Still, it is an interesting little volume.

It is revealing that the book is dedicated to Fannie Lou Hamer, of civil rights movement fame, and that included in the acknowledgments is the phrase: "To my students at Spelman College and the student movement in Atlanta, without whom this book could not have been written." A rather lengthy introduction explains much about the book. "Perhaps the most striking development in the South," begins Zinn, "is not that the process of desegregation is under way but that the mystique with which Americans have always surrounded the South is beginning to vanish." Having lived for seven years inside "what is often thought to be the womb of the South's mystery: the Negro community of the Deep South," admitting that the "Southern mystique hovered nearby even on yellow spring afternoons when we talked quietly to one another in the classroom," Zinn is prepared to say that "the mystique is dissolving, for me, and for others." The South has not lost its fascination, Zinn acknowledges, but he insists it is no longer mysterious.[29]

To explain this, says Zinn, it is necessary to talk about the two groups that have been at the center of the mystery, the whites and blacks of the Deep South. The mystery of the white southerner, Zinn suggests, comes from "a trait that he is presumed to possess in quantity and quality sharply distinct from that of everyone else. That trait is race prejudice." We should not get hung up on causation, because to do so baffles and immobilizes people. "Stop fumbling with the *cause* of prejudice except for those aspects on which we can operate." Atlanta, like the South, had basically said "never" to integration. Yet in the past seven years, the buses, public libraries (thanks in part to Zinn and his students), rail and bus terminals, department store cafeterias, public schools, colleges, some hotels, the police and fire departments, the parks, the county committee of the Democratic Party, even the Senate of the Georgia legislature, had all integrated. The key, concluded Zinn, to "the traditionally mysterious vault of prejudice locked inside the mind of the white Southerner," is that he cares, but not enough, or, to put it another way, "although he cares about segregation, there are things he cares about *more*." Among those things that the white Southerner cared about more than segregation: "monetary profit, political power, staying out of jail, the approval of one's immediate peers, conforming to the dominant decision of the community." (One is reminded of the white officer on the ship with Zinn on the way to Europe in World War II who did not want to eat sitting next to a black man—but he did want to eat.) What was needed, then, was "to decide for each group of whites in the community which value is more important and to plan a web of multiple tactics—negotiation, boycott, lawsuit, voting, demonstration—that will effectively invoke these priorities." In short, "It's time to clear from our minds that artificial and special mystique, so firmly attached to the Southern white, that has too long served as a rationale for pessimism and inaction."[30]

But what of the blacks? "There is a strange and damnable unanimity among segregationists, white liberals, and Negroes on one fervent belief," acknowledges Zinn, and that is "the mystery of *negritude*—the irreducible kernel, after all sociological peelings, of race difference." But there is "a magical and omnipotent dispeller of the mystery," insists Zinn, and that is simply contact. "Contact—but it must be massive, unlike those 'integrated' situations in the North, and it must be equal, thus excluding maid-lady relationships of the South—destroys the man-made link between physical difference and behavior." For race consciousness is hollow, according to Zinn; "its formidable-looking exterior is membrane-thin and is worn away by simple acts of touch, the touching of human beings in contact that is massive, equal, and prolonged." The specialness of the southern mystique vanishes, then, says Zinn, approaching one of his basic points in this book, "when one sees that whites and Negroes behave only like human beings, that the South is but a distorted mirror image of the North." We are both powerful and free enough "to retain only as much of the past as we want. We are all magicians. We created the mystery of the South, and we can dissolve it."[31]

In the first part of *The Southern Mystique*, entitled "Is the Southern White Unfathomable?" Zinn insists on reversing the usual mode of thinking about which comes first, thinking or acting. We now have enough actual experience of social change in the South, he says, to say confidently that "you *first* change the way people behave, by legal or extralegal pressures of various kinds, in order to transform that environment which is the ultimate determinant of the way people think." It was also surely one of the first times the civil rights movement was referred to as the "Second Reconstruction" when Zinn spoke of the "Second Reconstruction now transforming the South." He insisted, though, that there were two basic differences from the first: this time blacks were the leaders and whites the followers; and this time, except in rare instances such as Little Rock, Arkansas, and Oxford, Mississippi, "change is not coming at the point of bayonets but through a mammoth, internal convulsion within the South itself." Zinn spoke highly of famous historian C. Vann Woodward's pioneering work *The Strange Career of Jim Crow*, published originally in 1955. It was, he said, the most forceful historical attack on the notion that the South's racial mores were unchangeable. In his conclusion Zinn notes that he is being optimistic, "insistently optimistic."[32] That optimism was to become a guiding principle in his career and philosophy.

Part two, "The 'Mysterious' Negro," obviously argues that the Negro is not so mysterious after all. "The Negro will be inscrutable until we begin to scrutinize him." What Zinn calls for is integration, not just desegregation. "You have desegregation when the legal bars to racial contact are lifted," he explains. "You have integration when that contact actually takes place." He feels lucky, he says, that he has had the opportunity to work and to live over a period of years with his wife and family in a predominantly black community. "This kind of total immersion is not just educational, in the pallid sense of book learning; it is transforming, as real education should be." "A Negro seen casually at a distance is mainly a black person," Zinn suggests, while "a Negro *known* is a person with dozens of different characteristics, one of the least important of which is blackness." "Living together, working together, bring the fastest results in destroying race prejudice. And engaging in some common endeavor is an even more intensely productive experience." The sit-in movement is Zinn's major example. Things were changing, including at Spelman College. A poster headed "Young Ladies Who Can Picket, Please Sign Below" "combined perfectly the past and present of the Spelman girl." Martin Luther King Jr. himself, noted Zinn in one of the rare times he focused on a nationally known leader of the civil rights movement rather than the unknown legions, was the most famous and "a perfect example of the blending of the old and the new, of traditional Negro religion and modern philosophical thought, of emotion and intellect, of folk tradition and twentieth-century sophistication."[33]

Many would consider Zinn at his best when at his most personal. He had been "an observer, a friend, and an occasional participant" in the student movement, he said, picketing supermarkets, sitting in, desegregating the gallery of the state legislature, picketing the state capitol, marching downtown in a mass parade. But he had been arrested only once in Atlanta, and it had nothing to do with any of those actions. It was in January 1960, he recalls, a cold night, when, driving off the campus, he stopped to give a ride to a student going in the same direction. She was an honor student, recently returned from a year of study in Paris, France. Let Zinn pick up the story:

> We talked, rode on. I parked the car and we were still chatting when powerful headlights swept through the car. A patrol car stopped near us. Two white policemen ordered us out of the car and into the back seat of theirs. "If you're arresting us, what is the charge?" I asked. The older patrolman

turned to face us from the front seat. "You sittin' in a car with a nigger gal an' wantin' to know what's the charge?" We were taken to the police station and booked, charged with "disorderly conduct."[34]

The incident, concludes Zinn, "reveals the traditional mystique of race consciousness that the South is just beginning to overcome: a mystique that expresses itself in the rage which inflames some white Southerners who see a white and a Negro together as friends, a rage," Zinn predicted (perhaps too optimistically?), "which will fade as massive and equal contact becomes a fact in the Deep South." After recounting the follow-up to the story, including the release of Zinn and the student from jail and the dropping of the charges, Zinn concluded, "It was a Kafka-like episode, a relic perhaps for future historians."[35] Indeed.

Part three of *The Southern Mystique* is entitled "Albany, Georgia: Ghost in the Cage," and is an excellent example of both Zinn's personal involvement and his storytelling ability. "Nowhere does the South envelop you so completely as in the Black Belt," Zinn begins. All around Albany, Georgia, as in most of such states as Mississippi, Alabama, South Carolina, and Louisiana, "the mystique of the South is overwhelming, stifling, depressing." Zinn tells of a nineteen-year-old boy showing a burn on his arm and blood on his shirt from shotgun blasts that had grazed him and wounded another voter-registration worker near Albany; the young man asked wryly, "Why is Hollywood still producing Westerns instead of Southerns?" In December 1961 Zinn was drawn directly into the situation in Albany when he received a phone call from the research director for the Southern Regional Council, an Atlanta organization specializing in gathering data on race relations in the South. "You know there's trouble in Albany and we want a report on it," Zinn was told. "We'd like you to go down there for us. You see, we couldn't decide whether to send a white or a Negro, so we compromised." Says Zinn: "We both laughed, and I agreed to go."[36] Thus began Zinn's adventure in Albany, which provided the basis for his report, and this part of his book.

Again and again in Albany, white people made such statements to Zinn as "Albany has always had good race relations," or "Our colored folks have been satisfied," or "We have made considerable progress." Observes Zinn: "In a nation with ten thousand history teachers, memories remain poor; the same statements were made in Montgomery before the bus boycott, in Atlanta before the sit-ins, and all through the South in the days of slavery." Again showing his unorthodox approach to history—and moving toward a devastating critique of the federal government—Zinn raises the question

"Who is responsible for the atmosphere of brutality which pervades Albany, Georgia, and its surrounding Black Belt counties?" He did not mean, he clarified, "who is to blame for the long *history* of injustice in that area; for historians it is of scholarly interest, for others it is an empty exercise, to fix the responsibility for past sins." Instead, he is speaking of responsibility for their *continuance*: "When I speak of 'blame,' the intent is not to gain emotional satisfaction at finding a culprit, but to try to locate a focal point for constructive action in the future." That is to say, the central question should be "On whom will the pressure of indignation bring the maximum in results?" Of all the possibilities—blacks, whites, the local political power structure—"it is the government of the United States that maintains the widest gap between verbal declaration and action, between potential and performance." The government has not lived up to its moral pretensions, nor has it lived up to the Constitution. Noting that some people had begun comparing John F. Kennedy to Lincoln the Great Emancipator himself before Kennedy's assassination, Zinn suggests that to the blacks of Albany he seemed a reluctant emancipator indeed. The executive branch of government, he said, had retreated before the "Southern mystique," and had "abrogated a responsibility which was written into the Constitution by the Founding Fathers, and underlined in blood by the Civil War: to enforce constitutional rights in every corner of the Union, with all the ingenuity and, if necessary, the power, at its command." Ever since "Northern and Southern politicians ended Radical Reconstruction by a political deal in 1877," Zinn asserted, that responsibility simply has not been fulfilled in the Deep South. Indeed, when the passive role of the federal government in the Albany crisis did finally come to an end, it involved the Department of Justice initiating a large-scale criminal prosecution against eight black leaders and one white student in the Albany movement itself! Zinn said it reminded him of the World War I–era case involving government censorship of a motion picture: *The United States v. "The Spirit of '76."*[37] Zinn concluded:

> If there is a quality of harshness in my estimate of a federal government so often lauded by liberals, it may come from some of the things I heard and saw in the Albany area. I recall particularly driving from dirt road onto dirt road deep into the cotton and peanut land of Lee County to talk to James Mays, a teacher and farmer. He showed me the damage done by 30 bullets which hours before, in the middle of the night, had been fired through doors and windows and had crashed into the walls around the heads of 19 sleeping persons, most of them children. With the coming of dawn, he had quickly lettered a sign of protest and stood with it out on the

main road to Leesburg in front of a Negro school. It was clear that, although he was a member of a nation whose power stretched around the globe and into space, James Mays was on his own.[38]

"The South as a Mirror," the final part of *The Southern Mystique*, is in some ways the most interesting. For it is here that Zinn directly challenges the idea of southern exceptionalism. Instead of being different, Zinn argues, the South "is really the *essence* of the nation," containing, "in concentrated and dangerous form, a set of characteristics which mark the country as a whole." In short: "Those very qualities long attributed to the South as special possessions are, in truth, *American* qualities, and the nation reacts emotionally to the South precisely because it subconsciously recognizes itself there."[39] The conclusion, in which he summarizes the argument—and, of course, lists the characteristics of which he speaks—is worth quoting at length:

> Let me go back over my argument. The South is everything its revilers have charged, and more than its defenders have claimed. It is racist, violent, hypocritically pious, xenophobic, false in its elevation of women, nationalistic, conservative, and it harbors extreme poverty in the midst of ostentatious wealth. The only point I have to add is that the United States, as a civilization, embodies all of those same qualities. That the South possesses them with more intensity simply makes it easier for the nation to pass off its characteristics to the South, leaving itself innocent and righteous.
>
> In any truth which is knotted and complex, we can choose what strand we want to grasp. To pick out the South has the advantage of focusing attention on what is worst; but it has the disadvantage of glossing over the faults of the nation. It is particularly appropriate in this time, when the power of the United States gives it enormous responsibility, to focus our critical faculties on those qualities which mark—or disfigure—our nation. With this approach, the South becomes not damnable, but marvelously useful, as a mirror in which the nation can see its blemishes magnified, so that it will hurry to correct them. In effective psychotherapy, the patient is at first disturbed by self-recognition, then grateful for the disclosure. It is the first step toward transformation, and in the 1960s, this nation, with its huge potential for good, needs to take another look in the mirror. We owe this to ourselves, and to our children.[40]

Interestingly, it is not until the end of the book, in his brief "Bibliographical Notes," that Zinn describes *The Southern Mystique* as "primarily a speculative essay based on personal experience." Also, in giving a few of his sources, he describes Richard Hofstadter's *The American Political Tra-*

dition as "one of the great books written by this generation of historians," and admits that "what started as a germ of an idea based on observation and experience became strengthened as I began to read the literature of post-Freudian psychology and certain works of sociology and history." Among the works listed, specifically for the first part of the book, are those by Karl Mannheim, Robert K. Merton, Arnold M. Rose, Harry Stack Sullivan, Herbert Marcuse, Gordon Allport, and finally historians Stanley Elkins, C. Vann Woodward, and Dewey Grantham.[41]

Some reviewers of *The Southern Mystique* took note of Zinn's efforts at social science theorizing—and were not impressed. Charles A. Raines, for example, writing in the *Library Journal*, said that one would have hoped Zinn "could have relegated more substantial evidence to his thesis, and that he did not so often escape from or obscure his argument in generalities and the jargon of professional sociologists." Raines felt Zinn's "factual reportage is far more accurate and effectual than his sociological speculation." Finally, Raines suggested that Zinn's contention that southern characteristics were merely national characteristics writ large "only goes to prove that he is not a Southerner—that he has not experienced the Southern sun from the time of his birth, nor the Southern sense of guilt and defeat as did Faulkner and many others. If he had, the problem would appear far more difficult and frustrating."[42] Interestingly, a very brief note in the children's section of the *Library Journal* differed somewhat, suggesting that Zinn's "thoughtful presentation of the thesis that the ills of the South are symptomatic of a national prejudice is provocative reading for young people seeking to understand today's problems."[43] Ralph McGill, in the pages of the *Saturday Review*, was quite receptive to Zinn's position that it is appropriate to emphasize result over cause, and also said, "Mr. Zinn is quite right in saying that the mystique with which the South has so long surrounded itself is beginning to vanish."[44]

Perhaps significantly, *The Southern Mystique* was not reviewed in any of the standard journals of the historical profession. Easily the most interesting and important review it received, then, was the one written by noted African American literary figure, author of 1952's National Book Award–winner *Invisible Man*, Ralph Ellison. It appeared in the pages of *Book Week* (published by the *New York Herald Tribune*). The headline refers to Zinn's book as a "bold tract"—"Only massive contact can dissolve the racial myth, a bold tract argues." But one wonders if Ellison wrote the headline. His review is thoughtful, heavily philosophical, at times critical. Comparing Zinn to the carpetbaggers of the first Reconstruction, and his book to some of the important writings of that era, such as those of Charlotte Forten and Thomas Wentworth Higginson, was brilliant. While he disagreed with some of Zinn's procedures and conclusions, Ellison noted, he was "sympathetic with his attempt to do pragmatically what our best critical minds have failed even to recognize as important," that is, in the area of race relations specifically, to attempt to "forge, for himself at least, a fresh concept of man." Cleverly, and insightfully, Ellison wrote that "Howard Zinn is no Zen Buddhist; he is a passionate reformer, and his passion lends his book the overtones of symbolic action." Ellison wrote with apparent approval, "The assumption here is that social change is sparked by the concern of responsible individuals, and an overtone of individual salvation sounds throughout Mr. Zinn's book." He also felt Zinn's "rejection of the gradualists' assumption that a change in thinking must precede changes in behavior seems justified by the actual dynamics of recent social changes in the South." He felt he "must leave [it] to more qualified critics to assess the broader implications of Mr. Zinn's theoretical approach," but he was willing to say that he believed that Zinn's "effort to see freshly and act constructively is, despite all objections, overwhelmingly important." Perhaps ironically, one thing Ellison hit Zinn rather hard for was his "shrugging off the encumbrances of the past."[45]

Most readers of Ellison's review would probably not think he had been "overly critical," but he was concerned about that; his conclusion is worth quoting at length:

> If I seem overly critical of *The Southern Mystique*, it is by no means out of a lack of respect for its author and what he has attempted to do. His is an act of intellectual responsibility in an area that has been cast outside the range of intellectual scrutiny through our timidity of mind in the face of American cultural diversity. Mr. Zinn has not only plunged boldly into the chaos of Southern change but he has entered that maze-like and barely charted area wherein 20 million Negro Americans impinge upon American society, socially, politically, morally, and therefore, culturally. One needn't agree with Zinn, but one cannot afford not to hear him out. And once we read him—and we must read him with the finest of our attention—we can no longer be careless in our thinking about the Negro Revolution, for he makes it clear that it involves us all.[46]

For reasons to be explained further at a later point, Howard Zinn had essentially a year off to focus on his writing in 1963–64. The second book to emerge from that year—and from his experience of the South and the civil rights movement—was *SNCC: The New Abolitionists*, like *The Southern Mystique*, published in 1964.

"SNCC," of course, was the Student Nonviolent Coordinating Committee. Despite the word nonviolent in its name, SNCC was to become one of the most militant of the civil rights organizations. Zinn served for some time as an adult adviser to SNCC. His book, then, he admits freely, is not a history in a formal sense: "What I *am* attempting to do here is to catch a glimpse of SNCC people in action, and to suggest the quality of their contribution to American civilization." He made no pretension of distance—some SNCC people were his former students, many his friends. He considered these young people "the nation's most vivid reminder that there is an unquenchable spirit alive in the world today, beyond race, beyond nationality, beyond class. It is a spirit which seeks to embrace all people everywhere." Much of the book, he said, was based on firsthand information, "from being where SNCC people work, watching them in action, talking to them." But he had also done research of a more traditional type, including in the SNCC archives in Atlanta and the files of the Southern Regional Council. *SNCC* was dedicated to Ella Baker, described by Zinn as "more responsible than any other single individual for the birth of the new abolitionists as an organized group, and who remains the most tireless, the most modest, and the wisest activist I know in the struggle for human rights today."[47]

The historian especially is attracted to Zinn's title, and wants to know the basis of Zinn's comparison of the young radicals of SNCC in the 1960s to those who worked for the abolition of slavery in the pre–Civil War era. Zinn supplies that explanation throughout the book, but especially in his opening chapter, "The New Abolitionists." "For the first time in our history," he begins, "a major social movement, shaking the nation to its bones, is being led by youngsters." More a movement than an organization, he says, SNCC's youth "are clearly the front line of the Negro assault on the moral comfort of white America." To be with them in their work, he exclaimed, was "to feel the presence of greatness." All Americans owed them a debt for "releasing the idealism locked so long inside a nation that has not recently tasted the drama of a social upheaval," and for "making us look on the young people of the country with a new respect." Their greatness, according to Zinn, came from "their relationship to history." He estimated there were about 150 in SNCC by early 1964, and doubted there were ever that many dedicated abolitionists "who turned their backs on ordinary pursuits and gave their lives wholly to the movement."[48] Then, the heart of the matter:

These 150 . . . are the new abolitionists. It is not fanciful to invest them with a name that has the ring of history; we are always shy about recognizing the historic worth of events when they take place before our eyes, about recognizing heroes when they are still flesh and blood and not yet transfixed in marble. But there is no doubt about it: we have in this country today a movement which will take its place alongside that of the abolitionists, the Populists, the Progressives—and may outdo them all.[49]

Even if one feels that Zinn's prediction in 1964 was prophetic, and looks true from today's vantage point, it can still be seen in a passage such as this just how far he had moved with this book from mainstream historical writing. Indeed, he once again drew here from the works of social science theorists, specifically Erik Erikson. Noting that one condition of effective psychotherapy is that "the patient must begin to see himself as he really is," Zinn suggests that the country, "now forced by the young Negro to see itself through *his* eyes (an ironic reversal, for the Negro was always compelled to see himself through the eyes of the white man), is coming closer to a realistic appraisal of its national personality."[50]

Zinn certainly was able to see some substantial differences between the original abolitionists and the new ones of SNCC. The movement of the 1830s and 1840s had been led primarily by white New Englanders; the movement of the 1960s was led primarily by young southern blacks. The abolitionists of old mostly bombarded the South and the nation with words; the new abolitionists focused more on "physical acts of sacrifice." Modern mass communications, especially television, in some ways made the task of the new abolitionists easier, "for the nation, indeed the whole world, can *see* them, on the television screen or in newspaper photos—marching, praying, singing, *demonstrating* their message." Like the earlier abolitionists, the youth of SNCC "have a healthy disrespect for respectability; they are not ashamed of being agitators and troublemakers; they see it as the essence of democracy." But unlike them, the youth are not "middle-class reformers who became somehow concerned about others"; rather they "come themselves from the ranks of the victims," both because they are mostly black and because they are of working-class origin. Concluding his "New Abolitionists" chapter, Zinn emphasizes that the youth of SNCC are indeed radicals, that the word "revolution" occurs again and again in their speech, that though they "have no clear idea of a blueprint for a future society," they do "know clearly that the values of present American society—and this goes beyond racism to class distinction, to commercialism, to profit-seeking, to the setting of religious or national barriers against human contact—are not for them." "They are prepared to use revolutionary means against the old order," says Zinn, with obvious approval, including civil disobedience, demonstrations, nonviolent confrontation, and "direct action."[51]

Most of what Zinn does so effectively in *SNCC* is to string together an incredible number of powerful stories of the action at the cutting edge of the civil rights movement in the early to mid-1960s. We must limit the number of them here. John Peck, a participant in one of the "freedom rides," the eventually successful efforts to integrate interstate bus travel by the very act of traveling integrated on buses, tells of the arrival of his bus in Birmingham. He and several others were beaten severely. He awoke in an alleyway with blood flowing down his face. He was taken to a hospital, where he lay on an operating table for several hours while reporters plied him with questions and doctors took fifty-three stitches to close his head wounds. While waiting outside the hospital in the middle of the night for a friend to pick him up, he was told by police he must get off the street or be arrested for vagrancy. But when he went back into the hospital, a guard informed him that discharged patients were not permitted in the hospital. So he went back into the street. Fortunately, at that time, his friend arrived to pick him up.[52]

Perhaps the most effective stories to focus on here are the ones where Zinn himself was present. Both he and his wife, Roslyn, were present at SNCC headquarters in Greenwood, Mississippi, on an August night in 1963 when fifty-eight individuals, many of them teenagers, were released from jail. Obviously, they had been treated none too well. Said Zinn: "That night SNCC headquarters had the eerie quality of a field hospital after a battle." Eye problems from some dietary deficiency while jailed, an infected hand, a swollen foot—these were among the more obvious problems resulting from the fact that the youth had been denied medical attention while behind bars.[53]

Zinn's own obviously deep personal involvement perhaps lends credence to his speculations in a chapter entitled "The White Man in the Movement." The central question is: Can white people and black people truly live together as friends in the United States? Zinn's answer seems to be a cautious yes. The young people of SNCC, he insists, are proving it possible. "Never in the history of the United States has there been a movement where the lives, day by day, of Negro and white people are so entwined physically, intellectually, emotionally." But he acknowledges freely that it has not always gone smoothly. And he observes it to be easier with the young than with the old. There is no single correct path toward putting race behind us. It is easier to note some common mistakes. It is a mistake, for example, to think than one can forget completely about race— but also a mistake not to try. It is clearly a mistake "for a white person to play at being black," or to "romanticize the Negro, simply because in this period of our history, *he* is carrying the torch of American idealism." Zinn insists again here, as in *The Southern Mystique*, that "the key to a solution of the dilemma is contact—continued and massive contact among people of different races."[54]

Zinn also restates his criticism of the federal government. Noting that SNCC's chairman, John Lewis, was pressured into toning down his speech at the historic March on Washington in August 1963 because other civil rights leaders considered his criticism of the Kennedy administration unacceptable, Zinn firmly supports Lewis's views. "In literally thousands of instances," he insists, "Southern policemen and local officials have trampled on the Constitution with no interference, as if they were a law unto themselves, as if they were not in the United States, as if the Constitution did not apply to them, as if the power of the federal government was nonexistent." These things had happened openly, sometimes under the eyes of federal officials, yet the local authorities "have remained untouched by the law." This raises a broader theme that foreshadows one of Zinn's later books, *Declarations of Independence*. For there is another issue beyond race which is illumined by the civil rights struggle, and that is the problem of free expression in the United States. We have always assumed, writes Zinn, that because the First Amendment guarantees freedom of speech and press and peaceful assembly, "these are an iron-bound fact of national life." But it has not been so. Those who have "subjected the Bill of Rights to severe test" have often suffered: pacifists during World War I, Japanese Americans during World War II, Jehovah's Witnesses, Communists, and many others. "The rest of the country remained free mainly because it remained silent, or, when it spoke, stayed within acceptable limits." (Some might be reminded of the words of the 1970s song, "Know Your Rights," by the radical rock-'n'-roll band The Clash: "You have the right to free speech—as long, of course, as you're not dumb enough to actually try it!") Zinn concluded: "We are now learning that what is true in the South is also true, to a lesser extent, all over the country, that the guarantees of the Bill of Rights are often in the hands of the policeman, and that the national government offers the individual no effective protection against local abuse of the Constitution."[55]

Moving toward the conclusion of *SNCC: The New Abolitionists*, Zinn returned to the justification for his title. "Different from the old abolitionists in its predominantly Negro character, its greater reliance on action than words, its working from within the source of the evil rather than berating it from the outside," he acknowledged, still "SNCC retains the essence of what made for greatness in Garrison, Phillips, and their contemporaries." What was the essence? The answer is key to understanding the abolitionists, SNCC, and Zinn: "This is the recognition that agitation, however it offends one's friends and creates temporary strife, is indispensable to social progress as a way of breaking through an otherwise frozen status quo." Zinn even suggests that SNCC is "the closest thing we have in the United States to that militant mood of change which one finds in emerging nations abroad," and that "the nation should be grateful, because many of our mistakes in foreign policy might be corrected if we had a better understanding of the revolutionary spirit of Africa and Asia." In the case of both SNCC and those revolutionary movements, claims Zinn, what we have is "hungry, harried people" with "a militancy hard to purchase." "Also, such a movement is impatient with worries about ideology," for it "understands what it sees and feels—bread, land, a policeman's club, a friend's hand—and is impervious to sophisticated talk about doctrinal bogies."[56]

As with *The Southern Mystique*, the historical journals paid no attention to *SNCC: The New Abolitionists*. However, the most interesting review was by a person obviously very familiar with history and historians. Howard N. Meyer reviewed Zinn's book jointly with the important work on the Reconstruction era by Willie Lee Rose, *Rehearsal for Reconstruction: The Port Royal Experiment*, in the pages of *Book Week*. Meyer felt there was "an urgent necessity for the historians of today to assume a special responsibility in the field of race relations—not only in telling the truth about the past," as he felt Rose had done, but in "agitating for justice in the present," as he felt Zinn had done with his book on the Student Nonviolent Coordinating Committee. Meyer seemed to praise Zinn for his indictment of the U.S. Department of Justice, and concluded that "Professor Zinn's book is as valuable in dispelling illusions about the present as Mrs. Rose's is in respect to our myth-bound past."[57]

Ralph McGill jointly reviewed *The Southern Mystique* and SNCC for the *Saturday Review*. While he recognized Zinn as "a passionate idealist and partisan," and noted that one of his strengths was "an almost philosophic determination to express what is best about those whom he admires and those who are on his side," he also felt this led at times to "sentimentalizing and romanticizing"—in both books. And while he shared Zinn's admiration for the youth of SNCC, McGill felt it was "a little difficult to accept the author's conclusion that the federal government has been deliberately negligent in not using all its legal weapons. He generalizes too much."[58]

There is a logic to considering *The Southern Mystique* and *SNCC: The New Abolitionists* together—as McGill did—and at this point in our narrative of Howard Zinn's life and writings. For they both so clearly grew out of his teaching at Spelman College and his involvement in the civil rights movement. But the fact is, he had already left Spelman before the two books appeared in print. To be blunt, he was fired. "I was fired with a year's pay," recalls Zinn with no apparent bitterness, "to sweeten the firing." He had tenure, after all, and was the head of the department, so the year's pay was also probably an effort "to legitimize what was being done." Still, he "was fired on twenty-four hours notice."[59]

He talks about his firing, and some of the events that led to it, in *You Can't Be Neutral on a Moving Train*. Partly it came out of the discontent of the "Spelman girls" with the "benevolent despotism" of Spelman president Albert Manley. One student had used that term in an editorial in the student newspaper and had been chastised by the president himself for doing so. Manley was Spelman's first black president, but according to Zinn a cautious, conservative man, uneasy with the militant new currents sweeping through black campuses. Zinn felt the student needed and deserved his support, so he wrote a long letter to Manley saying that in his classes he had been emphasizing "the need for independent thought, for courage in the face of repression, and that any administrative effort to discourage freedom of expression was a blow at all of the values crucial to liberal arts education." Perhaps not surprisingly, Manley did not respond. When five other faculty members wrote to him with similar concerns, he still did not respond.

Zinn wrote an article for the *Nation* in August 1960 entitled "Finishing School for Pickets," in which he noted that "the traditional Spelman emphasis on turning out 'young ladies' was being challenged, that the new-type Spelman student was to be found on the picket line, or in jail." He later learned that Manley resented the article. The next specific crisis came when Spelman alumna Marian Wright—she of "Young Ladies Who Can Picket" fame, later to become founder of the Children's Defense Fund—visited the campus and spoke to students about the importance of young people becoming a force for social change. Shortly thereafter, a group of students addressed a petition to the Spelman administration respectfully acknowledging Spelman's "productive past," but suggesting that the college was "not preparing today's woman to assume the responsibilities of today's rapidly changing world." They asked for "first steps," in Zinn's words, "to create a new atmosphere, a liberalizing of the rules, modernization of the curriculum, improvement of library facilities." President Manley was not happy. He called in the student leaders and berated them for their actions; he also refused to allow the student newspaper to print the petition.[60]

Matters came to a head in the spring of 1963, when the Social Science Club, of which Zinn was the faculty advisor, held a meeting with some two hundred students and a dozen faculty in attendance; the subject was "On Liberty at Spelman." A large number of vigorous complaints were aired. Manley was not present, and when Zinn suggested during a faculty meeting that he should listen to a tape of the meeting, he refused. Says Zinn: "It was becoming clear that he saw me as in instigator rather than simply a supporter of the protests." And further: "When students begin to defy established authority it often appears to besieged administrators that 'someone must be behind this,' the implication being that young people are incapable of thinking or acting on their own."

After the faculty meeting, Zinn went to see Manley, hoping to clear the air—their families now lived close together, they visited occasionally, "and our relations had been friendly if somewhat formal." But Zinn kept a journal in those days, and his entry on this meeting shows that it did not go well. Manley kept wanting Zinn to be interested in students cheating on exams, stealing things in dormitories. Zinn said he was interested in those things, but there were more important things, including democracy on campus. Manley said at one point, "I have never been a crusader and I am not now." According to Zinn's journal: "At the end of the meeting I said, you put your finger on the heart of it when you said you aren't a crusader. Perhaps I am somewhat. But whatever we are, shouldn't we want to turn out students who have something of the crusader in them? No response." In April there was a testimonial dinner in honor of Manley's tenth year at Spelman. The speaker, the chairman of the Spelman trustees, perhaps gave a hint of what was coming when he said, again according to Zinn's journal: "A president is like a gardener—he must make sure things grow in their place—and if anything grows where it's not supposed to grow he must get rid of it."[61]

Two months later, in June, the semester over, students gone, the Zinn family was packed and ready to head north for the summer. Zinn asked them to wait for a moment while he checked his mail one last time. There was a letter from the Office of the President informing him that his appointment would not be renewed, that he was relieved of all duties as of June 30; the check for one year's salary was enclosed. Zinn was shocked, he recalls. "Despite the conflict, which had become intense, I had not expected this." Younger faculty tended to support Zinn, including Staughton Lynd, destined himself to become one of the important "New Left" historians, referred to by Zinn as "our campus neighbor and my departmental pal." Veteran faculty seemed hesitant to speak up. Some faculty mounted a campaign to reverse Manley's decision, but he was unbending. Says Zinn: "To visiting delegations he gave the reason he had not put in the letter. I was 'insubordinate.' (It was true, I suppose.)" Zinn considered fighting the decision. He talked to a lawyer and the American Association of University Professors.[62] Ultimately, he decided not to fight it. His reflections on that are interesting and worth quoting at length:

> By this time I was acutely conscious of the gap between law and justice. I knew that the letter of the law was not as important as who held the power in any real-life situation. I could sue, but the suit would take several years and money I didn't have. The A.A.U.P. [American Association of University Professors] would investigate, and some years later would issue a report citing Spelman College for violating my academic freedom, but this would mean little. I soon concluded that I did not want to tie up my life with this fight. In doing so, I was reluctantly bowing to reality. "The rule of law" in such cases usually means that whoever can afford to pay lawyers and can afford to wait is the winner, and "justice" does not much matter.[63]

That may sound somewhat cynical to some readers, but Zinn's final assessment of his Spelman years is anything but, largely because of his students. They, he said, had made his Spelman years "a loving, wonderful time." "Watching them change in those few years, seeing their spirit of defiance to established authority, off and on the campus, suggested the extraordinary possibilities in all human beings, of any race, in any time." This seems to reveal what is really important to Zinn, at least some of the things that are really important to him. And it also seems to suggest his optimism, a central element of his philosophy. He was even able, in retrospect, to inject a note of humor into the story of his firing. He quoted one of the many students who came to his support upon learning of his leaving Spelman. She wrote to President Manley of Zinn's unquestioned competence, but further said that he was "admired, respected, and loved by all of the Spelman students. . . . This man is not just a teacher, he is a friend to the students. He is someone that all students feel free to approach. . . . No person is insignificant to him." Noted Zinn, parenthetically, after that glowing praise: "Being fired has some of the advantages of dying without its supreme disadvantage. People say extra-nice things about you, and you get to hear them."[64]

Another advantage of being fired, in Zinn's case, was that it gave him time to focus on other things. The months following his dismissal from Spelman were some of the most intense in terms of his involvement in the civil rights movement, particularly with SNCC. But, as he said elsewhere, matter-of-factly, after briefly relating the story of his firing, "So, I had a year to write."[65] Zinn has always seemed to consider it natural to balance different activities, to keep up a schedule that would look impossible to most people. Two of the books to come from that "year to write" were *The Southern Mystique* and *SNCC: The New Abolitionists*. Another was *New Deal Thought*.

New Deal Thought was Zinn's fourth book, but his first editing project. One might be tempted to think that it was a follow-up to his first book on LaGuardia, but Zinn notes that it was not deliberately so; indeed, it was almost, he says, "an accident." He was leaving a meeting of the American Historical Association, he thinks in Washington, D.C., and found himself in the same cab going to the airport as Leonard Levy, another historian. They introduced themselves. Levy asked, "Didn't you win a Beveridge Prize for the book on LaGuardia?" Zinn acknowledged that he had, and Levy proceeded to inform him that he and Alfred Young were editing a series of volumes for the Bobbs Merrill Company, the American Heritage Series, and were looking for someone to do the volume on the New Deal. "Since you did LaGuardia, this should be a natural," Levy suggested. "So," says Zinn, "I agreed."[66]

Zinn does not regard *New Deal Thought* as one of his favorites among his fifteen books. Partly that seems to be because it was an edited volume rather than an authored one, but mostly it seems to be because "it's one of the few books I did which was sort of commissioned rather than me deciding I was going to write this kind of book," and "when you write something that was on somebody else's demand, it's not something that comes out of your powerful desire, it's probably not as good." But he did still regard it as "moderately useful," or maybe even "a valuable collection," and he was fond enough of his introduction for the volume as "a critique of the New Deal from a left-wing point of view," that he later reprinted it in his important 1970 volume, *The Politics of History* (significantly entitled "The Limits of the New Deal"). When it was suggested to him that the only problem with *New Deal Thought* was "There's not as much of you in it," he responded, "Exactly."[67]

But there is plenty of Zinn in that introduction. Indeed, editors Levy and Young noted in their foreword that although the book was about the 1930s, and drawn from the material of that era, "it is also a book for our own time, assembled by an editor who believes that the past should 'speak wisely to our present needs.'"[68]

Zinn insisted that though the New Deal's "accomplishments were considerable enough to give many Americans the feeling they were going through a revolution," while they "successfully evaded any one of a number of totalitarian abysses into which they might have fallen," and it is therefore not surprising that it "left a glow of enthusiasm, even adoration, in the nation at large," still, "when it was over, the fundamental problem remained—and still remains—unsolved: how to bring the blessings of immense natural wealth and staggering productive potential to every person in the land." When the reform energies of the New Deal began to wane around 1939, and the depression was over, "the nation was back to its normal state: a permanent army of unemployed; twenty or thirty million poverty-ridden people effectively blocked from public view by a huge, prosperous, and fervently consuming middle class; a tremendously efficient yet wasteful productive apparatus." It was "efficient because it could produce limitless supplies of what it decided to produce, and wasteful because what it decided to produce was not based on what was most needed by society but on what was most profitable to business." What the New Deal did, concluded Zinn, "was to refurbish middle-class America, which had taken a dizzying fall in the depression, to restore jobs to half the jobless, and to give just enough to the lowest classes (a layer of public housing, a minimum of social security) to create an aura of good will."[69]

Zinn himself acknowledges that his is a rather harsh estimate of New Deal achievements, but explains that it "derives from the belief that the historian discussing the past is always commenting—whether he realizes it or not—on the present"; because the historian is presumably a part of a "morally responsible public," his commentary "should consider present needs at the expense, if necessary, of old attachments." There is no use in debating "interpretations" of the New Deal today, says Zinn, for "we can no longer vote for or against Roosevelt. We can only affect the world around us." Although it is now the 1960s, not the 1930s, "some among us live very high, and some live very low, and a chronic malaise of lost opportunities and wasted wealth pervades the economic air." In short: "It is for today, then, that we turn to the thinking of the New Deal period."[70]

New Deal Thought does indeed contain a substantial amount of "the thinking of the New Deal period." It is extensive, and balanced. All the big names have excerpts from their work presented here, including Thurman Arnold, Henry Wallace, Rexford Tugwell, David Lilienthal, Harry Hopkins, Harold Ickes, Frances Perkins, John Maynard Keynes, and of course Franklin D. Roosevelt himself. Also included are some of those who thought the New Deal was going too far, such as Walter Lippmann and Raymond Moley, and some of those who thought it was not going far enough, such as John Dewey, W. E. B. Du Bois, Norman Thomas, Lewis Mumford, and Carey McWilliams.

Zinn's introductory paragraphs for each selection are quite good, in the information they provide, and in their balance. One almost needs to know Zinn's values, and look for them, to find them in these brief blurbs—but then one can, for they have been stated forcefully in the introduction. Two examples will suffice. In the first, Zinn is introducing FDR's famous San Francisco Commonwealth Club speech from September 23, 1932. This speech, Zinn acknowledges, "was the most daring in its exposition of a new economic and social philosophy." But he then notes that it was written by Adolf A. Berle, with some assistance from Rexford Tugwell, that Roosevelt never saw it until he opened it on the lectern, and that it "stretched Roosevelt's philosophy to its boldest limits," as evidenced by the fact that later in the campaign Roosevelt became increasingly "cautious and conservative," clearly "more concerned about winning the election than about laying down a comprehensive liberal philosophy." Somewhat ironic, then, that this speech "sounded that chord of idealism and fire which, to all later followers of the New Deal, represented the essence of the Roosevelt creed."[71]

In the second example, Zinn is introducing Robert C. Weaver's "The New Deal Is for the Negro." Obviously, this is an issue Zinn cares about passionately. He acknowledges there were "unmistakable overtures by the New Deal to the Negro." Certainly Eleanor Roosevelt made her sympathies clear, and Secretary of the Interior Harold Ickes appointed blacks to important posts in his department. "Most important, millions of poverty-stricken Negroes benefitted from the relief program, WPA, TVA, public housing, and other welfare measures of the New Deal, and as a result they turned, for the first time in American history, toward the Democratic Party." But Franklin D. Roosevelt himself, while "clearly sympathetic toward the Negro, . . . never gave the problem of civil rights the same high priority that he gave to economic recovery," and "not one civil rights law was passed while he was president."[72]

New Deal Thought apparently drew only two reviews. The one by H. M. Christman in the *Nation* was so brief and noncommittal as to be worthless to us here—though it did acknowledge the American Heritage Series as "excellent." The anonymous one in *Choice* was both more helpful and more critical. While the reviewer found Zinn's introduction "interesting and provocative," the conclusion was that Zinn, at times, "seems to be berating Roosevelt for not doing in the 1930s what needs to be done today."[73]

By the time *New Deal Thought* was published, in 1965, Zinn had already been teaching a year at Boston University.

NOTES

1. Howard Zinn, e-mail message to the author, December 3, 1996.

2. Ibid.

3. This paragraph is based on a letter to the author by William E. Leuchtenburg, dated August 31, 2000.

4. Howard Zinn, e-mail message to the author, January 4, 1997.

5. Howard Zinn, *LaGuardia in Congress* (Ithaca, N.Y.: Cornell University Press, 1959), pp. vii–ix.

6. Ibid., p. viii.

7. Ibid., pp. ix–x.

8. Ibid., pp. 1, 3, 15, 25–26, 34–35.

9. Ibid., pp. 51, 75.

10. Ibid., pp. 97, 107, 122, 135.

11. Ibid., pp. 138–39, 198.

12. Ibid., pp. 205–206.

13. Ibid., pp. 224, 226, 230, 235–37.

14. Ibid., p. 241.

15. Ibid., pp. 259, 269.

16. Ibid., p. 273.

17. August Heckscher, review of *LaGuardia in Congress* by Howard Zinn, *Saturday Review* 43 (February 13, 1960): 24; Belle Zeller, review of *LaGuardia in Congress* by Howard Zinn, *American Political Science Review* 54 (June 1960): 540.

18. Arthur Mann, *LaGuardia: A Fighter against His Times, 1802–1933* (Philadelphia: J. B. Lippincott Co., 1959).

19. Fred J. Cook, review of *LaGuardia in Congress* by Howard Zinn, *Nation* 190 (February 13, 1960): 149–50.

20. Wallace S. Sayre, review of *LaGuardia in Congress* by Howard Zinn, *Political Science Quarterly* 75 (June, 1960): 263–65.

21. John D. Hicks, review of *LaGuardia in Congress* by Howard Zinn, *American Historical Review* 65 (July 1960): 931–33. The review in *Bookmark* 19 (February 1960): 118, which also reviewed Zinn jointly with Mann, is anonymous, and so brief as to deserve no further comment.

22. Howard Zinn, *You Can't Be Neutral on a Moving Train: A Personal History of Our Times* (Boston: Beacon Press, 1994), p. 17.

23. Howard Zinn, e-mail message to the author, December 3, 1996.

24. Zinn, *You Can't Be Neutral on a Moving Train*, pp. 19–21.

25. Ibid., pp. 21–22.

26. Ibid., pp. 22–24.

27. Howard Zinn, e-mail message to the author, January 4, 1997.

28. Howard Zinn, interview, Boston, Mass., March 14, 1997.

29. Howard Zinn, *The Southern Mystique* (New York: Alfred A. Knopf, 1964), pp. 3–5.

30. Ibid., pp. 5–10.

31. Ibid., pp. 10–13.

32. Ibid., pp. 18–21, 36–37, 83.

33. Ibid., pp. 89, 97, 99, 104, 107, 127.

34. Ibid., p. 136.

35. Ibid., pp. 136–37.

36. Ibid., pp. 147, 149.

37. Ibid., pp. 151, 190, 197, 148, 204, 212.

38. Ibid., p. 213.

39. Ibid., p. 217.

40. Ibid., pp. 262–63.

41. Ibid., pp. 265–67.

42. Charles A. Raines, review of *The Southern Mystique* by Howard Zinn, *Library Journal* 89 (October 15, 1964): 3970.

43. Review of *The Southern Mystique* by Howard Zinn, *Library Journal* 89 (November 15, 1964): 4664.

44. Ralph McGill, review of *The Southern Mystique* by Howard Zinn, *Saturday Review* 48 (January 9, 1965): 52.

45. Ralph Ellison, review of *The Southern Mystique* by Howard Zinn, *Book Week* (*Sunday Herald Tribune*), November 8, 1964, pp. 1, 20, 22, 24. Notice that Ellison's review—more because of his prestige at that point than Zinn's?—was the lead review that week, beginning on and occupying the entire front page.

46. Ibid., p. 25. *The Southern Mystique* was also reviewed by T. H. Clancy in *America* 111 (October 24, 1964): 488, and noted briefly in *Nation* 199 (October 26, 1964): 284.

47. Howard Zinn, "A Note, and Some Acknowledgments," *SNCC: The New Abolitionists* (Boston: Beacon Press, 1964), n.p.

48. Ibid., pp. 1–3.

49. Ibid., p. 4.

50. Ibid., pp. 5–6.

51. Ibid., pp. 7–9, 13–15.

52. Ibid., pp. 42–43.

53. Ibid., p. 96.

54. Ibid., pp. 167–68, 181, 185.

55. Ibid., pp. 190, 192, 224–25.

56. Ibid., pp. 237, 270.

57. Howard N. Meyer, review of *SNCC: The New Abolitionists* by Howard Zinn, *Book Week* (*Sunday Herald Tribune*), December 6, 1964, pp. 18 and 20.

58. Ralph McGill, review of *SNCC: The New Abolitionists* by Howard Zinn, *Saturday Review* 48 (January 9, 1965): 52. Additional reviews or notices of *SNCC: The New Abolitionists* appeared in *America* 111 (October 24, 1964): 488 (by T. H. Clancy); *Christian Century* 81 (November 25, 1964): 1464 (by Allan R. Brockway); *Library Journal* 89 (October 1, 1964): 3766 (by Ruben F. Kugler); and *Nation* 199 (October 26, 1964): 284.

59. Howard Zinn, interview, Boston, Mass., March 14, 1997.

60. Zinn, *You Can't Be Neutral on a Moving Train*, pp. 37–39.

61. Ibid., pp. 39–41.

62. Ibid., pp. 41–43.

63. Ibid., p. 43.

64. Ibid., pp. 43–45.

65. Zinn, interview, March 14, 1997.

66. Howard Zinn, e-mail message to the author, January 4, 1997.

67. Zinn, interview, March 14, 1997.

68. Alfred Young and Leonard W. Levy, foreword to *New Deal Thought*, ed. Howard Zinn (Indianapolis: Bobbs Merrill, 1965), p. vii.

69. Howard Zinn, introduction to *New Deal Thought*, pp. xvi–xvii.

70. Ibid., p. xvii.

71. Ibid., p. 45.

72. Ibid., pp. 324–25.

73. H. M. Christman, review of *New Deal Thought*, ed. Howard Zinn, *Nation* 204 (April 17, 1967): 508; review of *New Deal Thought*, ed. Howard Zinn, *Choice* 4 (June 1967): 474.

THREE

YOU CAN'T BE NEUTRAL
ON A MOVING TRAIN
1964–1973

Howard Zinn's move from Spelman College, where he received his first full-time teaching appointment in 1956 and taught until 1963, to Boston University, where he began in 1964 and taught until his retirement in 1988, provides an excellent opportunity to take a closer look at Zinn the teacher. His teaching always stimulated strong responses, but by no means uniform ones; remember the two students mentioned in the preface who said, "The course is useless" and "Howard Zinn should be immortalized"—and they were responding to the same course! One of the strongest endorsements of Zinn as a teacher, in part because of who it comes from, was made on the dust jacket of his 1994 book, *You Can't Be Neutral on a Moving Train*. Pulitzer Prize–winning African American novelist (*The Color Purple*) Alice Walker said:

> What can I say that will in any way convey the love, respect, and admiration I feel for this unassuming hero who was my teacher and mentor, this radical historian and people-loving "trouble-maker," this man who stood with us and suffered with us? Howard Zinn was the best teacher I ever had, and the funniest. Here is a history and a history maker to give

us hope; especially the young to whom he has always committed so much
of his life.[1]

Marian Wright, now Marian Wright Edelman, another of Zinn's Spelman
students who went on to achieve prominence, spoke of him as the "most
influential teacher I've ever had."[2]

Zinn's own views on his teaching are perhaps even more revealing.
Remember that he had thought so highly of David Donald as a teacher in
part because he "was impressed by teachers who would allow themselves
to be moved by things that they were talking about." Certainly the evidence
is clear that this is a description of Zinn's teaching as well. Not long after
he was fired at Spelman, Zinn wrote to Boston University (BU), where he
"had once given a lecture on what was happening in the South." Speaking
specifically about the fact that his training was in history but he wound up
teaching more political science, especially at BU, he says, "They [BU]
invited me to join the political science department. They apparently didn't
care that I was really a historian, but I didn't care really what department I
was in, 'cause I knew I was going to teach the way I was going to teach
anyway." Clarifying further, he adds, "I always believed in playing a kind
of guerilla warfare with administration. No matter what the title of the
course was, no matter what the description in the catalog was, I would just
teach what I wanted to teach."[3]

Perhaps in part because of this attitude—but perhaps even more at
Spelman because of their need in such a small department for people to be
flexible in what they taught—Zinn taught remarkably diverse courses over
the years. At Spelman, he taught courses in American history, American
government, Russian history, Chinese history, and a course called Civil
Liberties. "And who knows what else?"[4] Russian and Chinese history?
Probably a surprise to many readers. But the fact is, Zinn was a postdoctoral fellow in East Asian Studies at Harvard University in 1960–1961, and,
in addition to his teaching at Spelman, served as director of Non-Western
Studies at Atlanta University in 1961–1962. At Boston, he regularly taught
a course that started out being called Civil Liberties, but was then changed
to Law and Justice in America; usually this was offered in the fall semester.
In the spring term, he would teach Introduction to Political Theory. He also
taught a senior seminar on Marxism and anarchism and a graduate seminar
entitled the Politics of History. Usually, then, his teaching load was six
hours, or two courses, per semester. Many teachers had to teach nine hours,
he said, but he had so many students that it allowed him to get away with

six. So many students? Between two hundred and four hundred usually, with the tendency toward the higher figure more and more frequently as he became better known over the course of his twenty-four years at BU.

He chose the rather vague title Law and Justice in America, he admitted freely, "so I could do whatever I wanted in there."[5] He agreed with many students that most textbooks were boring, so basically he never used one, in that course or any other. Instead, he would put together a selection of diverse readings. In Law and Justice in America, for example, he would use Arthur Miller's play *The Crucible* when talking about McCarthyism; *Johnny Got His Gun* by Dalton Trumbo or *Born on the Fourth of July* by Ron Kovic when dealing with war; Langston Hughes's poetry or Richard Wright's *Black Boy* when covering race; as well as excerpts from Emma Goldman's anarchist autobiography, Studs Terkel's oral histories, and Howell Rains's *My Soul Is Rested* (an oral history of the civil rights movement). In Introduction to Political Theory, Zinn would use the same eclectic, unorthodox approach, sometimes pairing Plato with Daniel Berrigan, for example, or Machiavelli with Henry Kissinger. In either of these courses, or any other, Zinn's approach to the classroom experience was similar:

> So, my style, as you know, is informal, and I came into class with notes, quotations, and papers. And I sort of tried to gauge the situation, and I let students interrupt me to ask questions, I let them know that they should, because my argument and my principle was if you can't speak when you want to speak, then you've really lost some of your freedom of speech. And so I always had discussion and always had questions, and I never ended the class with my talk. I deliberately chose classes that lasted an hour and a half, so I could give a forty-five minute lecture and have time for questions and discussion.[6]

It was an approach that worked, obviously, at least in terms of drawing power. Zinn became one of the most famous and popular professors at BU, so that as his enrollment approached four hundred, and there was no meeting place on the campus big enough to accommodate such a class, his classes would meet in a commercial theater down the street! "I always taught in the morning," he recalled, "and when my class was over, they would clean up the theater, and prepare it for the first moviegoers of the day."[7]

But did all of those students enroll because Zinn's courses were so good? Cynics would think not, and even one of Zinn's colleagues and friends in the political science department had his doubts. Asked about grading, specifically how he graded students when he had such large classes, Zinn replied, "I graded it, I did that with hate," then laughed. He explained, "I hated grading, that was the worst part." He did not give exams, but rather had his students write papers. A typical project consisted of getting involved with a community organization in the Boston area—one example was the American Civil Liberties Union—or creating an organization of their own—one example of this was a group of students who set up a bail fund and raised money and helped indigent prisoners who were spending extra time in jail only because they did not have the money to bail themselves out; another, a group who created a project helping veterans with Agent Orange claims. Then students would write a paper about their experience. Zinn also required students to keep journals, which supposedly consisted primarily of their day-to-day reactions to the class sessions and the readings. These, since they were each personal and individualistic, were less a burden to read than essay exams, for example, where they would all be writing the same thing.[8] Not exactly orthodox, but still perhaps not a problem—except that real traditionalists, of course, questioned Zinn's requiring students to get involved in organizations outside the university as a part of a university course.

The real problem came with the grades assigned. The colleague who spoke critically of Zinn here was Murray Levin, who suggested that Zinn's philosophical leanings toward anarchy showed themselves in his teaching. "He does not set standards," said Levin. "There is no discipline nor is there any emphasis on grades. He feels those students who care and want to learn, will, and those who do not, won't." Levin said that when Zinn first began teaching at Boston, he was known for assigning more work than anyone else in the department, "then suddenly he began accepting photographs instead of final exams. I've asked him about it a million times and I still don't understand why he is like that now," Levin concluded. "Maybe he has become more of an anarchist over the years." Zinn did not seem to care about what other professors thought. He even acknowledged some of the criticism. "I know a lot of people do not agree with my methods of teaching and I know a lot of students take my course as a gut," he once said candidly. "If they mean because it's easy, they're right. I don't give my students much work. I want them to obtain certain things from my courses. And it's not the facts that they retain—that's not important. It's the atmosphere, the mood they come away with. And that's what stays with them."[9] Elsewhere, Zinn attempted to justify his policy of never failing anyone in ideological terms. Because he "knew that grades were subjective," and did not "want to punish anybody," he "wanted students to know from the very beginning that you can't flunk Zinn's course," he said. Then: "I wanted the word to get around that even if they disagreed with me, I didn't want the threat of a bad grade to stand in the way of freedom of speech in the class. Word would get around, you're not going to get punished, you're not going to get a low grade because you disagree with Zinn."[10] But surely radicals in the academic world do not wish for radicalism to be equated with low (or no) academic standards. Human nature being what it is, student nature being what it is, word also must have gotten around that you could not flunk Zinn's course even if you did not work very hard. Indeed, even if you did not work at all, for asked what he did on those occasions when students simply did not do the work, he said he just gave them an incomplete.

Clearly, there are aspects of Zinn's teaching fated to be controversial at any university, in any era. We have seen him being fired from Spelman. A professor whose self-described stance is that of being involved in guerilla warfare with the administration was likely to get in trouble at Boston University as well. And Zinn did. When it was suggested that if he had not had tenure at BU, he might have been in danger of being fired again, he responded with his typical humor and bluntness, "Oh, oh, oh—in danger is a euphemism; without tenure, I would have been sacked, assassinated, history." This raises the subject of the long confrontation between Howard Zinn and the president of Boston University for much of his tenure there, John Silber. Silber, according to Zinn—and, admittedly, many others—was "ruthless in dealing with people who disagree with him. With people who came up for tenure, unanimous recommendations from every single faculty committee, wonderful student evaluations, and they were out." Noting that the problems under Silber at BU raised such broad concerns about higher education that they were even written up in such places as the *Chronicle of Higher Education*, Zinn responded quickly, "That's right. Silber became nationally known as the number one martinet." But then he admitted, "Depending on your point of view, I mean, some people looked upon him as 'he's the kind of guy we need, a tough guy.' Parents, a lot of parents, saw Silber as just the person they wanted to discipline their unruly students." Apparently, Zinn was regularly denied graduate assistants to help him with the massive amount of grading he had in those large classes because of Silber: "He was infuriated because I had so many students listening to me—the poisonous things I was saying. So he wrote a letter to the chairman of the department saying, if Zinn would cut his class down to seventy students, I'll give him a teaching assistant." The logic of that might escape some. Said Zinn, "The logic of that is bizarre. But Boston University under John Silber is a bizarre place."[11]

The antagonism between Silber and Zinn was mutual. In his book *Straight Shooting: What's Wrong with America and How to Fix It*, Silber had a subsection of a chapter entitled "Poisoning the Wells of Academe." Is there any surprise that Howard Zinn was considered a "well-poisoner" by Silber? But Silber certainly did not make a very strong case. The only specific issue he chose to challenge Zinn on was a different understanding of Martin Luther King's philosophy. This was Zinn's home turf, so to speak, and his position stood up well under Silber's attack. "There is no reason to believe that Zinn is a more reliable exponent of King's views than King himself," wrote Silber.[12] Well, no, but there is reason to believe that Zinn is a more reliable exponent of King's views than Silber.

Most of Silber's and Zinn's attacks on each other came within the context of Boston University. Apparently one persistent problem was Silber's denial of raises for Zinn. One year Zinn's department recommended him for a $1,000 raise. Next it was approved by the dean. Then the president eliminated it entirely! Zinn signed his contract, but attached a note. "Considering my record of teaching and publication, this action is at first puzzling," he said. "Then, noting my strong criticism of the Silber administration in the past, and John Silber's tendency to go into tantrums when criticized, one is led to reasonably conclude that his veto of my salary raise is a petty act of revenge." Zinn noted that Silber had vetoed numerous other departmental recommendations for raises, but suggested that this was clearly not an economy measure, since his own large salary and "rent-free mansion" remained intact. If, as it appeared, Silber was indeed "misusing his authority by manipulating salary raises to punish critics," Zinn suggested that "this is a serious violation of ordinary standards of decency and fairness, and should be remedied by the university community." That remedy? "The corrective for abuse of presidential power is the same in the university as in the nation—removal from office." Zinn apparently sent copies of this document to his department head, dean, the chairman of the BU Board of Trustees, and the chairman of the BU chapter of the American Association of University Professors.[13] One might agree fully with Zinn here—yet also anticipate that he would have trouble with his salary for the next year as well!

A graduate student interviewed Silber in 1979 and asked him directly about his denial of raises to Zinn, even suggesting this might be part of an effort to push Zinn out at BU. Silber responded: "He has to decide if he thinks he has a higher market value in the academic community some place else. He ought to look at it. I'm not aware that he has received an offer from any other place. I think he is paid all he can get in the academic market-place." "Do you feel he's not worth any more than he's making?" asked the student. "I don't think he's worth that," replied Silber. Asked why, Silber said he did not think Zinn's "standards of scholarship" were very high. He gave as an example the same difference of opinion between himself and Zinn about Martin Luther King's philosophy. Asked for others, he said there were "many"—but he could not think of any more. In further parts of the interview, Silber referred to Zinn as "irrational" and even "totali-tarian."[14] But then Silber was inclined to make outrageous charges. He ran for governor of Massachusetts in 1990, against William Weld, who won; Silber once described Weld as a "back-stabbing son of a bitch" and an "orange-headed WASP."[15] (Zinn was part of a group, by the way, called Concerned Faculty and Students of Boston University, who prepared a dev-astatingly critical "Factbook on John Silber" during his gubernatorial cam-paign; Zinn notes that it was a close election, and thinks the "Factbook" may have helped defeat Silber.)[16] A person who met Silber at a reception for recipients of BU Trustee Scholarships in 1978—she was the recipient of one of the scholarships herself, and had never met Silber or Zinn—made the mistake of mentioning that she was enrolled in a course taught by Zinn. Silber's "pleasant demeanor changed to anger," she said. "He raised his voice, and said that Mr. Zinn is a charlatan, a sham, and a liar," and "I was wasting my time taking his course."[17]

Even more incredibly, Silber once accused Zinn of arson. In the memory of one faculty member, it was a meeting of the School of Educa-tion faculty, and Silber said: "When Howard Zinn and a group of students tried to set a light to 147 Bay State Road, President Christ Janer [Silber's predecessor] had the students arrested and, because one did not arrest fac-ulty, failed to include Professor Howard Zinn. I would have arrested Howard Zinn and let the students go free as I consider him to be respon-sible for the students [*sic*] behavior." Silber did apologize for this accusa-tion, explaining that he had unintentionally connected two disparate events, and called the mistake "unfortunate." He made that apology in the context of a general meeting of the BU faculty on December 18, 1979, a meeting at which the faculty voted 456 to 215½ for his dismissal! (Half-time and unpaid honorary faculty were given half-votes.)[18] He was not dismissed.

Zinn felt so strongly about Silber that he became a part of a group on campus that called itself the Ad Hoc Committee for a True University and published a pamphlet entitled "Who Rules B.U.?" It featured such articles as "Erosion of Democracy at BU," and in one, entitled "What We Want," the number one "DEMAND" was that "BU become a democratic university, with students, faculty, employees making the critical decisions which affect their lives, and administrators carrying out these decisions."[19] Zinn also worked actively against Silber when he ran for governor in 1990. Notice that this was two years after Zinn's retirement. And he still felt so strongly about Silber that when Silber finally resigned as president of Boston University—only to become its chancellor, and eventually Governor Weld's "education czar," chairman of the Massachusetts Board of Education—and lots of people were saying lots of nice things about him, as people will do when someone retires, Zinn came out of retirement to write a scathing letter to the editor of the *Boston Globe*. It was dated March 30, 1996, and began by suggesting that the *Globe*'s coverage of Silber's retirement "seemed to come right out of Silber's huge public relations apparatus." It must have been written by someone who "knows nothing about the history of Silber's reign at B.U." For you would never know from the coverage that Silber was a "petty dictator who created an ugly atmosphere of intolerance on campus." Zinn insisted Silber had treated students with contempt, established censorship of campus publications, held down salaries of others while enriching himself, gotten rid of faculty whose political views he did not like, harassed anyone who participated in any kind of demonstration, and so on. Silber had been "more a police chief than an educator," contended Zinn, and the values he taught by example included "greed and ruthlessness." Silber was a "businessman obsessed with money. A poor educator, mean, destructive."[20]

Zinn believes, probably correctly, that if he had not already been tenured before Silber's arrival as president, he would have lost his job. The story of how he secured tenure is a delightful one. It was 1967. Zinn was already involved in early anti–Vietnam War protests. Some faculty expressed opposition to tenure for Zinn, considering his protest activity an embarrassment to the university. But his student evaluations were good, and his fifth book was being published that spring, so the department voted for tenure. It was also approved by the dean and the president. All that was needed now was a vote of the Board of Trustees. Their meeting that spring coincided with a Founders Day dinner, an elaborate affair at Boston's Sheraton Hotel. The speaker was Dean Rusk, one of the strategists of the Vietnam War. A group of antiwar students came to Zinn to ask him to speak at a demonstration in front of the hotel. He thought of his tenure decision the board was making that day. But he felt he could not say no. He spoke. As he spoke, several limousines drove up and unloaded tuxedoed guests, including Rusk and the trustees. They "stopped for a moment to take in the scene," in Zinn's words, then went on into the hotel. A few days later, Zinn received a letter from the Office of the President. "As I opened it," he recalls, "I thought of that other letter of 1963 from the office of another president." But this one said, "Dear Professor Zinn, I am happy to inform you that you have been awarded tenure." Explains Zinn: "So the trustees had voted me tenure in the afternoon, then arrived in the evening for the Founders Day dinner to find their newly tenured faculty member denouncing their honored guest."[21]

Perhaps it is best to let someone else have the last word on the Silber versus Zinn saga. It is not a favorable word for Silber. Daniel Gross, who has written for *New York*, the *New Republic*, and the *New York Observer*, published an article in *Lingua Franca* in 1995 entitled "Under the Volcano: Boston University in the Silber Age." A thorough investigation of the situation, Gross's piece presents both sides, and more, on Silber's controversial presidency. But when it mentions Zinn, it seems to do so in a favorable manner. Zinn is described as "until his retirement from BU in 1988 . . . a happy warrior against Silber's excesses." And Silber is quoted as having said, "The more democratic a university is, the lousier it is." He is also presented as having proudly resisted academic trends such as Afrocentrism, radical feminism, multiculturalism, structuralism, and deconstruction. And Gross concludes, à la Zinn, that "Boston University does indeed resemble a Third World dictatorship in many respects," and that "acting in the best tradition of kleptocracy, Silber has enriched himself while the university struggled financially," making himself by 1993 the highest-paid college president in the country. Silber successfully dissolved the faculty union at BU in 1986, drove out "many outstanding scholars and engaging teachers," and actually created a separate Department of International Relations "to skirt the political science department," because several of its members, including of course Howard Zinn, had been resistant to his will. Finally, Gross points out that Zinn, who published numerous books and taught large classes, retired in 1988 making "only $41,000, far below the university average for someone with nearly twenty-five years' experience."[22]

There are plenty of positive things to say about Zinn's teaching. Even Levin, the colleague who was somewhat critical of Zinn's academic standards, said, "The thing I admire most about Howard is that he is the only faculty member I have ever met with substantial political convictions and who lives by them." One of the students who profiled Zinn emphasized, among other things, Zinn's accessibility to students. At the time she wrote, his office hours were from 2:00 to 4:00 each afternoon, "but he is there almost every day until 6:00, talking with students. He is always willing to help a student and never makes one feel that he is wasting his time." She quotes a student who assisted Zinn speaking of his "great respect and true love for people," how he was "never condescending," and "treats men and women exactly the same, all with the utmost respect."[23]

Another student did one of those profiles of Zinn. Hers presented her own brief questions and Zinn's long answers, and is thus very valuable. Asked, for example, "What is the ultimate understanding that you want people to have by explaining history the way you do?" Zinn responded by revealing much about his philosophy, his teaching, himself:

> I guess I want them to understand—first—there's no such thing as objective history. Because history is always slanted in some way or another, and I want to be very forthright about my slant—that I want to see history from a standpoint of the people of the world who have been mostly on the underside of things. I want them to see the shape of the world as it has been created by the people in power and what that did. I want them also to get a picture, which I think is missing in most texts, of those people who have struggled, fought, organized, and defied authority, because I really want to encourage people to do that themselves. To me, the most important thing you can do in education is try and teach people not to accept authority, and not to think that somebody is going to take care of them, that some great savior is going to come along and save us all. Lincoln, Washington, Roosevelt, Reagan. . . . It's up to us. I want to create a different kind of hero and heroine, you might say. When you go to elementary school you hear your John Paul Jones, military heroes, "Don't fire until you see the whites of their eyes." I want people to be excited, the way I was when I learned about Eugene Debbs [sic], Emma Goldman, Harriet Tubman, about people who were not big shots or Supreme Court justices, but who showed courage and did remarkable things. Basically, that is what I want to accomplish.

When the student said, "You must have to deal with negative reactions, expressing your point of view," and asked, "What are some of the hassles, so to speak, that you've had to deal with? Was it much worse in the past than it is now?" Silber came up again in Zinn's response. "It all depends on where you are," Zinn began. "Boston University is one of the most harassing places." He smiled, then continued, "Have you heard of our president—John

Silber? I mean, it's like living in Lybia [*sic*]." Zinn laughs, but said, "Really." Personally, he insisted, "you're harassed more psychologically if you don't fight back." He admitted he has always had to contend with administration: "Wherever you teach the administration is never happy with a teacher who supports the students when they strike," so they give you a hard time. "Silber never wanted to give me raises. He tried to fire me once when I supported the secretaries who were out on strike."

Finally, asked, "What do you ultimately want your students and the American people to know?" Zinn said with apparent passion:

> I want them to know that they are capable of thinking things through for themselves, and capable of coming to their own judgements about right and wrong. Also, that the experts, the authorities, the people in power, the newscasters, and the teachers, should not be looked upon as authorities on important moral issues. People have to think for themselves and do for themselves. This is not something that is secured by a constitution, a president, or a congress; it is secured by people acting directly on their own lives.[24]

The concept of compartmentalizing life, of separating out the professional from the personal—the view, for example, that it is acceptable to condemn the war in Vietnam as a private citizen, but that must be kept out of the classroom—is clearly alien to Howard Zinn. David Barsamian interviewed him for the *Progressive* in 1997. He was speaking specifically of his Spelman years in this response, but he could have been speaking of his teaching in general.

> I learned that the most important thing about teaching is not what you do in the classroom but what you do outside of the classroom. You go outside the classroom yourself, bring your students outside, or have them bring you outside the classroom, because very often they do it first and you say, "I can't hang back. I'm their teacher. I have to be there with them." And you learn that the best kind of teaching makes this connection between social action and book learning.

Barsamian also asked Zinn a question about his 1994 memoir, entitled *You Can't Be Neutral on a Moving Train*. "Why did you pick a title like that?" "To confuse people, so that everybody who introduces me at a lecture gets it all wrong, like, *You Can't Be Training in a Neutral Place*," Zinn began humorously. Then, in his real answer, he revealed not only the title of the book (and of this chapter), but again much about his teaching:

The title came out of my classroom teaching, where I would start off my classes explaining to my students—because I didn't want to deceive them—that I would be taking stands on everything. They would hear my point of view in this course, that this would not be a neutral course. My point to them was that in fact it was impossible to be neutral. *You Can't Be Neutral on a Moving Train* means that the world is already moving in certain directions. Things are already happening. Wars are taking place. Children are going hungry. In a world like this—already moving in certain, often terrible directions—to be neutral or to stand by is to collaborate with what is happening. I didn't want to be a collaborator, and I didn't want to invite my students to be collaborators.[25]

Certainly in Howard Zinn's life he has made that "connection between social action and book learning" that he considered "the best kind of teaching." Though he looked back fondly on his years at Spelman College, it did not take long for him to become involved after his move to Boston University—both within and without the university. The first "cause" he began to devote extensive time to after moving to Boston was Vietnam. As usual for him, he did it with both his actions and a book.

The year Zinn was fired from Spelman, 1963, was the year of the March on Washington, the peak event of the civil rights movement; John F. Kennedy's assassination and Lyndon Baines Johnson assuming the presidency; and publication of *The Feminine Mystique* by Betty Friedan. The year he began teaching at Boston, 1964, saw the Civil Rights Act, Johnson being elected president in his own right, and the Gulf of Tonkin resolution, which essentially gave the president a sweeping mandate to conduct the operation in Vietnam as he saw fit—the first U.S. combat troops arrived there in 1965. As has so often been the case with Zinn, we first notice his response to an issue through his writings. In January 1966 he published an article in the *Nation* under the title "Vietnam: Means and Ends," and in the next month one in *Commonweal* entitled "Negroes and Vietnam." (Martin Luther King was to combine the civil rights movement and the anti–Vietnam War movement some time later.) In February 1967 came another article in the *Nation*, this time bluntly called "Vietnam: The Logic of Withdrawal."

Later in 1967, in the spring, Zinn managed to produce a little book already under the same title: *Vietnam: The Logic of Withdrawal*. Asked a question about which of his books he was proudest of or thought might have had the most impact, he began his answer, logically, with *A People's History of the United States* and *The Politics of History*. But the next one to come up was *Vietnam: The Logic of Withdrawal*. It was, he said, one of those "other books I felt good about because they were very pointedly aimed at something that was happening in our country." It went through eight printings within a short time, he recalls; he thinks it sold about fifty thousand copies.[26] Zinn's friend and fellow historian Staughton Lynd also considered *Vietnam* second in importance to the *People's History*.[27]

It was a small book, but a big subject. Zinn dedicated it, significantly, "To the People of Vietnam." Zinn was able to draw from many different elements of his training and experience in writing it, including his work in Asian history, his own wartime experiences, even his involvement in the civil rights movement. All this enabled him to produce a powerful work, especially considering the context of 1967. President Johnson had begun the process of massive escalation of American forces in Southeast Asia, with the number already approaching half a million, and the first major demonstrations against the war took place that year in such cities as New York and San Francisco. There was also the march on the Pentagon.

Zinn began with this sentence: "Vietnam, it seems to me, has become a theater of the absurd." He proceeded to support that statement with a series of brief, numbered points, a writing tactic he used frequently. Here is the first one: "By late 1966, the United States was spending for the Vietnam war at an annual rate of twenty billion dollars, enough to give every family in South Vietnam (whose normal annual income is not more than several hundred dollars) about $5,000 for the year." He added: "Our *monthly* expenditure for the war exceeds our *annual* expenditure for the Great Society's poverty program." Some of his other points seemed even more effective in supporting his claim about absurdity. Zinn had come away from his World War II military experience, he said, with several conclusions, one of which was "that innocent and well-meaning people—of whom I considered myself one—are capable of the most brutal acts and the most self-righteous excuses, whether they be Germans, Japanese, Russians, or Americans." Later, he added, he "was trained as a historian and learned that our country is *capable* of moral absurdities." He gave several examples, focusing on the Spanish-American War. "My conclusion," he wrote, "was not that the United States was more evil than other nations, only that she was *just* as evil (although she sometimes had more finesse)." Furthermore, "It does not take too much study of modern history to conclude that nations as a lot tend to be vicious."[28]

"Because I think perspective is so important," wrote Zinn, "I am going to start as far away from the American environment as possible, looking at the Vietnam war from Japan." He told about traveling there and finding the Japanese people "virtually unanimous in their belief that United States policy in Vietnam was not just a bit awry, but profoundly wrong." Some were even willing to say: "You are behaving in Asia as we once did."[29]

Next Zinn attempted "A View from Within: The Negro." Noting that African Americans had largely supported World War II because of its strong element of antiracism, he then insisted that it was fundamentally different in Vietnam. "The foe is not an Anglo-Saxon racist but a mass of poor, dark-skinned peasants who resemble in many aspects of their lives the Negroes of the American rural South." The charge most often flung at the Johnson administration by blacks in connection with Vietnam was summed up in a single word: hypocrisy.[30] (Some readers might recall the title of a movie about the extensive yet problematic involvement of blacks in Vietnam: *No Vietnamese Ever Called Me Nigger.*)

After the view from Japan, the view from black Americans, next Zinn attempted "The View from History: What Nation Can Be Trusted?" His basic answer, not surprisingly, was none. In the United States, we do not need proof of the iniquities of other nations, he noted, but "our memory somehow fails when it comes to our own history." The basic problem is worldwide: nationalism, patriotism, chauvinism, whatever. But in our case it is aggravated by other factors, including the still-recent experience of World War II in which it seemed clear to us that the struggle was between total good and total evil, and of course we were the total good. "It is a matter of faith with most Americans that our policies in international relations are designed to further the values we cherish at home: liberty, justice, equality"—all those ideals spelled out in the Declaration of Independence and the Bill of Rights. The connection between national and international ideals has even been compressed into a simple phrase: the free world. We are the leaders of the free world. But have those values actually been furthered by our foreign policy since World War II? Zinn thinks not, and again used his device of brief numbered paragraphs to make his point. Here is one: "Actively helping to overthrow the legally elected Arbenz government in Guatemala in 1954, and then supporting the various dictatorships which succeeded it."[31]

Zinn increasingly became, over the course of his writing, a master of the art of quotation; many readers of his *People's History* considered that one of its greatest strengths. The point, of course, is that if the common people make their own history, they should be allowed to tell it as well. It is very effective when Zinn quotes Donald Duncan, a master sergeant of the

U.S. Special Forces in Vietnam (the Green Berets), who resigned from the Army early in 1966, saying he considered "anti-Communism . . . a lousy substitute for democracy." He told about the torture techniques he and his men learned to use to extract information from the Vietnamese, then concluded: "We weren't preserving freedom. There was no freedom to preserve. To voice opposition to the government meant jail or death. Neutralism was forbidden or punished. We aren't the freedom fighters. We are the Russian tanks blasting the hopes of an Asian Hungary."

But Zinn's own words can be powerful as well, as when he questions how we can possibly support such a regime as that in place in South Vietnam. To some, he notes, it needs no justification, for "anything is preferable to Communism—even a dictatorship based on a wealthy elite controlling impoverished masses." But most American liberals cannot accept this, and seek "a third way, so that our foreign policy can satisfy the aims of liberty and justice, and the rest." But what they are unable (unwilling?) to grasp is that this cannot be imposed from the outside. "Refusing to accept these limits to what an outsider can do, the United States engages in a giant pretense; it announces that reform is on the way, then it entrusts the carrying out of that reform to those very people who constitute the right-wing elites of wealth—those who have most to lose by change." Anticipating his fundamental conclusion, that the only appropriate course of action for the United States is to immediately withdraw from Vietnam, Zinn writes that "it seems clear that the billions of dollars, the tens of thousands of lives lost in Vietnam, cannot be justified by what we are doing for social change there." If we assume that our "basic bundle of values" consists of life and liberty, "we might agree that sometimes liberty may be sacrificed for life, or life for liberty. But if we are giving up *both*, then nothing is left in the bundle. And if so, then we had better withdraw from the scene."[32]

A chapter entitled "Violence: The Moral Equation" had appeared as an article in the *Nation* and would later be reprinted in Zinn's *The Politics of History*. It includes some of Zinn's strongest language. After stating that "the United States must be included as a nation which, like the others, will use any means to gain its ends," he lists—twenty-six numbered paragraphs this time!—"some of the means being used in Vietnam by this liberal nation." They are ugly, and include deaths and maimings of many innocent civilians. Zinn then concludes: "This list . . . is only a tiny *known* part of an enormous pattern of devastation which, if seen in its entirety, would have to be described as one of the most evil acts committed by any nation in modern times." Part of the problem is the very nature of the war. Whereas in World War II the bombing deaths of civilians resulted from "terrible mistake[s] in judgment," "*In Vietnam, . . . the bombing and shelling of civilians constitutes the war.*" The Vietcong, supposedly the enemy, "are indistinguishable from any Vietnamese peasant. Indeed, they *are* Vietnamese peasants. This is guerrilla warfare, in the countryside, and the guerrillas are part of that countryside." Thus the United States is "bombing villages, inundating whole areas with bombs, destroying rice fields, spreading chemicals and fire over huge sections of South Vietnam—which we claim to be defending."[33]

There are, suggests Zinn at this point, only two major arguments remaining. One is that while we should perhaps stop or diminish our offensive activity in Vietnam, we should maintain a military presence there to support a South Vietnamese government that is fighting a defensive war against outside aggressors. The other is that even if it is true that we are fighting a counterrevolutionary war rather than a defensive one, and even if we are killing innocent Vietnamese on a large scale, we must continue, even increase, our military actions "because a gigantic issue is at stake which requires this sacrifice: Communism vs. freedom."[34] Zinn attempts to demolish these arguments in his next two chapters. "It was very clear to all sides," he writes in one important passage, "in those years when the United States began its intervention in Indochina, that there was only one party engaging in 'external aggression' and 'external attack' in Vietnam: the French." And what the United States was doing was massively helping the French to reestablish control over a former colony; this was, said Zinn, a "simple fact of recent history."[35] And when the French pulled out, after their defeat at Dien Bien Phu in 1954, we jumped in and became "the only ones who matched the accusation of 'outside aggression.'"[36] The other argument, about stopping Communism, Zinn notes, is sometimes called the "domino theory," coming from a statement in April 1954 by President Dwight D. Eisenhower: "The loss of Indochina will cause the fall of Southeast Asia like a set of dominoes." Zinn notes that this is very similar to the Munich analogy, and that when it is looked at closely, it falls apart. He also notes, with perhaps a touch of both humor and bitterness, that Robert Scalapino had preferred to see it as a game of checkers, with China doing the jumping, then concludes: "Others might call the game Monopoly and put the onus on the United States; my own temptation is to call the whole business Russian roulette."[37]

Too much of the discussion on Vietnam has centered on the question of whether we can "win," suggests Zinn, and not enough on whether we *should*

Howard Zinn and his wife, Rosyln (1976). (Photo courtesy of Howard Zinn.)

Left: Howard Zinn and his wife, Rosyln (1985). (Photo courtesy of Howard Zinn.)
Right: Howard and Rosyln Zinn and their children, Myla and Jeff. (date unknown).
(Photo courtesy of Howard Zinn.)

Howard and Rosyln Zinn and their children, Myla and Jeff. (1981). (Photo courtesy of Howard Zinn.)

Howard Zinn speaking at an anti–Vietnam War rally on Boston Commons. (May 1971). (Photo courtesy of Howard Zinn.)

Howard Zinn being arrested at an anti–Vietnam war demonstration. (Reprinted from *Ordfront Magasin—Bokmassan 1998*.)

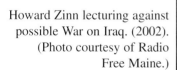

Howard Zinn lecturing against possible War on Iraq. (2002). (Photo courtesy of Radio Free Maine.)

Rosyln Zinn, Howard Zinn, Noam Chomsky, and Carole Chomsky. (2002). (Photo courtesy of Howard Zinn.)

Staughton Lynd, Alice Lynd, and Rosyln Zinn. (date unknown, but obviously a fairly recent photo). (Photo courtesy of Howard Zinn.)

win. "'Victory' for the United States in the cold war has too often meant the maintenance of a repressive oligarchy in power, ignoring the needs of the population, and holding on by its teeth to a brass ring held by an American general." For some readers in 1967, this conclusion by Zinn was probably one of the hardest to swallow: "Right now, for Vietnam, a Communist government is probably the best avenue available." The perspective of history suggests, he says, that "a united Vietnam under Ho Chi Minh is preferable to the elitist dictatorship of the South, just as Maoist China with all its faults is preferable to the rule of Chiang, and Castro's Cuba to Batista's."[38] "We should keep in mind that, at this point in history, Communism is only part of a much broader movement—the rising of hungry and harassed people in Asia, Africa, Latin America (and parts of the United States)," insists Zinn. For if we forget this, we try to crush an insurrection in one place, and apparently succeed, only to find another—"whether Communist or Socialist or nationalist or of indescribable character"—springing up elsewhere. "We surround the world with our navy, cover the sky with our planes, fling our money to the winds, and then a revolution takes place in Cuba, nearby." Our tendency is to "see every rebellion as the result of some plot concocted in Moscow or Peking," but "what is really happening is that people everywhere want to eat and to be free and will use desperate means, and any one of a number of social systems, to achieve their ends."[39]

If the worry about withdrawing, as it seemed to be with some, was about American prestige, wondered Zinn, "does it not seem likely that the result of withdrawal would be a net *gain* in prestige?" To reenforce this point, Zinn quotes respected scholar of international relations Hans Morgenthau, himself wondering, "Is it really a boon to the prestige of the most powerful nation on earth to be bogged down in a war which it is neither able to win nor can afford to lose?" "The sanity of unilateral withdrawal," concludes Zinn, "is that it makes the end of the war independent of anyone's consent but our own. It is clean-cut, it is swift, it is right."[40]

The last chapter of *Vietnam: The Logic of Withdrawal* Zinn entitled "A Speech for LBJ." It is brilliant; but it is not unfair to suggest that it is also a perfect illustration of just how far from mainstream historical writing Zinn is. We mean primarily here in terms of methodology. But in terms of what he has President Johnson say in this imaginary speech, it is also probably outside the mainstream of American thinking as of early 1967. The speech incorporates all the arguments we have summarized above, and concludes, "My fellow Americans [*That* certainly sounds like Johnson!], good night and sleep well. We are no longer at war in Vietnam."[41]

It may have been unorthodox, but that proposed speech for Johnson became a focal point in the response to Zinn's book. A group in New York asked for and secured permission from Beacon Press to run the speech as an ad in the *New York Times*, followed by the statement "Mr. President, we want you to give this speech and take the action indicated" therein—also followed by "many, many signatures."[42] Wes Lawrence, a columnist for the *Cleveland Plain Dealer*, editorialized, "Howard Zinn, professor of government at Boston University, who served as a bombardier in World War II, has written a speech for Lyndon Johnson which, if he delivered it, would make the President one of the great men of history, in my opinion."[43]

The response to this book was the broadest of any of Zinn's writings so far. Most of it was positive, but, not surprisingly, not all. At one extreme, for example, was the accusation that Zinn was a Communist. "Howard Zinn and the Communists have been saying the same things for a very long time," said someone named Nord Davis Jr., of Hollis, New Hampshire. He reproduced a couple of news items that seemed to look favorably on the antiwar movement in general and the 1969 moratorium in particular as "proof" to justify painting Zinn with the Communist label—though neither of the items he reproduced mentioned Zinn. An accompanying biographical sketch of Zinn by a Francis X. Gannon also emphasized Zinn's supposed Communist connections; he was a sponsor, for example, of the "National Student Strike for Peace, which was led by Communist Bettina Aptheker."[44]

It is not surprising that Zinn's Vietnam book elicited divided response —the war itself obviously elicited diverse and strongly felt responses as well. Some reviewers, for example, praised Zinn for presenting a "clearly argued case for what most critics of the Vietnamese war believe but will not say—that America should withdraw *now*." That same critic, while noting certain weaknesses in Zinn's argument, including that he "promises far more for withdrawal than it can provide," concluded that "his argument may succeed in persuading us that it is the least of the available evils."[45] Perhaps the most positive review of all appeared in the *New York Times*. *Vietnam: The Logic of Withdrawal* was referred to as a "slim, closely reasoned" book, presenting a "compact, accurate history of the United States' involvement in Vietnam." Zinn's analysis of the Japanese view of the war was regarded as "particularly probing," and his chronicling of the devastating impact of the war on Vietnamese civilians "a powerful moral argument."[46]

Other reviewers were more critical, some nastily so. The *Times Literary Supplement*, for example, noted sarcastically that Zinn's experience as a bombardier "gave him an interest in history but, as his book shows, little talent for it." (This seems not only nasty, but illogical—where is the evidence that Zinn's interest in history came, especially exclusively, from his having been a bombardier?) Zinn "knows what he thinks," the brief review continued, "but he does not contribute to the argument." Also, "There is not much logic in *The Logic of Withdrawal*." Collin Clark vented his spleen on Zinn and his book in a brief note in the *Library Journal*. The book, he said, had "about the thoroughness of a half-hour television documentary," and was "a brief, angry, personal scrapbook, which has a right to exist, but will do little good." Libraries were advised, finally, "to spend their money, and readers their time, on books of more substance." Finally, Saville R. Davis, writing for the *Christian Science Monitor*, placed Zinn among those "who would denounce what they call professional and obsessive anti-communism." These people, according to Davis, are "so driven by the counter-obsession—anger or righteous condemnation of their own government—that they close their eyes to things the Communists are doing, or think them somehow different, and not deserving of even-handed verdicts." Finally, and snidely: "If you are a pamphleteer (like Howard Zinn . . .), you simply make your own history; it is what you say it is."[47]

The reviews of *Vietnam: The Logic of Withdrawal* may not have been the most important responses it elicited. In Zinn's files are personal letters from both of Massachusetts' U.S. senators, Edward M. Kennedy (noncommittal—the strongest phrase was "very interesting") and Edward W. Brooke (he expressed "great respect" for Zinn), as well as one from Alaska's senator Ernest Gruening. Gruening was actually responding to Zinn's earlier essay bearing the same title as the book, and said he considered it "extremely thoughtful," so much so that he had it inserted in the *Congressional Record* of February 3, 1967, along with his own comments critical of the war.[48] (Gruening and Sen. Wayne Morse of Oregon had been the only two members of the Senate to vote against the Tonkin Gulf Resolution in 1964.) Edwin Newman devoted his commentary on NBC News on July 5, 1967, to Vietnam in general and Zinn's book in particular. He did an excellent job of summarizing Zinn's position and suggested that the book should get a healthy debate started, but except for the attention he gave it possibly suggesting a positive view, he was careful not to endorse it.[49]

Very important to Howard Zinn, obviously, were his students; he openly acknowledged efforts to impact their attitudes, get them involved. His files are bursting with hundreds of letters that suggest, among other things, that he succeeded. One seems especially relevant here for considering Zinn's views on Vietnam, and their impact. The former student began modestly, "I don't expect that you remember me." He had taken several courses with Zinn in 1966 and 1967, and had been "greatly stimulated" by Zinn's views on "many subjects—especially Vietnam and civil liberties." He was now on a "two-year vacation—all expenses paid," he said, meaning he was in the Army and leaving for Vietnam the next month. The painful soul-searching is evident as he continues: "I have for a long time found myself in a quandry [sic] as to whether I could fight in an immoral and purposeless conflict or whether I could refuse to serve." Obviously, he was "disillusioned at the course that the nation is now pursuing. I cannot however avoid paying back this state a debt that I owe." Anticipating hopefully his return, and concerned about "what will I be when I return," he concluded, "Firstly I will feel that I owe the state nothing more," and "Secondly I will feel even more alienated than I do now for having to fight an unjust war." He anticipated that it would be "difficult to reach a reproachment [sic] with a state that has made me both a murderer and a hypocrite." This former student did not like the idea of "undermining the military," as it seemed to him many radical students did. "It is not the war machine that is at fault," he felt. Rather, "It is ourselves who are at fault for not adequately overseeing the politico-military and economic complexes which cause the military arm to be employed without our consent." He knew he was not going to Vietnam "merely because a few generals decided it was to be," but rather "because millions of Americans let it happen and now can't easily halt this fait accompli." In his final paragraph, he said he hoped to speak with Zinn when he returned. "Perhaps I will be fortunate enough to be enrolled in another of your courses or to work with you on some project by which we can state and act on what we are for and not merely attack what we are against."[50] A powerful document, probably reflective of more deep thought than most of the young men who went off to Vietnam experienced—but then Zinn clearly encouraged that kind of process in his students.

He also encouraged it, and promoted vigorously his views of Vietnam, in a commencement address at Brandeis University in 1968. Eloquently, passionately, Zinn related the recent assassination of Robert F. Kennedy to what was going on in Vietnam. Our nation, he said, "is once more engaged in an orgy of mourning which must certainly be one of the great acts of hypocrisy in world history." For "one by one the leaders of the nation are stepping forward to the television cameras to declare their revulsion against senseless violence," that is, the killing of Kennedy, but these were, after all, the "leaders of a nation which for the past three years has been engaged in senseless violence not just against one individual, but against millions of people." Consistent with the theme of his Vietnam book, Zinn concluded: "If the nation really wants to show its concern over violence, let it stop the orgy of mourning and speeches—let it even stop the charade of negotiations—let it announce to the world that as a sign of its concern it is now beginning the orderly withdrawal of U.S. forces from Vietnam."[51]

For what it is worth, thirty years later, Zinn had not changed his mind—and still had that passion. Indeed, he clearly felt that the antiwar movement had not only been right but had been instrumental in finally getting the United States out of Vietnam. Reflecting briefly in the pages of the *Progressive* thirty years after the notorious Tet offensive of 1968 in Vietnam, Zinn first recalled his trip with Jesuit priest Daniel Berrigan to North Vietnam to pick up the first three captured American pilots to be released by the North Vietnamese. Even Robert McNamara, as secretary of defense one of the "masterminds" of the war, now agrees that Vietnam was "a shameful episode in our nation's history." But not, insisted Zinn, because it could not be won. The destruction we wreaked there was "morally indefensible, win or lose." None of the reasons given to explain what we did—"stopping the spread of communism, defending an ally, fulfilling our 'treaty obligations'"—could really stand up under close examination. "And even if any element of that explanation had been true," Zinn questioned, "would it have justified the mass slaughter of Asian peasants and the deaths of 58,000 Americans, to say nothing of all those left blind, maimed, and paralyzed on both sides?" Clearly, Zinn's answer was no. And he insisted, based on public opinion polls, that the answer of most Americans was no as well, for in August 1965, 61 percent of those polled approved of American involvement in Vietnam, while by May 1971, that same percentage considered our involvement wrong. Thirty years later, what have we learned from Vietnam that might be of use today? Zinn suggested two major answers: "That with the indiscriminate nature of modern military technology, all wars are wars against civilians, and are therefore inherently immoral." (As an example, Zinn wrote, "The 'good war' against Saddam Hussein, [i.e., the Gulf War] has succeeded . . . in bringing about the deaths of hundreds of thousands of Iraqi children, according to U.N. reports.") And the second lesson: "That no political leaders should be trusted when they urge their people to war."[52]

Zinn says one of the reasons he liked *Vietnam: The Logic of Withdrawal* was because it was short—"I like books that are 100 to 125 pages," he said. But he was also obviously quite proud of the fact that it "was much used by the movement, went through eight printings, etc." The next book he mentioned when he was talking about his favorites was also a short one, and was to become his best-seller (at an estimated 75,000 copies), second only to the *People's History*.[53] It was entitled *Disobedience and Democracy: Nine Fallacies on Law and Order*, and was published in 1968. In general, it, too, was related to Vietnam. But more specifically it was a response to a little booklet by Supreme Court justice Abe Fortas entitled *Concerning Dissent and Civil Disobedience*. The booklet was part of what Zinn called the "current rush back to 'law and order.'" But he knew it was widely distributed, that Fortas's views probably reflected the majority of the Court, that "what Mr. Fortas says is important."[54]

"What I will suggest in this essay," Zinn stated in his introduction, "is that Mr. Fortas's brief on dissent and civil disobedience is exactly that sanctification of law which proved a failure in the two greatest crises in American history." He was referring to the American Revolution, when "we had to go beyond British and colonial constitutions in order to gain independence," and the Civil War, when "we had to go beyond our own constitutional limits in order to end slavery." After noting that Fortas's views were important, Zinn said, "If he misled us, that would be very serious." And Zinn felt that Fortas had indeed "misled us," on nine specific counts. "These nine fallacies, I believe, are not only harmful to the liberty of dissident minorities, but stifling to the growth of democracy for the majority of Americans."[55] Before spelling out the "nine fallacies," Zinn generalized as follows in perhaps the most important paragraph of this important little book:

> For the crisis of our time, the slow workings of American reform, the limitations on protest and disobedience and innovation set by liberals like Justice Fortas, are simply not adequate. We need devices which are powerful but restrained, explosive but controlled: to resist the government's actions against the lives and liberties of its citizens; to pressure, even to shock the government into change; to organize people to replace the holders of power, as one round in that continuing cycle of political renewal which alone can prevent tyranny.[56]

At the heart of *Disobedience and Democracy*, obviously, are the "nine fallacies." Each deserves exact quotation, with a few accompanying elaborative comments.

"First fallacy: *that the rule of law has an intrinsic value apart from moral ends. (By 'moral ends' I mean the needs of human beings, not the mores of our culture.)*" Most of us do have some commitment to the rule of law in general, Zinn acknowledges, and our reasons for that go deep into the past, at least to the Magna Carta. But, "To assume that because some laws may serve democratic purposes all laws must always be obeyed, is to give a blank check to government—something that citizens in a democracy should never do." Zinn insists that "there is no evidence that violations of law in the spirit of civil disobedience lead to a general contempt for all laws," as some fear. He agrees, however, that "there is some truth . . . to the notion that acts of civil disobedience have a proliferating effect." As an example, he suggests that the civil disobedience of the civil rights movement may have had "a stimulating effect" on the anti–Vietnam War movement. "But that is not a *general* breakdown of law and order; that is a spread of organized protest against wrong. And such an effect," concludes Zinn, "is to be welcomed in a country seeking improvement." But, "If we justify one act of civil disobedience, must we not justify them all? If a student has the right to break the conscription law, does this not give the Klan the right to disobey the Civil Rights Acts?" In answering this objection, Zinn emphasizes that there is a fundamental distinction between speech and action; all speech should be tolerated, but not all action. A bigot has the right to express his bigotry, but not to violate the civil rights of another citizen. Zinn suggests that part of our problem is that we have become so far removed from our own revolutionary tradition, and from the reality of suffering among other people; thus, "we consider as unpardonable transgressions of law and order what are really mild acts, measured against the existing evils." As examples he cites students occupying a university building "in protest against that University's longtime policy of pushing black people from their homes while it accumulated enormous wealth," black Mississippians occupying government property "in protest against their poverty," and a young person burning a draft card as "protest against a government which drops bombs on villages, destroys crops, kills thousands in war." Civil disobedience, concludes Zinn, "is not just to be tolerated; if we are to have a truly democratic society, it is a *necessity*." He is not addressing himself to the government, he notes, but to his fellow citizens. "If enough of them will act according to their conscience, the government will have to change its laws and its policies." Our job as citizens is to "hold conscience above law," "so as to continually close the gap between law and justice."[57]

"Second fallacy: *the person who commits civil disobedience must accept his punishment as right.*" But *why* should the citizen accept the result of a law or court decision he considers immoral, Zinn asks, "To support 'the rule of law' in the abstract? We have just argued [in answering the first fallacy] that to support a wrong rule of law does not automatically strengthen the right rule of law, indeed may weaken it." Sanctification of the law, argues Zinn, sometimes subordinates more important values. He tells of the jailing of Ralph Abernathy and hundreds of others in June 1968 after they set up their tents in Washington to demonstrate their needs, and of the *New York Times* editorializing that, by submitting peacefully to arrest, the protestors showed that it is possible to have strong dissent, even civil disobedience, "without endangering the foundation of law and order on which the rights and liberties of all Americans rest." Fortas may have liked that conclusion; Zinn did not. Such an attitude, he argues, places "law and order" above "human welfare." "Law and order remained intact. But where was justice for the poor?" Zinn felt the jailings should have led to *more* civil disobedience. "The sportsmanlike acceptance of jail as the terminus of civil disobedience is fine for a football game, or for a society determined to limit reform to tokens," Zinn concludes. But, "It does not suit a society which wants to eliminate long-festering wrongs."[58]

"Third fallacy: *that civil disobedience must be limited to laws which are themselves wrong.*" The primary problem here, says Zinn, is that such a position allows no distinction between bad laws and bad conditions. Poverty, racism, and the war in Vietnam—"the most persistent and basic evils of our time," according to Zinn—could not be opposed by civil disobedience by this standard. "If a law has been passed registering what is wrong, you may violate it as a protest; if no law has been passed, but that same wrong condition exists, you are left without recourse to any protest as vigorous as an act of civil disobedience." Obviously, this is not acceptable, says Zinn; traffic laws, trespass laws, and tax laws would be examples of laws that could justifiably be the focus of civil disobedience to protest those intolerable conditions.[59]

"Fourth fallacy: *that civil disobedience must be absolutely nonviolent.*" Civil disobedience, says Zinn, should be defined as "the deliberate violation of law for a vital social purpose." This leaves open the possibility of violating laws which are immoral whether constitutional or not, laws which themselves are not at issue as well as those that are—and it leaves open also the question of the means of disobedience. Certainly Zinn does not attempt to make a case for violence. "To me one of the cardinal principles in any moral code is the reduction and elimination of violence," he writes. But he points out that violence has sometimes brought about positive social change, and that some of the people usually marshaled to support total nonviolence indeed did not. Henry David Thoreau, while fundamentally nonviolent, did support John Brown in his attempt to seize arms and instigate a slave rebellion. Even Gandhi once said, "I do believe that where there is only a choice between cowardice and violence I would advise violence." Violence clearly should be used only as a matter of last resort, insists Zinn: "It would have to [be] guarded, limited, aimed carefully at the source of injustice, and preferably directed against property rather than people." The reasons for such criteria are, first, moral: "that violence is in itself an evil, and so can only be justified in those circumstances where it is a last resort in eliminating a greater evil, or in self-defense." And second, the reason of effectiveness: "The purpose of civil disobedience is to communicate to others, and indiscriminate violence turns people (rightly) away." We should insist on the principle, says Zinn, that "all victims are created equal." Such a conclusion is "self-evident" from the Declaration of Independence, and "this means that violence to any man must be equated with violence to any other." Finally, says Zinn, "I insist only that the question is so open, so complex, that it would be foolish to rule out at the start, for all times and conditions, all of the vast range of possible tactics beyond strict nonviolence."[60]

"Fifth fallacy: *that the political structure and procedures in the United States are adequate as they stand to remedy the ills of our society.*" Noting that Fortas had presented as his primary evidence for belief in the adequacy of our present system the progress made by blacks in the civil rights movement (obviously a movement that had utilized massive civil disobedience to accomplish what it had!), Zinn quotes as refutation the 1968 report of the National Advisory Commission on Civil Disorders (the Kerner Commission): "The political system . . . has not worked for the Negro as it has for other groups." And, "This is our basic conclusion: Our nation is moving toward two societies, one black, one white—separate and unequal." Fortas had referred to "the all-important access to the ballot box," but Zinn notes that "the ballot box creates no access to foreign policy." Elaborating further, he says, "It is one of the ironies of the American system that the closer we get to matters of life and death—that is, to questions of war and peace— the less does democracy function." Vietnam, he insists, was a good example, for the people had voted in 1964 for the "candidate who rejected the idea of escalating the war in Southeast Asia. He won, and then escalated the war." We need, Zinn concludes, "new methods of social change beyond the obviously unsuccessful present ones. We need to experiment, to find political techniques which are more effective and less costly than either traditional politics or spontaneous violence." Finally, "It is precisely because the ballot box and other standbys of high school civics are insufficient that the citizen in a democracy needs the weapon of civil disobedience."[61]

"Sixth fallacy: *that we can depend on the Courts, especially the Supreme Court, to protect our rights to free expression under the First Amendment.*" This one is largely self-explanatory. Zinn quotes effectively from Mark Twain: "It is by the goodness of God that in our country we have those three unspeakably precious things: freedom of speech, freedom of conscience, and the prudence never to practice either of them." Zinn is especially hard on Fortas on this point, noting he was part of the seven-to-one majority in a Supreme Court decision holding that a draft card–burner must be punished for his protest—yet "how Fortas has assured us we are safeguarded in our right to protest!" In conclusion, Zinn insists that civil disobedience—"protest *beyond* the law"—is so precious in part because "whatever the law says in theory, as applied by the federal courts, including the Supreme Court, in practice, it is not a dependable shield for free expression." The Court's record on this issue, contends Zinn, is far too "erratic."[62]

"Seventh fallacy: *that our principles for behavior in civil disobedience are to be applied to individuals, but not to nations; to private parties in the United States, but not to the United States in the world.*"[63] Zinn lashes out at the double standard such a position creates, and is especially effective in relating it to Vietnam.

"Eighth fallacy: *that whatever changes are taking place in the world, they do not require a departure from the traditional role of the Supreme Court playing its modest role as a 'balancer' of interests between state and citizen.*" Zinn contends that during great crises in the nation in the past—the Revolution, the Civil War, labor in the 1930s, the civil rights movement—"the traditional workings of the government, including the decisions of the courts, had to be supplemented by much more vigorous activity." He then argues that "the present situation of this country is another time of great crisis, when drastic change, even revolutionary change is needed—and that these times require modes of expression, forms of protest, stretching civil disobedience to wider limits." His illustrations focus on race, poverty, and especially foreign policy, again because "this is the area of policy least vulnerable to the electoral process." Zinn concludes by giving some advice to the Supreme Court. It "needs to rule on the most fundamental questions posed to it, rather than on the narrowest," he argues. It also "should not assume the political branches (President, Congress) are most competent to determine certain questions, and therefore the Supreme Court should not interfere." (His major example, of course: Vietnam.) Finally, and most important, "The Court should consider that its special duty is to protect those natural rights 'life, liberty, and the pursuit of happiness' which are the most fundamental purpose of government, above and beyond any specific Constitutional provisions." In short, says Zinn, "The courts should stand for the law sometimes, for justice always."[64]

"Ninth fallacy: *that we, the citizenry, should behave as if we are the state and our interests are the same.*" Zinn draws on John Locke's *Second Treatise on Government* and the Declaration of Independence to refute this final fallacy. Governments, those sources insisted correctly, are instituted for certain ends, including the protection of life, liberty, and the pursuit of happiness. Whenever a government becomes destructive of those ends, it is the right of the people to alter or even abolish it. "The government is not synonymous with the people of the nation; it is an artificial device, set up by the citizens for certain purposes," concludes Zinn. "It is endowed with no sacred aura; rather, it needs to be watched, scrutinized, criticized, opposed, changed, and even overthrown and replaced when necessary."[65]

Indeed, argues Zinn, "More important perhaps than all of Fortas's specific fallacies is the spirit underlying them: a spirit of awed respect for the state and its organs (President, Congress, the Supreme Court)." That, he insists, "is not the spirit of a dynamic democracy, sensitive to the need for change in a changing world; it is the stagnant atmosphere of the past, artificially perfumed with enough rhetoric to build our confidence." But we should not be taken in. "Our times require not the spirit of McKinley and Grover Cleveland, nor even Holmes and Wilson, but the spirit of Tom Paine, of Frederick Douglass, the spirit of Thoreau, of Eugene Debs." In short, "Let the state worry about its power. The record in history of our government—of all governments—is a record of violence, cruelty, callousness, intrusion. We, the citizenry, had better augment our own power, because we are the most dependable defendants of our own liberty."[66]

Obviously, much of *Disobedience and Democracy: Nine Fallacies on Law and Order* is a critique of Abe Fortas's views of civil disobedience. But emerging from it is a positive principle or code or theory that Zinn states eloquently near the end. He feels that "revolutionary changes are needed," but suspects that "classical revolutionary war in our country is not feasible." Thus, citizens must "accept, utilize, control the disorder of civil disobedience, enriching it with countless possibilities and tactics not yet imagined, to make life more human for us and others on this earth." Zinn's final paragraph is worth quoting in full:

> It is very hard, in the comfortable environment of middle-class America, to discard the notion that everything will be better if we don't have the disturbance of civil disobedience, if we confine ourselves to voting,

writing letters to our Congressmen, speaking our minds politely. But those outside are not so comfortable. Most people in the world are hungry, have no decent place to sleep, no doctor when they are sick; and some are fleeing from attacking airplanes. Somehow, we must transcend our own tight, air-conditioned chambers and begin to feel their plight, their needs. It may become evident that, despite our wealth, we can have no real peace until they do. We might then join them in battering at the complacency of those who guard a false "order," with that healthy commotion that has always attended the growth of justice.[67]

Disobedience and Democracy was published in the midst of the incredible year of 1968. It was the year of the Tet offensive in Vietnam, the assassinations of both Martin Luther King Jr. and Robert F. Kennedy, the "police riot" against protestors outside the Democratic National Convention in Chicago, and the eventual election of Richard M. Nixon to the presidency. The response of reviewers to Zinn's little volume was doubtless influenced by the climate of the times. Even a reviewer for such a respectable publication as the *New Republic* practically destroyed the credibility of his review by referring shallowly to "the romanticism of enthusiasts like Mr. Zinn about the virtues of confrontation for its own sake."[68] Saville R. Davis, once again reviewing a Zinn book for the *Christian Science Monitor*, was also keenly aware of the crisis flavor of 1968. "This is not a bland subject," he wrote of the confrontation between Fortas and Zinn, "at a time when it has been argued out on the streets for five tumultuous years with the result, in the Nixon years ahead, still acutely uncertain." But Davis then settled down and wrote an insightful, if critical, review. "One would not look to Supreme Court justice Abe Fortas for guidance on civil disobedience, nor to author and teacher Howard Zinn, a passionate advocate of disobedience, for direction on how to preserve the American system of law," he suggested. "But let each one define his position and then lean toward the other, and the occasion is instructive. It is also going to make partisan readers on each side more uncomfortable." Davis suggested that "at first glance Mr. Zinn sounds like a troublemaker. A second look confirms it; he is a professional." But Davis also saw value in Zinn's work, and even suggested a "possible accommodation" between Fortas and Zinn, "the anguished statement continually made by Martin Luther King Jr. toward the end: that, unless American society paid far more attention to nonviolent protests, large segments of the community would turn to violence."[69]

Carl Cohen, a philosophy professor at the University of Michigan, provided the most thoughtful review of *Disobedience and Democracy*, in the

Nation; he considered it "a most extraordinary book." He did not find Zinn's views entirely correct or even consistent, and was convinced that he was mistaken on certain issues. "Yet the book is splendid—crisp and biting, reflective and insightful, sympathetic and humane. It deserves to be very widely read and very thoughtfully discussed." Zinn's work, felt Cohen, was "so effective in opening our eyes and our minds that we profit more [even] from considering his mistakes than from the muddy and superficial truths often encountered elsewhere." Including perhaps the pages of Justice Fortas's book? Apparently so, for Cohen insisted that Fortas, though "a man of generous inclinations and considerable mental power, is bested again and again [by Zinn]—shown to have been inconsistent, careless, occasionally shallow, or unfair." Finally, and perhaps unusually in a book review, Cohen gave "three cheers" for *Disobedience and Democracy*. First, a cheer for "a short, punchy book, written in a prose that is plain and beautiful. Zinn writes with a directness and candor rare among scholarly men. Just reading the book is a pleasure." The second cheer was for "Zinn as a perceptive critic of the American scene. He is a merciless enemy of hypocrisy and cruelty. . . . He is bitter, but not without hope. . . . He is good for us." The final cheer was for "an author who comes through to his reader as a compassionate and gentle man, deeply anguished by the wrongs our nation does in his and all our names."[70]

Thirty years after the publication of *Disobedience and Democracy*, historian Charles Angeletti still believed that "Zinn on civil disobedience is truly revolutionary, groundbreaking—far more important (theoretically) than has been acknowledged. Bad timing on his part. The paradigm didn't (doesn't) allow for it."[71]

As for Zinn, if he read Cohen's review at all—for he was constantly busy at this time, teaching, protesting, working on his next book—he probably liked best the part about not being without hope. His next book ends on a hopeful note as well.

> So here is something for us to do: we can begin the withdrawal of allegiance from the state and its machines of war, from business and its ferocious drive for profit, from all states, all bullying authorities, all dogmas. We can begin to suggest, and to act out, alternative ways of living with one another. It is possible, barely possible, that we can be a *cause* of change, that coming generations will have a new history.[72]

That is the final paragraph of *The Politics of History*, published in 1970. Many years later, Zinn acknowledged that the book came out of the events of the 1960s, and was an attempt "to represent what I was trying to do at the time, to be a historian in the movement and of the movement, and to theorize about the function of the historian and the uses of history."[73]

The Politics of History is clearly one of Zinn's most important books, probably the most important of all the ones we have considered thus far, and in a sense the culmination of all the ones we have considered thus far. Certainly if one is seeking to assess Zinn as a historian, his impact on the historical profession, on history and how it is done, *The Politics of History* and *A People's History of the United States* stand out. Zinn himself lists *Politics* right after the *People's History* when talking about his own favorites among his fifteen books, especially in terms of the impact he thinks they might have had. He thinks *The Politics of History* "had the greatest effect on history teachers. Because I was really speaking for those historians, especially young historians, who were looking for some corrob-oration of what they were feeling, they didn't want to be a traditional, neu-tral historian playing at objectivity, but wanted to be engaged." So the book "dealt with those issues as well as giving illustrations with some specific essays on substantive events in history."[74]

That is a pretty good description of *The Politics of History*. The dedi-cation read "To, for, with Roslyn," and the acknowledgments included the phrase "To Myla and Jeff, for being themselves," suggesting the continuing importance of Zinn's wife and children in his life and work. There is a page at the front of the book devoted to this quotation from Denis Diderot, writing of Voltaire: "Other historians relate facts to inform us of facts. You relate them to excite in our hearts an intense hatred of lying, ignorance, hypocrisy, superstition, tyranny; and the anger remains even after the memory of the facts has disappeared." It is significant that Zinn would choose that quotation, obviously, and suggestive of the approach to history he hoped to take, and encourage others to take. In his introduction, Zinn tells of the death in 1968 of America's leading entrepreneur of political but-tons, whose own button had always read, "I don't care who wins. My busi-ness is buttons." To Zinn, that symbolizes the historian as "passive reporter, studying the combatants of yesterday, while those of today clash outside his window. His preferences are usually private. His business is history." But whether it *should* be that way is the question underlying Zinn's book: "In a world where children are still not safe from starvation or bombs, should not the historian thrust himself and his writing into history, on behalf of goals in which he deeply believes? Are we historians not humans first, and scholars because of that?"[75]

Recalling Rousseau's accusation, "We have physicists, geometricians, chemists, astronomers, poets, musicians, and painters in plenty, but we have no longer a citizen among us," and noting that since the eighteenth century that list of specialists has grown to include sociologists, political scientists, psychologists, and historians, Zinn concludes, "The scholars multiply diligently, but with little passion." The passion he spoke of, he clarified, was "the urgent desire for a better world." That urgent desire, he contended, "should overcome those professional rules which call, impossibly and callously, for neutrality." It is not his aim "to disengage history from the classical effort to be scientific," Zinn insists, "but rather to reaffirm the ancient humanist aims of the scientists (before military needs began to command so much of their talent), and to catch up with the new understanding in science about what 'scientific' means." Nor is it his aim to argue for a uniform approach to the writing of history, and certainly not for the banning of any kind of historical work. Then what is it? "Its aim is, by encouragement and example, to stimulate a higher proportion of socially relevant, value-motivated, action-inducing historical work." Finally, he certainly does not call for tampering with the facts. "My point," he says forcefully, "is not to approach historical data with preconceived answers, but with preconceived questions." Accuracy is a prerequisite, of course, he acknowledges, but "history is not praiseworthy for having merely achieved that. Freud once said some people are always polishing their spectacles and never putting them on."[76]

The Politics of History is divided into three parts. Zinn's own words best describe what he is trying to do in each. Part one, "Approaches," and part three, "Theory and Praxis," "are *about* the writing of history." Essays in these sections "proceed from a discussion of the uses of knowledge in general to historical consciousness in particular." In them, says Zinn, he tries to argue for "the notion of the historian as an actor." This requires discussing many of the problems that fall, professionally speaking, within "the philosophy of history," including determinism, causality, present-mindedness, analytical versus speculative approaches, narrative versus theoretical approaches, what history is really *for*, and what the responsibility of the historian is. In one of these essays Zinn suggests some criteria for a radical history. In part two Zinn presents "essays *in* history," specifically "Essays in American History," under three main headings: class, race, and nationalism. This part, in Zinn's words, "represents an attempt to begin to meet those criteria for a radical history." Though they are diverse, they have a common purpose: "to participate a bit in the social combat of our time." Finally, and central to understanding this book (and Zinn): "My chief hope is to provoke more historical writing which is consciously activist on behalf of the kind of world which history has not yet disclosed, but perhaps hinted at."[77]

The first essay in part one is entitled "Knowledge as a Form of Power." In the context of 1970, it was powerful; perhaps it still is. "Is it not time that we scholars began to earn our keep in this world?" Zinn begins. And, turning the common cliche among academicians, "publish or perish," on its head, Zinn asserts, "We publish while others perish." Knowledge is indeed power, he says, including the "knowledge industry" of academe, and it "can be used, as traditionally, to maintain the status quo, or (as is being demanded by the student rebels) to change it." Clearly, Zinn leaned toward the student rebels. Still, he was not "trying to obliterate all scholarship except the immediately relevant," he insisted; it was just a matter of proportion. We are troubled, said Zinn, "because the new urgency to use our heads for good purposes gets tangled in a cluster of beliefs which are so stuck, fungus-like, to the scholar, that even the most activist of us cannot cleanly extricate ourselves." These beliefs are expressed by such phrases as "disinterested scholarship," "dispassionate learning," "objective study," and "scientific method." All together, felt Zinn, they added up to "the fear that using our intelligence to further our moral ends is somehow improper." Therefore, "we mostly remain subservient to the beliefs of the profession although they violate our deepest feelings as human beings, although we suspect that the traditional neutrality of the scholar is a disservice to the very ideals we teach about as history, and a betrayal of the victims of an un-neutral world." So Zinn sets out to examine the arguments for a supposedly neutral scholarship. "If there is to be a revolution in the uses of knowledge to correspond to the revolution in society," he says (having already stated that "revolutionary changes are required in social policy"), "it will have to begin by challenging the rules which sustain the wasting of knowledge."[78] He proceeds to challenge five such rules.

"Rule 1. *Carry on 'disinterested scholarship.'*" But, "There is no question . . . of a 'disinterested' community of scholars," insists Zinn, "only a question about what kinds of interests the scholars will serve." Ironically, he notes, "Scholars have often served narrow governmental, military, or business interests, and yet withheld support from larger, transcendental values, on the ground that they needed to maintain neutrality."[79]

"Rule 2. *Be objective.*" But objectivity, as usually understood in the scholarly world, is a "myth," insists Zinn. Too many scholars are confused about "the proper distinction between an ultimate set of values and the instruments needed to obtain them." The values, Zinn suggests, may well be subjective (i. e., "derived from human needs"), but the instruments must be objective (i. e., "accurate"). In short, "Our values should determine the *questions* we ask in scholarly inquiry, but not the answers."[80]

"Rule 3. *Stick to your discipline.*" But specialization, notes Zinn, "has become as absurdly extreme in the educational world as in the medical world," something that is natural "when education is divorced from the promotion of values." To work on any real problem, a problem that matters today, such as "how to eliminate poverty in a nation producing eight hundred billion dollars' worth of wealth each year," one would have to cross disciplinary lines from history to economics to political science, and the academic establishment discourages that.[81]

"Rule 4. *To be 'scientific' requires neutrality.*" But, "This is a misconception of how science works," Zinn insists, "both in fact, and in purpose." Scientists do, after all, have values, it is just that they "decided on these so long ago that we have forgotten it." Those values include saving human life and extending human control over the environment to increase the happiness of men and women. "Somehow the social scientists have not yet gotten around to accepting openly that their aim is to keep people alive, to equitably distribute the resources of the earth, to widen the areas of human freedom, and therefore to direct their efforts toward these ends."[82]

"Rule 5. *A scholar must, in order to be 'rational,' avoid 'emotionalism.'*" But, suggests Zinn, while emotion can distort, it can also enhance. Can we describe something like war or slavery unemotionally? Should we even try? "Reason, to be accurate, must be supplemented by emotion," Zinn concludes, paraphrasing Reinhold Niebuhr.[83]

Wrapping up this critique of what the academic world traditionally has done, what it is like, Zinn insists he is merely suggesting "that scholars, on their own, reconsider the rules by which they have worked, and begin to turn their intellectual energies to the urgent problems of our time." The true task of education is to abjure stale knowledge, Zinn paraphrases Alfred North Whitehead, and then, quoting him: "Knowledge does not keep any better than fish." In Zinn's own words: "We need to keep it alive, vital, potent." Then, one of those paragraphs from Zinn that must be reproduced in its entirety:

> Specifically, we might use our scholarly time and energy to sharpen the perceptions of the complacent by exposing those facts that any society tends to hide about itself: the facts about wealth and poverty; about tyranny in both communist and capitalist states; about lies told by politicians, by the mass media, by the church, by popular leaders. We need to

expose fallacious logic, spurious analogies, deceptive slogans, and those intoxicating symbols and concepts which drive people to murder (the flag, communism, capitalism, freedom). We need to dig beneath the abstractions so that our fellow citizens can make judgments on the particular realities beneath political rhetoric. We need to expose inconsistencies and double standards. In short, we need to become the critics of the culture rather than its apologists and perpetuators.[84]

"Let us turn now from scholars in general to historians in particular," Zinn begins his next chapter, "History as Private Enterprise." Indeed, he does turn to history! And history as traditionally done fares none too well. "For a long time, the historian has been embarrassed by his own humanity," Zinn asserts. "Touched by the sight of poverty, horrified by war, revolted by racism, indignant at the strangling of dissent, he has nevertheless tried his best to keep his tie straight, his voice unruffled, and his emotions to himself." Oh, yes, "he has often slyly attuned his research to his feelings, but so slyly, and with such scholarly skill, that only close friends and investigators for congressional committees might suspect him of compassion." Historians seem to worry "that a deep concern with current affairs may lead to twisting the truth about the past." Zinn acknowledges that it might, but is clearly more worried that "nonconcern results in another kind of distortion, in which the ore of history is beaten neither into plowshare nor sword, but is melted down and sold." For the historian, he concludes, "is a specialist who makes his living by writing and teaching, and his need to maintain his position in the profession tends to pull him away from controversy (except the polite controversy of academic disputation) and out of trouble."[85]

Zinn notes with obvious approval the exceptions to the rule of scholarly caution among historians—they "have been glorious." Charles Beard's *An Economic Interpretation of the Constitution*, W. E. B. Du Bois's *Black Reconstruction*, Matthew Josephson's *The Robber Barons*, Arthur Weinberg's *Manifest Destiny*, C. Vann Woodward's *The Strange Career of Jim Crow*, and, not surprisingly, Richard Hofstadter's *The American Political Tradition* were among his favorite examples.[86]

Asked, late in his life, how he came to be so fascinated by history and its impact on social, political, economic, and related developments, Zinn replied in a manner consistent with those sentiments expressed many years before: "By reading Upton Sinclair and Charles Beard and John Steinbeck, becoming politically aware, and concluding that in order to understand what was going on in the world and in this country—Fascism, Communism, capitalism, democracy—history was an essential starting point."[87]

But certainly the dominant mood in historical writing in the United States as of 1970, Zinn insists, "avoids direct confrontation of contemporary problems, apologizes for any sign of departure from 'objectivity,' spurns a liaison with social action."[88]

"At the bottom of the fear of engagement, it seems to me," writes Zinn, "is a confusion between ultimate values and instrumental ones." Unyielding dedication to certain instrumental values—to specific nations, organizations, leaders, social systems, religions, or techniques, "all of which claim their own efficacy in advancing the ultimate values"—"creates powerful pressures for hiding or distorting historical events." On the other hand, to start our historical enquiry with frank adherence to a small set of *ultimate* values—"that war, poverty, race hatred, prisons, should be abolished; that mankind constitutes a single species; that affection and cooperation should replace violence and hostility"—"places no pressure on its advocates to tamper with the truth." Elaborating that point further, Zinn insists that the problem of lying is not the most serious one, for if a historian lies, "someone will soon find him out." But, "If he is irrelevant, this is harder to deal with. We have accepted truth as criterion, and we will rush to invoke it, but we have not yet accepted relevance."[89]

This was a chapter surely designed to grab and shake any reader trained traditionally as a historian. As it moved toward its close, Zinn insisted that "the earth has for so long been so sharply tilted on behalf of the rich, the white-skinned, the male, the powerful, that it will take enormous effort to set it straight." The very selection of a topic for study he considers "the first step in the weighting of the social scales for one value or another"; the problem should first and foremost be a *present* problem, not some dead one of the past like the tariff controversy of the 1820s. Finally, "Teachers and writers of history almost always speak warmly (and vaguely) of how 'studying history will help you understand our own time,'" says Zinn. But what this usually means is that "the teacher will make the point quickly in his opening lecture, or the textbook will dispose of this in an opening sentence, after which the student is treated to an encyclopedic, chronological recapitulation of the past." In effect, then, the student is told: "The past is useful to the present. Now you figure out how."[90]

Part one concludes with the central chapter, "What Is Radical History?" "Historical writing always has some effect on us," it begins. "It may reinforce our passivity; it may activate us. In any case, the historian cannot choose to be neutral; he writes on a moving train." (That passage eventually gave Zinn the title of his memoir: *You Can't Be Neutral on a Moving*

Train.) "I start, therefore," Zinn writes from that moving train, in an absolutely crucial sentence, "from the idea of writing history in such a way as to extend human sensibilities, not out of this book into other books, but into the going conflict over how people shall live, and whether they shall live." "I am urging value-laden historiography," he asserted bluntly. "I can think of five ways in which history can be useful." It should be adequate here to simply list them:

1. *We can intensify, expand, sharpen our perception of how bad things are, for the victims of the world.*

2. *We can expose the pretensions of governments to either neutrality or beneficence.*

3. *We can expose the ideology that pervades our culture—using "ideology" in Mannheim's sense: rationale for the going order.*

4. *We can recapture those few moments in the past which show the possibility of a better way of life than that which has dominated the earth thus far.*

5. *We can show how good social movements can go wrong, how leaders can betray their followers, how rebels can become bureaucrats, how ideals can become frozen and reified.*[91]

In part two, Zinn presents a substantial number of "Essays in American History" that attempt to begin to meet those five criteria for radical history. The ones under the heading "Class" draw heavily from his LaGuardia and New Deal work; the ones under the heading "Race" grow out of his civil rights work; and the ones under the heading "Nationalism" primarily emphasize Vietnam. Approximately half the chapters in *The Politics of History* had seen print previously, primarily as articles; that was true of most of the essays included in part two.

But of the four chapters in part three, "Theory and Praxis," only one had seen print previously, and none deal with material that has occupied our attention so far. This is material that is exceptionally important in understanding Zinn as a historian. His aim, he said, was "to look at what the academic historians and philosophers do when they deal with the 'philosophy of history.'" Zinn's work here is far more readable than most traditional philosophy of history, it should be said. And it should also be said that philosophy of history as traditionally done fares poorly indeed in Zinn's hands. "I will argue that they [philosophers of history] seem to have lost their way without realizing it, because they have forgotten the humanistic goals of historical work." Or, "If they are not lost," he continued, "it is because they are content to wander aimlessly so long as it is 'interesting' or in respectable company." He went on to explain that he put "interesting" in quotation marks "because we have weakened the word by neglecting its denotation as some *interest* to be gained or lost, beyond mere curiosity."[92]

Typically, when Zinn takes on the problem of meaning in history, he is interested in escaping "the whole scene of scholarly discussion by drawing attention to the consequences *in action* of historical writing." The meaning of a writer, then, "will be found not just in what he intends to say, or what he does literally say, but in the effect of his writing on living beings." Similarly, "An idea fulfills its meaning at the moment when, by its effect on others, it becomes an act." By writing history, then, "we are engaging in an act which (through the reader) has consequences, large or small, on behalf of humane values or in opposition to them."[93]

Exploring the question of freedom versus determinism, Zinn is similarly practical in his emphasis. "As if" is his key phrase. "Acting as if we are free is a way of resolving the paradox of determinism and freedom, of overcoming the tension between past and future." The past, he insists, "suggests what can be, not what must be. It shows not all of what is necessary, but some of what is possible." Some of the great leaps humans have made in history have been the responsibility of those who acted "as if." The abolitionists, for example, acted "as if they would arouse a cold nation against slavery," and "Castro and his tiny group in the hills behaved as if they could take over Cuba." "Freedom brings Responsibility," Zinn reminds us. (Indeed, "Freedom and Responsibility" is the title of the first chapter in this last part of the book.) But "responsibility," like "freedom," can remain an abstract notion. "It takes on meaning only when the historian recognizes that his writing of history is an act, thrust into the world, for which he is responsible." And responsibility in history can have meaning only in immediate activity. "It is an old and useless game among historians to decide today whether Caesar was good or bad, Napoleon progressive or reactionary, Roosevelt a reformer or a revolutionist. In a recounting of past crimes, it is senseless to ask: Who was guilty then? unless it leads directly to: What is our responsibility now?"[94]

As he moves specifically into the portion of *The Politics of History* concerned with philosophy of history, Zinn deals first with the historians and then with the philosophers. Firmly, he asserts that "the first question to be asked by anyone philosophizing about any activity is: What is it for?"

He takes a look at the 1965 book *History: The Development of Historical Studies in the United States*, by John Higham with Leonard Krieger and Felix Gilbert. He acknowledges its importance. It "represents the professional historians' considered summary of the state of historical writing in the U.S. at that time." But he also considers it "an inadvertent summary of the formalism and academic detachment that mark much of American historiography today." It evidences a "mood of satisfaction with the position of historiography since the mid-1950s," says Zinn, but this mood is "based on the improvement of the historian's professional position rather than on any notable contribution made by historians to American society." It is worthless to point to the growth of membership of the American Historical Association and the quantity of its activities. A "much more pertinent" question would be: "In what way have the activities of the American Historical Association and its members focused historical knowledge on the solution of the problems pressing in on America and the world in the 1950s and 1960s?"[95]

Zinn quotes Higham's reference to certain historians having an "overdeveloped" commitment to the present, then reacts vigorously, wondering how there could possibly be such a thing as an overdeveloped commitment to the present, if, in the words of Alfred North Whitehead, "the present is all that there is." "What else is there to be committed to but present and future, with life itself the highest value?" Zinn wonders. "The past is dead," he asserts. "Surely, it is useful, as a cadaver is useful to an anatomist, and interesting, as souvenirs and photos are, but we cannot be 'committed' to it in any sense and still call history a humanistic rather than a necrophilic endeavor." "Past-mindedness," Zinn clearly feels, is both impossible and undesirable. "I suspect that the historian who stresses 'past-mindedness' is really telling us that *his* present value is the appreciation of history as a profession," writes Zinn, with what seems an almost painful degree of truth, "that his concerns are academic rather than social, that the 'discipline' of history is competing with other disciplines, rather than joining them to solve social problems." Furthermore, "When historians refuse to let their deepest values (rather than their professional ones) guide their work, the result is often a set of empty arguments about methodology, a spurious 'theorizing' which races around in the academic stratosphere with no particular destination." As to the debate between narrative and explanatory history, Zinn does not much care, for "if our starting point is: How can history serve man today? then it doesn't matter if the method is narrative or explanatory." Either can be useful or useless.[96]

Similarly, addressing the problem of generalization in history, Zinn insists that the key is whether the generalizing is useful. Too often, he says, it is not; rather, "it is as if two lovers are sitting on a hillside in a critical moment of their relationship when matters need to be resolved, and one of them says: 'I've been thinking: every time we've met, it was a Tuesday.'" It is perfectly appropriate, Zinn concedes, that historians be modest about the potential impact of their work; what is inexcusable is the attitude that such impact should not even be their purpose. The traditional response of the historian, he says, is: "I am adding to your stock of knowledge about the world. My job is not to help you act. But take comfort. The sheer increase in knowledge of the past will *somehow* help you." Clearly, Zinn believes that is not enough. Finally, on the subject of generalization, Zinn addresses the 1963 volume edited by Louis Gottschalk entitled *Generalization in the Writing of History*, and concludes that the collection itself is "a striking illustration of the accuracy of at least one generalization: that historians (with few exceptions) do not have as a major concern whether their generalizations will be useful to help solve the problems of our time." Indeed, "the academic historian is the blind scholastic of our time, hardly deserving of emulation by young people entering the field of history, if those young people care about the world."[97]

Zinn is not much gentler when he turns from the historians to the philosophers. Given his fundamental premise "that the past should be studied in such a way as to help us move towards certain obviously desirable goals," there are a number of valuable jobs that philosophers *might* do. As ethicists, they could help clarify the historian's thinking about values. As logicians, they could check the work of the historian in proceeding from premise to conclusion. As analysts of language, they could help the historian express more clearly and accurately both factual and theoretical statements. But instead, "much of the discussion of philosophy of history that has taken place in the United States in the past decade has been trivial, pretentious, tangential."[98]

Taking up specifically the debate over "explanation" in history, Zinn suggests that "the entire discussion falls within the realm of Tolstoy's definition of history as 'a deaf man replying to questions which nobody puts to him.'" He refers primarily to the confrontation between Carl Hempel and his leading critic, William Dray. Once, Zinn agrees with a criticism Dray makes of Hempel, but concludes that "the point Dray makes is both incontestable and trivial." But he is even more critical of Morton White's 1965 work, *The Foundations of Historical Knowledge*. White, notes Zinn, is "one of the foremost Americans in the field," yet his book is also "a good illustration of the impotence characteristic of recent work in the philosophy of history." White's main concern seems to be "with historians, not with history, with language and not with life, with a description of what historians do, not a set of critical judgments about whether they are doing the world any good, or how they might start doing such good." Zinn quotes George Lichtheim: "Philosophy does not change the world: it interprets it and thus reconciles the world to itself." And this, he concludes, is the real meaning of White's "glaring attention to what historians actually do, his interpretation of how they speak about the past," while at the same time showing a "scrupulous unconcern, in an entire book on the philosophy of history, for any *live* human problem."[99]

Zinn concludes *The Politics of History* with a chapter on causation. The chapter includes an excellent case study of different theories of causation of the American Civil War. But Zinn shows that he considers much of this debate, and any other that raises "questions about the past whose answers are useful only to the past," a waste of time. Both philosophers and historians, he insists, "tend to deal with theoretical questions of history, to the advantage of dead scholarship and the disadvantage of living people." He quotes approvingly from *What Is History?* by E. H. Carr: "Good historians, I suspect, whether they think about it or not, have the future in their bones. Besides the question: Why? the historian also asks the question: Whither?"[100]

In 1990, twenty years after its original publication, a second edition of *The Politics of History* appeared. Zinn made no changes in the text itself; he did write an instructive new introduction. The concerns of the original volume "remain alive," he insisted therein. Interestingly, he used the occasion of the republication of *Politics* to show one major example of "where history can be useful." Noting that the Reagan-Bush administration's praise of the so-called free enterprise system counted on a general "historical amnesia," Zinn proceeded to show that the government had been dominated by essentially conservative economic policies from the 1790s all the way to the Great Depression. But "free enterprise" had never been free; rather, it had always been controlled by private wealth with the collaboration of the government. The system had never worked very well for the poor even in times of so-called prosperity. And it had collapsed in 1929 and brought hunger and homelessness to a large part of the American people. Quoting Bush that "there is no place in American public life for philosophies that divide Americans one from another on class lines and that excite conflict among them," Zinn suggested that the apparent premise of that statement that "the excitation of class conflict in this country came from 'philosophies' and not from the reality of class division, the existence of very rich and very poor," could also use a little "historical corrective."[101]

Zinn insisted again that objectivity is a myth. He praised Peter Novick's recent book on that subject, *That Noble Dream: The "Objectivity Question" and the American Historical Profession*, saying that Novick "punctures again and again the pretenses of historians to 'objectivity,' the claim that they have no purpose beyond recapturing the past 'as it really was,'" and quoting approvingly Novick's words: "It seems to me to say of a work of history that it is or isn't objective is to make an *empty* observation; to say something neither interesting nor useful." And in an interesting and rare moment, he showed concern about one review of *The Politics of History* from all those years ago, the one by Christopher Lasch.[102]

This provides an opportunity to see what Novick and Lasch said about Zinn. Novick quoted Zinn saying that "the closest we can come to that elusive 'objectivity' is to report accurately *all* of the subjectivities in a situation." He then quoted Communist historian Herbert Aptheker's review of *The Politics of History*: "A 'slave-oriented' historiography of slavery does not merely 'fill out the picture' of that institution; it *is* the picture. That is, if one wants to know what the institution of slavery was he must go to the slave, to those who endured it; there is the *objective* picture of that institution." But Zinn and Aptheker, along with other leftist historians of the era, agreed, said Novick, that "acknowledged identification with those on the bottom of society was at worst no more distorting, or inconsistent with objectivity, than unacknowledged identification with those on top." Novick placed Zinn, along with Staughton Lynd and Jesse Lemisch, into a group of leftist historians who were "countercultural and with a more activist orientation." This was in contrast with another group of left historians, including Eugene Genovese and Christopher Lasch, many of whom were of Communist background, somewhat better established, and more traditionally scholarly in their orientation. Novick spoke of the "strong moralistic tone" of Zinn and others of his camp who sought to make history immediately useful. Finally, he noted that the reviewers of *The Politics of History* "could not decide whether he [Zinn] was embracing or seeking to escape from relativism," and specifically noted how in Lasch's review he "heaped scorn on Howard Zinn's ethical and presentist criteria for choosing which truths to emphasize."[103]

What else did Lasch say that caused Zinn to single out his review even some twenty years later? It turns out it was not even a review of Zinn's book, but rather an essay entitled "On Richard Hofstadter." Lasch did lash out at "drastic simplification of issues" and "strident partisanship," but he made clear in a footnote that the primary "New Left" historian he had in mind was not Zinn, but Staughton Lynd, specifically his 1968 book, *Intellectual Origins of American Radicalism*. And in his one mention of Zinn, his reference was to an essay entitled "Abolitionists, Freedom-Riders, and the Tactics of Agitation," not *The Politics of History*. Still, Lasch's words were strong ones. He quoted Zinn asking historians to decide "from a particular ethical base what is the action-need of the moment, and to concentrate on that aspect of the truth-complex which fulfills that need," and then concluded snidely: "In the face of such critics, the consensus historians need no defense." Lasch also read the New Left's emphasis on "conflict" as a criticism of Hofstadter's "consensus" approach in *The American Political Tradition*.[104] Zinn insisted that he was mistaken in doing so, at least in relation to Zinn's own work; we have already seen Zinn's admiration for Hofstadter. "In fact," said Zinn in his 1990 introduction to *Politics*, "I agreed totally with the existence of a consensus between the competing dominant groups in our society, but insisted that outside that consensus there was an opposition not given proper attention by historians."[105]

The Politics of History drew major reviews in both the *Annals of the American Academy* and the *American Political Science Review*. Interestingly, Donald B. Rosenthal, writing for the *Annals*, noted that though Zinn taught in a political science department, "it is obvious from this volume that much of his training and academic interest has been in the field of American history." Rosenthal considered Zinn's book "forcefully written," but at the same time was concerned about the author's "occasional stridency." He also insisted there was "a certain ambiguity" in Zinn's stance: "Though he presents variants of the same basic list of ultimate values in several places, for example, 'the need to abolish war, race hatred, poverty, and destructive competition,' he brushes aside too readily the problems of harnessing social activism to the realization of those values." Most of the ends Zinn espoused were already universally proclaimed in political rhetoric, said Rosenthal, but generally evaded in political reality; Zinn did not help show how to bridge this gap. Finally, "Zinn's call for socially committed history is neither grounded in a clear definition of social ends, nor is it related to a distinct vision of appropriate political means. Rather, like the abolitionists with whom he appears to identify himself, Zinn's approach is essentially a passionate appeal to ultimate values transcending historical circumstance."[106]

Philip Green, of Smith College, reviewed Zinn's volume for the *American Political Science Review*. It was a very thoughtful and very positive review. *The Politics of History* was an "excellent collection," according to Green, to be praised, among other reasons, for its exposure of objectivity as "only a mask with which we hide the real social consequences of what we are doing and saying." Green responded especially positively to the "uniform excellence" of Zinn's selected essays on American history. "It is in these essays that Zinn both particularizes his critique of status quo apologetics and—what is more rarely done—offers his own, competing version of history in the service of social change rather than history in the service of the current world and national division of powers." Green considered Zinn "brilliant" in his critique of traditional approaches to radicalism in history: "[Zinn] reveals American history-writing at its most complacent and methodologically inept in its treatment of the American radical tradition, as he shows that our historians have followed the pattern of psychoanalyzing the *latent motives* of radicals, but unquestioningly accepting the *manifest statements of principle* of the ruling class—and of the historians themselves!" Finally, Green also praised Zinn for his contribution to the insight that a society "is to be judged not by the power and freedom available to its best-off citizens, or even to the average citizen, but by the kind of life available to its *outsiders*." Green considered Zinn part of a group including Jesse Lemisch, Stephan Thernstrom, Michael Parenti, and others in this regard, and concluded his review: "It may be time for the practitioners of this kind of scholarship to come together and create their own standard texts to spread their unconventional wisdom."[107] It is not known whether Zinn's book published ten years later, in 1980, *A People's History of the United States*, satisfied Green in this regard.

Four more reviews of *The Politics of History* deserve briefer mention. "The world has become such a dangerous place, and its problems so great, that the historian can no longer afford the luxury of writing history as a mere intellectual exercise," begins Julian F. Jaffe in the *Library Journal*, sounding almost like Zinn himself. Jaffe goes on to suggest that Zinn's approach is "neither new nor radical in that many historians are using this approach today," but he is especially impressed by the way Zinn develops his thesis in "13 outstanding essays on various crises and issues in American history."[108]

Other basically positive reviews appeared in the *New York Times Book Review* and the *Christian Science Monitor*.[109] Finally, a brief and strange little review appeared in the pages of *America*. The reviewer recognized Zinn's theme as the "utilization of history as an instrument for today's problems." But then the strange part. Noting that "radical history" essentially means "the historian's obligation to expose the inequities and injustices of the past, to propound 'truth' and to relate all of these to our time," the reviewer mentioned how these issues had split the American Historical Association at its 1969 meeting, "when the 'radical' historians attacked the 'establishment' historians." He then concluded by predicting, of *The Politics of History*: "This work is likely to prove a portent of this year's gathering, where nobility will be deemed noxious and radicalism termed relevant. Even historians become hysterical."[110]

It is hard to know exactly what those last two sentences mean. Is nobility somehow the opposite of radicalism? Who is being called hysterical? Zinn and the radicals? In any case, Zinn was certainly not hysterical. Intense, yes; hysterical, no. Though it is easy to see how he could have been in those days, as active as he was. We have noted his dedication of *Politics* to his wife, and the continuing importance to him of family. In his 1994 memoir, he wrote, "I must confess that my revolutionary ardor has often been limited by my desire to get home to my wife and kids." The specific context for that remark was Zinn's participation in a 1968 trial in Milwaukee. Fourteen people had gone into a draft board there, taken thousands of documents, and burned them in a symbolic protest of the war in Vietnam. Zinn was called in as an "expert witness," but when he began to tell about the history of civil disobedience in America, presumably the subject on which he was an expert witness, the judge pounded his gavel and said, "You can't discuss that. This is getting to the heart of the matter!" Noted Zinn wryly as he looked back on this incident: "He was right. Courtrooms are not places where one is allowed to get to the heart of the matter." But at that point in the trial, Zinn was frustrated, and blurted out, "Why can't I say something important? Why can't the jury hear something important?" That angered the judge, who threatened Zinn with contempt of court. Zinn then responded, "An IBM machine could make this decision if the question is only did they do this." The judge pounded his gavel again, more forcefully this time. Recalled Zinn: "I could have gone on, I suppose, dramatically adding my civil disobedience to that of the defendants, but my courage stopped at that point." And then the confession about revolutionary ardor *in re* family.[111]

When it was suggested to him that the remark seemed to speak to family being important to him, he spoke honestly, at some length, and in a manner with which many activists who have struggled to balance activism and family could identify:

Yes, but probably not important enough, in the sense that there were times when I probably neglected them. I probably wasn't around as much for my children as I would have been if I wasn't politically active. But I was conscious of that—there was always conflict. Always tension. Always a meeting. "How many meetings did you go to this week?" And "Can't you stay home?" And like during the Vietnam War, I was going all over the country. Invited to speak here and there. "Do you have to say yes to everything?" So, sometimes I'd make the decision one way and sometimes I'd make the decision the other way. Sometimes I'd make the decision for my family, and feel guilty that I'd copped out on something where I should be. Sometimes I'd make the decision in favor of going to something political and feel guilty.[112]

In 1970, the very year of publication of *The Politics of History*, Zinn was involved in another trial; this time it was his own. By the spring of that year, feelings about the war in Vietnam had become, in Zinn's words, "almost unbearably intense." He chose to become part of a group of some one hundred people to block the road carrying draftees off to military duty at the Boston Army base. It was "a symbolic act, a statement, a piece of guerrilla theatre." They were all arrested, of course, "and charged, in the quaint language of an old statute, with 'sauntering and loitering' in such a way as to obstruct traffic." Most pled guilty, paid their fine, and moved on. Zinn and seven others insisted on a jury trial. They represented themselves in court that fall. They were allowed to speak about the war, the reasons they opposed it, and the tradition of civil disobedience. But the judge, addressing the jury, said it did not really matter, that the only issue was whether they did indeed block traffic. So they were found guilty, and sentenced to seven days or a $21.00 fine. Five paid the fine, and Zinn was ready to do the same, but felt obligated to join the two who refused. The judge gave them forty-eight hours, presumably hoping they would change their minds. In the meantime, Zinn had been invited to Johns Hopkins University in Baltimore to debate philosopher Charles Frankel on the issue of civil disobedience. But the debate conflicted with his scheduled reappearance in court. Deciding it would be "hypocritical for me, an advocate of civil disobedience, to submit dutifully to the court order and thereby skip out on an opportunity to speak to hundreds of students about civil disobedience," he went to Baltimore. The morning after the debate, he called his wife, Roslyn, from the Washington, D.C., airport. "The news on the radio says you cannot be located and there's a warrant out for your arrest," she informed him. But when he arrived in Boston, he felt compelled to go directly to a scheduled class at BU—after all, it was Law and Justice in America, and one of his topics was civil disobedience. A number of his students were shocked to see him. "You're wanted by the police! Aren't you supposed to turn yourself in?" He said he would, after class. But he did not have to, for when he walked outside, two detectives, accompanied by a nervous university official, were waiting for him. He was taken before the judge and given an opportunity to pay his fine. He refused, and was immediately handcuffed and taken to Boston's Charles Street Jail, in Zinn's words "an old dungeon of a building, long ago condemned as unfit even for prisoners." That night, he did not get much sleep: "The talk, sometimes shouts and screams, in the cellblock, the lights on all night, the cockroaches racing around my bunk, the constant clanging of steel doors." So he made up his mind that first night was his last one—he would pay the rest of his fine and get out. "Besides, my cellmate thought there was something wrong with me when he learned I could get out by paying a few dollars and chose to stay. Also, I had an engagement in Oregon to talk about the war. And— maybe above all—the cockroaches!"[113]

It was fairly unusual for Zinn to assign any of his own writings in his classes. But in 1988, his last year of teaching at BU, he was still using some passages from *The Politics of History* in a graduate seminar entitled Politics and History. And his syllabus described that seminar in a manner entirely consistent with the contents of the book. "We want to read about, think about, talk about the uses of history for political purposes," stated the syllabus, "and discuss the methodological and philosophical problems involved in such writing." But also, typically Zinn, "we want to produce actual pieces of writing which involve historical research and also have a political objective." And these writings were not just for the students to share with each other, but rather "real writing sent out into the world" as articles for magazines, columns for newspapers, letters to editors, pamphlets, or "any other form which would be useful for public education."[114]

Education that went beyond the classroom—Zinn was constantly involved in that kind of activity himself. In the early 1970s, much of it involved the notorious Pentagon Papers. These were a top secret, classified study, with accompanying documents, of U.S. involvement in Vietnam. They revealed blunders, misjudgments, and lies. Daniel Ellsberg, a former Department of Defense analyst now opposed to the war, began to leak them to the *New York Times* in 1971. Ellsberg and Zinn were friends. They had been a part of the same affinity group during the massive spring 1971 demonstrations against the Vietnam War in Washington. Noam Chomsky, noted linguist and radical critic of American foreign policy, was also a part of that group. Arnold Tovell, editor at Boston's Beacon Press, publisher of several of Zinn's books, was "very much against the war" (Zinn's words).[115] So Beacon Press decided to publish, in 1972, a four-volume edition of the Pentagon Papers, and asked Zinn and Chomsky to edit a fifth volume, a collection of essays commenting on the papers.

The title page of that fifth volume carried the words "critical essays." It was an accurate description. Zinn and Chomsky in their preface made no apologies for that—they felt people had heard enough of the government's view. Noting that the Pentagon Papers had become "public property" in 1971, against the wishes of the government, Zinn and Chomsky concluded: "This seems only proper when we consider that for seven years this government has been carrying on a war of annihilation in Indochina against the wishes of the people there, and now against the wishes of the American people, too." Ellsberg, and others who had laid out for public scrutiny the story of American war policy, have "exposed the coldness of mind, the meanness of spirit, behind that policy." But as a sign "that this country, born with thrilling phrases about freedom, has not been truly free, there was peril for those who informed the American people of the decisions that sent their sons to war." Prosecution had begun of both Ellsberg and Anthony Russo, who had helped him with the secret photocopying of the documents. But Zinn and Chomsky, of course, defended the photocopying and release of the documents. Of Ellsberg and Russo they wrote: "It was they who defied the doctrine of secrecy, showing that true patriotism which asks dedication not to one's government, but to one's country and countrymen." Noting that most of their essayists were American, but that one was Vietnamese and several were French, Zinn and Chomsky explained that they "wanted to include the view point of these people who have felt and suffered most from the policies of the United States, as well as to draw upon the prior French experience with the anticolonial revolution in Indochina." Finally, the editors made clear what they hoped the essays in their volume would accomplish: "Most of all, we hope they supply what the government documents lack, some sense of the human consequences of this war, so that now Americans will devote time and energy to stopping the unforgivable American assault on the land and people of Southeast Asia."[116]

Editing the volume of critical essays was not Howard Zinn's last involvement with the Pentagon Papers; he was also involved in the trial of Ellsberg and Russo, as an expert witness. He studied the documents extensively, and flew to Los Angeles for the trial. Staying at the oceanfront home of Leonard Weinglass, one of the attorneys for the defendants, Zinn managed to make a pleasant time of it, taking walks on the beach, and even spending one evening in a local club listening to "two of my favorite jazz and blues musicians, Sonny Terry and Brownie McGee." When he was called into court for his testimony, Zinn spoke for several hours on the history of the Vietnam War. "It was," he said, "like teaching a class, but with much more at stake." After his history lesson, Weinglass asked him if he felt the documents in the volumes were injurious to the "national defense." Zinn answered that there was nothing in them that could be harmful to the United States militarily speaking, but that there was certainly embarrassing information since it revealed how the government "had lied to the American public." Pushed further on the concept of "national defense," Zinn suggested that "a proper definition of the term was defense of the people, not of special interests." The "secrets" disclosed in the Pentagon Papers, according to Zinn, "might embarrass politicians, might hurt the profits of corporations wanting tin, rubber, oil, in far-off places. But this was not the same as hurting the nation, the people." The prosecutor did not cross-examine Zinn; he wanted only to establish that Zinn was a friend of Ellsberg, a fact which he established by holding up a police photo of the two together in a 1971 demonstration in Boston. After all the testimony, summations, and the judge's charge, the jury began its deliberations. But a few days later, the judge called them back into the courtroom and declared a mistrial. Noted Zinn: "The Watergate scandals were coming to light. The Nixon administration had engaged in illegal wiretaps. In an attempt to discredit Dan Ellsberg, it had sent a team to burglarize the files of his psychiatrist. It had even sent men to beat him up when he spoke at an antiwar rally." Based on such irregularities, the judge had little choice, Zinn felt. "The case of the Pentagon Papers was ended," he exulted. But he insisted on one further point in his account of this story: "The members of the jury were interviewed afterwards, and it was clear that Dan Ellsberg and Tony Russo would not have been convicted."[117]

NOTES

1. Howard Zinn, *You Can't Be Neutral on a Moving Train: A Personal History of Our Times* (Boston: Beacon Press, 1994), dust jacket.

2. Ibid.

3. Howard Zinn, interview, Boston, Mass., March 14, 1997.

4. Ibid.

5. Ibid.

6. Ibid.

7. Ibid.

8. Ibid.

9. This paragraph is based on a paper, "A Profile on Howard Zinn," by a student named Darcie F. Lubart, date illegible, found in Zinn's own files in the office he retains as a professor emeritus at Boston University. It should be noted that in the context of the paper it is not always clear when Levin is speaking and when the student is speaking. It seems the comments about standards, discipline, grades, learning, and photographs are the student's effort at a paraphrase of Levin, and that the one about asking him a million times is an actual quote; it is clear that the words attributed to Zinn the student actually intended to attribute to Zinn. Note: Henceforth, documents from these files are referred to as Howard Zinn Papers.

The State Historical Society of Wisconsin has a collection called "Howard Zinn Papers, 1956–1970," in the Social Action Collection of its Archives Division. The Magar Library at Boston University has this entire collection on microfilm. Its focus is primarily on Zinn's early involvement in the civil rights movement. For example, his research materials which led to the book *SNCC: The New Abolitionists* are included.

10. Zinn, interview, March 14, 1997.

11. Ibid.

12. John Silber, *Straight Shooting: What's Wrong with America and How to Fix It* (New York: Harper and Row, 1989), pp. 104–105.

13. Howard Zinn Papers. Unfortunately, this document is undated.

14. John R. Silber, interview by Laura Barrett, December 3, 1979, Howard Zinn Papers.

15. Patrick Collins, "They're Education's Odd Couple," *NewStandard*, January 11, 1997, http://www.s-t.com/daily/01-97/01-11-97/aO11o005.htm.

16. A copy of the "Factbook," dated August 1990, is in the Howard Zinn Papers; Zinn expressed his view that it helped defeat Silber in an interview, March 13, 1997.

17. Brief, signed statement by Hazel M. Hopkins, dated February 1980, Howard Zinn Papers.

18. Several documents relating to this incident are in the Howard Zinn Papers. Zinn also relates it briefly on pp. 193–194 of *You Can't Be Neutral on a Moving Train*.

19. Howard Zinn Papers. Unfortunately, there is no date on the pamphlet, but it appears to have been published in 1978.

20. A copy of the letter was supplied to the author by Zinn.

21. Zinn, *You Can't Be Neutral on a Moving Train*, pp. 184–85.

22. Daniel Gross, "Under the Volcano: Boston University in the Silber Age," *Lingua Franca* 3 (November/December 1995): 44–53.

23. Lubart, "Profile," Howard Zinn Papers.

24. Wendy Gillespie, "Howard Zinn: A Profile," November 23, 1987, Howard Zinn Papers.

25. David Barsamian, "The *Progressive* Interview: Howard Zinn," *Progressive* (July 1997): 37–40.

26. Zinn, interview, March 14, 1997.

27. Staughton Lynd, e-mail message to the author, August 6, 2000.

28. Howard Zinn, *Vietnam: The Logic of Withdrawal* (Boston: Beacon Press, 1967), pp. 1–6.

29. Ibid., pp. 9, 14.

30. Ibid., pp. 22–23.

31. Ibid., pp. 28–31.

32. Ibid., pp. 42–50.

33. Ibid., pp. 51, 59, 60–61.

34. Ibid., p. 66.

35. Ibid., p. 70.

36. Ibid., p. 80.

37. Ibid., p. 88.

38. Ibid., pp. 97, 101.

39. Ibid., p. 103.

40. Ibid., pp. 108, 115–16.

41. Ibid., p. 125.

42. Letter to Beacon Press from John E. Thorne, February 12, 1968, and letter to Thorne from Arnold C. Tovell, Editor, Beacon Press, February 20, 1968. Both documents are in the Howard Zinn Papers.

43. Wes Lawrence, "A Plea for Withdrawal," *Cleveland Plain Dealer*, April 6, 1967. Copy in the Howard Zinn Papers.

44. Both documents are found in the Howard Zinn Papers.

45. David P. Gauthier, review of *Vietnam: The Logic of Withdrawal* by Howard Zinn, *Canadian Forum* 47 (November 1967): 182–84.

46. Review of *Vietnam: The Logic of Withdrawal* by Howard Zinn, *New York Times Book Review*, June 11, 1967, p. 38.

47. Review of *Vietnam: The Logic of Withdrawal* by Howard Zinn, *Times Literary Supplement,* May 25, 1967, p. 431; Collin Clark, review of *Vietnam: The Logic of Withdrawal* by Howard Zinn, *Library Journal* 92 (February 15, 1967): 784; and Saville R. Davis, review of *Vietnam: The Logic of Withdrawal* by Howard Zinn, *Christian Science Monitor*, May 25, 1967, p. 7. A brief review in *Choice* 4 (December, 1967): 1180, was a moderately positive one. Another brief one in the *New Yorker* 43 (September 9, 1967): 179, was noncommittal.

48. Howard Zinn Papers. Attached to Gruening's letter are the appropriate tear sheets from the *Congressional Record*.

49. A copy of the transcript of the comments is to be found in the Howard Zinn Papers.

50. Letter to Howard Zinn from Howard Haverbach (?), October 19, 1968, the Howard Zinn Papers.

51. Notes for this speech are in the Howard Zinn Papers.

52. Howard Zinn, "Lessons of Vietnam—30 years after the Tet offensive," *Progressive*, January 26, 1998, http://secure.progressive.org/mpzinnjan98.htm.

53. Zinn, interview, March 14, 1997; Howard Zinn, e-mail message to the author, January 14, 1997.

54. Howard Zinn, *Disobedience and Democracy: Nine Fallacies on Law and Order* (New York: Random House, 1968), p. 5.

55. Ibid., pp. 5–6.

56. Ibid., p. 7.

57. Ibid., pp. 8, 12–14, 22, 25–26.

58. Ibid., pp. 27, 30–31.

59. Ibid., pp. 32, 36, 38.

60. Ibid., pp. 39, 41–42, 46, 48–52.

61. Ibid., pp. 53, 55–57, 62, 67–68.

62. Ibid., pp. 68, 75, 78, 87.

63. Ibid., p. 87.

64. Ibid., pp. 101, 105–106, 115–16.

65. Ibid., pp. 117–18.

66. Ibid., pp. 118–19.

67. Ibid., pp. 123–24.

68. Simon Lazarus, review of *Disobedience and Democracy: Nine Fallacies on Law and Order* by Howard Zinn, *New Republic* 159 (December 7, 1968): 33.

69. Saville R. Davis, review of *Disobedience and Democracy: Nine Fallacies on Law and Order* by Howard Zinn, *Christian Science Monitor* (January 16, 1969): 11.

70. Carl Cohen, review of *Disobedience and Democracy: Nine Fallacies on Law and Order* by Howard Zinn, *Nation* 207 (December 2, 1968): 597, 599–600. A brief review in the *Library Journal* 94 (January 15, 1969): 176, was not very helpful, but did say "Recommended for libraries." Reviews were also written by William B. Gould for *Commonweal* 90 (April 25, 1969): 178; and J. G. Deutsch for the *New York Times Book Review*, February 16, 1969, p. 18.

71. Letter to the author from Charles Angeletti, August 9, 1998.

72. Howard Zinn, *The Politics of History* (Boston: Beacon Press, 1970), p. 368.

73. Howard Zinn, e-mail message to the author, February 2, 1997.

74. Zinn, interview, March 14, 1997.

75. Zinn, *The Politics of History*, p. 1.

76. Ibid., pp. 1–2.

77. Ibid., pp. 2–3.

78. Ibid., pp. 5–9.

79. Ibid., pp. 9–10.

80. Ibid., pp. 10–11.

81. Ibid., p. 11.

82. Ibid., p. 12.

83. Ibid., pp. 12–13.

84. Ibid., p. 13.

85. Ibid., p. 15.

86. Ibid., pp. 16–17.

87. Howard Zinn, e-mail message to the author, October 17, 2002.

88. Zinn, *The Politics of History*, pp. 16–17.

89. Ibid., pp. 20–22.

90. Ibid., pp. 27, 29, 30.

91. Ibid., pp. 35–36, 42, 45, 47, 51.

92. Ibid., p. 290.

93. Ibid., pp. 279–80.

94. Ibid., pp. 280–86.

95. Ibid., pp. 289–91.

96. Ibid., pp. 294–95, 300, 303.

97. Ibid., pp. 304, 308–309, 313, 315.

98. Ibid., pp. 320–21.

99. Ibid., pp. 321, 330, 341, 342, 351.

100. Ibid., pp. 364, 352, 363.

101. Howard Zinn, *The Politics of History*, 2d ed. (Champaign: University of Illinois Press, 1990), pp. xi–xiv.

102. Ibid., pp. xvii–xviii, xi.

103. David Novick, *That Noble Dream: The "Objectivity Question" and the American Historical Profession* (Cambridge: Cambridge University Press, 1988), pp. 426, 428, 431, 436, 437.

104. Christopher Lasch, "On Richard Hofstadter," *New York Review of Books* 20 (March 8, 1973): 12. The Zinn essay on the abolitionists and the freedom riders appeared in *The Antislavery Vanguard*, ed. Martin Duberman (Princeton, N.J.: Princeton University Press, 1965), and was closely related to his book *SNCC: The New Abolitionists*.

105. Zinn, *The Politics of History*, 2d ed., pp. xi, xviii.

106. Donald B. Rosenthal, review of *The Politics of History* by Howard Zinn, *Annals of the American Academy* 393 (January 1971): 174–75.

107. Philip Green, review of *The Politics of History* by Howard Zinn, *American Political Science Review* 64 (December 1970): 1281–83.

108. Julian F. Jaffe, review of *The Politics of History* by Howard Zinn, *Library Journal* 95 (June 1, 1970): 2152.

109. L. B. Stevens, review of *The Politics of History* by Howard Zinn, *New York Times Book Review*, September 20, 1970, p. 39; and Courtney R. Sheldon, review of *The Politics of History* by Howard Zinn, *Christian Science Monitor*, July 30, 1970, p. 5.

110. Clarence Leonard Hohl Jr., review of *The Politics of History* by Howard Zinn, *America* 123 (November 28, 1970): 468.

111. Zinn, *You Can't Be Neutral on a Moving Train*, pp. 152–53.

112. Howard Zinn, interview, Boston, Mass., March 13, 1997.

113. Zinn, *You Can't Be Neutral on a Moving Train*, pp. 142–44.

114. Syllabus, Politics and History, spring 1988, Howard Zinn Papers.

115. Howard Zinn, e-mail message to the author, January 14, 1997.

116. Noam Chomsky and Howard Zinn, eds., *The Pentagon Papers: Critical Essays* (Boston: Beacon Press, 1972), pp. ix–x.

117. Zinn, *You Can't Be Neutral on a Moving Train*, pp. 159–61.

FOUR

YOU CAN'T BE NEUTRAL ON A MOVING TRAIN

1973-1988

M ore than the Daniel Ellsberg trial ended in 1973. That year also saw the end of both the U.S. draft and U.S. bombing in Southeast Asia, and the signing of the Paris Peace Accords, basically mandating unilateral withdrawal of American troops in exchange for the return of American prisoners of war held in North Vietnam.

Typically, Howard Zinn had already begun to move on to other things. In 1973, for example, his next book came out. Entitled simply *Postwar America*, it was a volume in the History of American Society series edited by Jack P. Greene of Johns Hopkins University. But it is about post–World War II American society only in the broadest sense, and it certainly is not mainstream American historical writing à la 1973. Mostly Zinn is concerned with war and race, disobedience and democracy—increasingly his dominant themes. Zinn's dedication was a clue to what was coming: "To Dave Dellinger who has worked so hard, through all the years covered in this book, against war, against injustice—always with that rare combination of revolutionary courage and concern for all human beings." Dellinger, of course, was a noted antiwar activist, pacifist, advocate of revolutionary nonviolence.

Looking back to that period in his life and the country's history, Zinn recalls that he saw the book as "an opportunity, in the early seventies, to sum up my views on recent American history." He remembers the first chapter as "especially important" to him, "because it was the first 'revisionist' account, as far as I knew, of World War II, sharply questioning its status as a 'good war.' I called that chapter 'The Best of Wars' (anticipating in a certain way Studs Terkel's *The Good War*)."[1]

Jack P. Greene acknowledged the nature of Zinn's volume in his editor's preface. While he considered it an "extraordinarily powerful and moving reading of the recent American past," it was certainly "not a conventional work of American history, not the traditional success story, not a chronicle of the social, material, political, and diplomatic achievements of the American nation over the past quarter of a century." Nor was it "objective," in the sense historians usually mean. Rather, it was "polemical," "passionate," and "a stinging indictment of the dominant groups within American society"—here the social history—"for their failure to live up to the principles on which this nation was founded." Then, back to what the volume was not; it was "obviously not the product of despair." For Zinn found hope, first in the black revolution then in the revolution of the young, the "possible beginnings of a sweeping revolution in values and behavior with the potential to mobilize the American public." This revolution, and "the painful failures of American society—more especially those of its predominant liberal credo," provided the central themes to Zinn's look at postwar America.[2]

Greene's introduction is helpful, but Zinn speaks so well for himself. In his introduction, entitled "The American Creed," he asserts, as he already has in *The Politics of History* and elsewhere, that "any book of history is, consciously or not, an interpretation in which selected data from the past is tossed into the present according to the interest of the historian." And that interest, "no matter how much the historian's mind dwells on the past, is always a present one." His own interest in this volume, he said, was to explore just two questions, and to do so "in the hope that the reader will be stimulated to take a more active part in the making of an American history different from what we have had so far." The two questions were "First, why did the United States, exactly as it became the most heavily armed and wealthiest society in the world, run into so much trouble with its own people?" (Explaining, Zinn wrote: "From the late fifties to the early seventies, the nation experienced unprecedented black rebellion, student demonstrations, antiwar agitation, civil disobedience, prison uprisings, and a widespread feeling that American civilization was faltering, or even in decay.") And second, "What are the possibilities, the visions, the beginnings, of fresh directions for this country?" Running through these two questions, and obviously through the book, "is the theme of an American creed at odds with itself." American history, in short, "is a long attempt, so far unsuccessful, to overcome the ambiguity in the American creed, to fulfill the principles of the Declaration of Independence."

Zinn commented in an interesting way on the now-standard distinction between *consensus* and *conflict* in American history and American historical writing. The consensus interpretation, he acknowledged, stated "a profound truth about our society, that its great 'progress' and its political clashes have kept within severe limits." But he also noted what was missing in the consensus analysis: "the persistent strain of protest that shows up repeatedly in American history . . . —the voices, the ideas, the struggles of those who defy the American working creed, who will not let the nation forget the rhetorical promises, who keep alive the vision, the possibility of a society beyond capitalism, beyond nationalism, beyond the hierarchies that are preserved in a man-eat-man culture." It was the existence of this strain that justified the work of the conflict school of American history, "which insists that Americans not forget the black abolitionists, the Wobblies, the Socialists, the anarchists, that we keep in mind Tom Paine, John Brown, Emma Goldman, Eugene Debs, Malcolm X."[3]

Zinn began the discussion of his first question in his opening chapter, "with Hiroshima, in 1945, when an entire city was annihilated by American technology in a burst of righteous brutality, with no protest from the American public." He raised his second question in his final chapter "with the scene at Bunker Hill, 1971, when veterans of the Vietnam War assembled to protest similar brutality in Indochina." In between, he noted how Americans entered the post–World War II era "with great confidence in their system, and with quadrupled power and wealth to back up that confidence," but how in the 1960s that confidence began to break down, "as crisis after crisis—in race relations, in the distribution of resources, in foreign policy —indicated that something was terribly wrong." And what was really disturbing was that "the troubles of American society could no longer be attributed to departures from the liberal creed—to youthful imperialism or southern racism or corporate exploitation or political witch-hunts." Instead, we had to begin to question whether that liberal creed itself was faulty.[4] Zinn clearly felt that it was.

It is the faith in this working creed that has now begun to waver—faith in achieving racial equality through constitutional amendments, statutes, and Supreme Court decisions; faith in the system of corporate profit as modified by trade unions and the welfare state; faith in due process, the Bill of Rights, the courts, and the jury system as the means of securing justice and freedom of expression for every American; faith in voting, representative government, and the two-party system as the best way in which to guarantee democracy; faith in police to keep peace at home and protect the rights of all, and in soldiers and bombs to keep law and order abroad; faith in what is perhaps the crucial element in the modern system, in the idea that a paternalistic government will take care of its citizens without their day-to-day exercise of judgment or criticism or resistance.[5]

"This book intends to show how this faith has been mistaken," Zinn said bluntly, "how, in the twenty-five years since World War II, the working creed of the American system has produced a crisis of culture and politics." But then, hopefully, "it also intends to show that out of this crisis has come at least the beginning of an attempt to act out what was promised, two centuries ago, in the Declaration of Independence."[6]

How well did Zinn accomplish his objectives? The answers, as evidenced in reviews of *Postwar America*, varied widely. Interestingly, for the first time, the *Journal of American History* assigned a reviewer to one of Zinn's books; not surprisingly, that reviewer was unimpressed. But first, more of Zinn's book itself.

Hiroshima, asserted Zinn, "was, despite all the earnest self-searching after the fact, the final affirmation of the ability of the best of civilizations—that of liberal, rational, enlightened Judeo-Christian society—to commit the worst of war's acts." And "the decision apparatus on the dropping of the atomic bomb was a perfect example of that dispersed responsibility so characteristic of modern bureaucracy, where an infinite chain of policy-makers, committees, advisers, and administrators make it impossible to determine who is accountable." Finally, Hiroshima "was not an unfortunate error in an otherwise glorious war." Rather, "it revealed, in concentrated form, characteristics that the United States had in common with the other belligerents—whatever their political nomenclature." The first of these characteristics was "the commission and easy justification of indiscriminate violence when it serves political aims." The second was "the translation of the system's basic power motives into whatever catchall ideology can mobilize the population—'socialism' for socialist states, 'democracy' for capitalist states, 'the master race' for Fascist states." The common denominator for all of them, concluded Zinn, has been "the survival of the system in power. . . . What dominated the motives for war among all the belligerents were political ends—power, privilege, expansion—rather than human ends—life, liberty, the pursuit of individual and social happiness."[7]

World War II, according to Zinn, "did not end, but rather sustained, the Fascist notions that war is a proper mode of solving international political problems, and that, once a nation is at war, any means whatsoever justify victory." He saw the "saturation bombing of Vietnamese villages by American bombers dropping napalm and cluster bombs, which are deliberately intended for people, not bridges or factories," as being perfectly in accord with this kind of thinking. Indeed, though he is concerned with America after 1945 in his book, Zinn looks back to the origins of World War II, and insists it was a challenge to the national power of the United States, "which meant the power and the prestige of those who held office and wealth in America," that led the country into the war, not the welfare of the American people or any other people. The "bald assertion of power as the justification for American involvement," as, for example, Henry Luce had made in his famous 1941 essay "The American Century," was of course avoided in the language of Franklin D. Roosevelt and other national leaders. Yet "after the war the phrase 'world responsibility' became the prime euphemism for what the British had called 'empire.'" Zinn even carries this kind of critique so far as to suggest that "the UN organization reflected the nationalist interests of the big powers rather than the dreams of freedom that many thought the war would make real."[8]

Zinn sounds almost cynical at times in this volume, not really a characteristic one associates with him ordinarily.

Most often, in the so-called cold war following World War II, the United States spoke of stopping Communism or saving the free world. Zinn's continued analysis of American foreign policy, however—including subheadings "Intervention," "Economic Penetration," "Militarization," and "Vietnam"—all take place in a chapter called "Empire." Throughout, Zinn's central point is that "the rhetorical values of American liberalism are in contradiction with its operating values, which actually determine policy for the policy-makers." But "nowhere was this discrepancy clearer than in America's policy toward Southeast Asia."[9]

Moving his analysis to the domestic scene following World War II, in a chapter entitled "Democracy and Profit," Zinn insists that although the most widely used descriptions of America involved such phrases as "free society," "democratic state," "affluent society," "people of plenty," "Fair Deal," "New Frontier," and "Great Society," the reality was that "the resources of the richest nation on earth were still irrationally allocated to the production of war goods and luxury goods; urgent social needs, like housing, health care, schools, were considered secondary in importance." Also, "at the top of the economic scale was enormous wealth, at the bottom, poverty—and hunger." Indeed, Zinn insisted, the "power of corporations and the drive for profit have always been more real than the chatter about a 'welfare state,'" and the "rule of special interests in politics has always been more real than the glib talk about 'representative government.'" Approaching the end of this chapter, Zinn asks, "What is it in the working creed of liberalism that has acted to defeat rhetorical promises from the days of Jefferson to the decades after Roosevelt?" His own answer emphasizes three factors: nationalism, the profit motive, and "the failure of the political system to go beyond a spurious representation to something approaching self-determination."[10]

Consistent with emphases in most of his work, Zinn devoted chapters in *Postwar America* to "Solving the Race Problem" and "Justice." Not surprisingly, he felt the race problem had by no means been solved as of 1970, indeed that "one great lesson" was just beginning to be understood: "that the premise of liberal reform, that 'someone,' the white reformer, would solve the problems of the black man, was false." Thus, especially among young blacks, "the most essential element of a real democracy had begun to take hold—that an oppressed people can depend on no one but themselves to move that long distance, past all defenses, to genuine dignity." Just so with justice. Free speech, free press, free assembly, due process of law—"these are presumed to be the unique qualities of American society that mark its superiority over all other systems." But Zinn's conclusion is that this is like all other elements of the liberal creed, "impressive in theory, weak in reality." It was a "persistent historical reality" that the judicial system of the United States was "biased against the poor, the radical, the peculiar."[11]

Unusual, in Zinn's work, was the use of pictures. But they were used in a powerful manner here. The section of pictures included bloodied freedom riders, victims of an American napalm bombing attack in Vietnam, a sobbing young woman kneeling over the lifeless body of one of the four students killed by the National Guard at Kent State University in Ohio (an incident Zinn called "one of the most shocking examples of official violence against assemblies of citizens"),[12] veterans of the Vietnam War protesting against that war, and abject slums in Washington, D.C., with the Capitol building in the background.

Even when one differs with Zinn's interpretations, one is usually impressed by the power of both his language and his logic. In at least two places in *Postwar America*, he seems to go beyond the boundaries of common sense. The American space program, including the very establishment of the National Aeronautics and Space Administration and specifically the 1969 Moon landing, he could see only as a waste of resources. Indeed, it was "perhaps the most flamboyant evidence of how enormous resources can be squandered for nationalist purposes," he insisted. He believed that "patriotic zeal, the compulsion to be first in putting a man on the moon—with flag—operated to support the allocation of vast sums of money for national pride rather than for men and women."[13] But does this not overlook at least two basic truths? First, the scientific value of the expenditures on the space program. Zinn calls this "dubious." Perhaps the evidence is more clear today than it was when Zinn wrote that there have been significant spin-offs, valuable to many if not all people. And second, the spirit of adventure, for lack of a better term. If the human race loses that, are we not in even more trouble in the long run than we are with underallocations for admittedly crucial social programs in the short run?

In all fairness, Zinn should be allowed to say a bit more for himself in this area. He clearly still felt the same way twenty years after the Moon landing. In a later book, he wrote of watching a television show on the occasion of that anniversary. "I heard a black woman poet, Maya Angelou, struggle, politely but with obvious frustration, against three famous male writers who spoke enthusiastically about spending more billions to send men to the moon and to Mars," he recalled. "Against them, she seemed to be climbing the steepest mountain," Zinn continued. "She kept saying, Yes, I am excited, too, about exploring space, but where will we get money to help the poor people, black and white and Asian, here at home?" Obviously, Zinn's sympathies were with Angelou. He seemed on more solid ground when he concluded this discussion by contrasting government social spending with defense spending, saying the old anger about class that he grew up with "returns when I read that the U.S. Defense Department proposes to spend $70 *billion* for still another war plane (a moral monster, called the Stealth Bomber) while the government cuts subsidies for public housing and 2 million Americans, including hundreds of thousands of children, have no place to live."[14]

The second problematic area is justice, specifically jails and prisons.

Zinn wants to abolish them. It is certainly necessary to agree with him that the system of justice in America seems terribly unbalanced in favor of the rich, that there have been terrible instances of brutality in American jails and prisons, and that the system sometimes seems more productive of crime than its cure. But he goes further. He acknowledges that "liberal America" has worked to ameliorate conditions in prisons, also to reduce sentences, lower bail, replace capital punishment by life imprisonment (later, of course, changed back), and introduce better visiting privileges. "But," he asserts, still accurate, "virtually no one in high public position has called for an end to the system of punishment, has challenged the idea that the proper response to a hurtful act is to hurt the person who committed the act." While there were arguments before the Supreme Court to abolish the death penalty as "cruel and unusual punishment," Zinn continued, "there was no loud call from any quarter to end the 'usual' punishment, no argument that jails—which deprive freedom [*sic*] on its basic level—are inherently cruel and should be eliminated."[15] Perhaps there has been no such suggestion because such a situation in modern America seems impossible to most people, even absurd. Is that just because most people are not as radical as Howard Zinn? As idealistic? Are those two fundamentally the same? Obviously, we must emphasize alternatives to incarceration, try to improve prisons so that they might rehabilitate rather than lead to further crime, and again outlaw the "cruel and unusual" death penalty. But can we really imagine, even in our most idealistic moments (not the same as unrealistic moments), a society so perfect that no one will ever fall through the cracks, so to speak, that we will never have to lock some individuals away to protect ourselves, our society, from them, indeed from themselves? We should work, as Howard Zinn has done much of his life, to improve society. But it is hard to believe that even with our best efforts we will be able to abolish prisons any time soon. Zinn's next book, *Justice in Everyday Life*, will provide an opportunity to explore these issues further.

Zinn concludes his view of justice in *Postwar America* with one of his patented series of brief paragraphs, this time a list of "new notions of law and justice [which] have begun to appear." One of these was the realization that the "'rule of law' merely codifies, standardizes, and legitimizes all the basic injustices of pre-modern times—the maldistribution of wealth, the tyrannical abuse of power, the widespread use of violence, the authoritarian control over private human relationships and even over the mind itself." Another was "that the grossest injustices stem not from the violations of the law, but from the workings of the law." By which Zinn meant that "the illegal abuses of individuals are insignificant compared with those committed by business corporations for profit and government representatives for power." Still another was "that the judicial system itself is not neutral, but is a branch of government and represents the interests of government, not of the governed." One more: "that the exterior dignity and quiet of the courts and the judicial process conceal the social reality just outside the courtroom doors: the fierce day-to-day economic struggle to keep alive; the violence of the social order."[16]

Typically, Zinn's final chapter, "Bunker Hill: Beginnings," ends on a hopeful note. But it is a hope based on the necessity of action. He finds the action of a group of Vietnam veterans against the war at Bunker Hill powerfully symbolic of the rebirth of the American revolutionary spirit that had expressed itself at Bunker Hill some two hundred years before. The veterans were protesting the war, but they were part of something much broader, "a great, loose, tangled movement in postwar America—of men and women, white and black, of all ages and backgrounds—that was trying, against overwhelming odds, to change the institutions, the human relations, the ways of thinking that had marked American society for so long." America has had reform movements, even radical movements, in the past, Zinn acknowledged, but, he insisted, "never anything quite like this one, where in one decade, protests against racism, against war, against domination by males, reverberated one against the other, to produce a widespread feeling that the traditional liberal solutions were not enough." Instead, these people felt (and Zinn clearly agreed with them) that fundamental changes were needed, "not just in America's political and economic institutions, but in its sexual and personal and work relationships, in the way in which Americans thought about themselves and about one another." Zinn considered the Montgomery bus boycott "the event that may be considered the starting point of the period of resistance and rebellion in postwar America." He was not unrealistic here; he realized, for example, that "most students were politically inactive most of the time during the late sixties," and that even among the ones who were active, "there were strong strains of either escapism or cynicism." But when he asked the question, "Was a revolution—at least the first stirrings of one— taking place in postwar America?" he clearly felt the answer was yes, and he just as clearly found hope in that. In his final two sentences he returned to the promise of the Declaration of Independence, and to the need to act to make that promise real: "To work for the great ends of the Declaration of Independence, for life, liberty, and the pursuit of happiness, did not mean looking for some future day of fruition. It meant beginning immediately to make those ends real."[17]

We have noted that for the first time with *Postwar America* the journal of the mainstream Organization of American Historians, the *Journal of American History*, deigned to review a Howard Zinn book. The reviewer was James T. Patterson, of Brown University. He was devastating, or at least attempted to be. He noted first that Jack P. Greene, the editor of the History of American Society series, had said that each of the volumes in the series would "outline in broad strokes . . . the main thrust of American economic, social, and cultural development and the interaction between that development and American political and public life." Then he continued: "Zinn, an activist who makes no pretense of objectivity, does no such thing." Instead, he begins with a New Left critique of U.S. foreign policy, then moves on to "sharp assaults" on both American political and judicial institutions, and concludes "by calling for a humane new socialism, the demise of the nation-state, the abolition of prisons, and the end of authoritarianism in personal and familial relationships." Zinn's "polemic" might reassure activist students, Patterson acknowledged, and might even shock the "few students, if any, who have never before encountered his point of view." (Surely Patterson exaggerated here; remember Zinn's own comment about "most students" in the 1960s.) And then: "Though repetitive and occasionally dull, his book may assist professors who are seeking examples to document the nasty side of postwar American life." An ambiguous recommendation, at best. But, "Teachers looking for social history should turn elsewhere." Nothing ambiguous about that. Patterson proceeded with a long list of subjects one might expect to find in a social history of post–World War II America that were ignored or minimized by Zinn, including women, family life, marriage and divorce, juvenile delinquency, other demographic trends, religion, ethnic relations, cultural trends, both immigration and internal migrations, the nature of life in northern cities and suburbs, and both class divisions within the black community and racial tensions within the civil rights movement. "In place of analysis," Patterson asserted, "Zinn relies on unbalanced assertions or on time-worn phrases." Finally, whatever one might think of the rest of Patterson's review, his last sentence is surely correct: "To Zinn, it is not the past but the future that counts."[18]

"Polemical" was an adjective that came to the mind of the reviewer for *Choice* as well. Also "impassioned" and "jaundiced." "Not recommended to anyone in search of an objective, balanced account of postwar America," the anonymous reviewer concluded, while acknowledging that it was "a good précis of 'new left' sentiments over the past quarter century."[19]

Peter Michelson was more thoughtful in the pages of the *New*

Republic. "If it is true, as one wit said, that a liberal is a radical with a wife and two kids, then that tells us a whole lot about the millstone around the neck of American radicalism," he began. Did he have Howard Zinn in mind? Probably not. But it reminds us of Zinn's struggle to balance personal and political commitments. *Postwar America*, Michelson suggested, "helps give us perspective on the melodrama of American liberalism, and in so doing gives us a sense also of the dilemma of American radicalism." While "ostensibly a history, the book is really a political argument indicting the domestic and international power drift of an American liberalism in the service of capitalism." Indeed, Zinn's "valuable service" is his "incisive analysis of history, showing how liberalism has served the interests of corporate capitalism under the rhetorical banner of preserving the 'free world.'" But, "for all the sharpness of its critique, the book suffers finally from political romanticism, the sort of wishful thinking that reveals the frustrating dilemma of American radicalism." What did he mean? "Bracketing American history with Bunker Hill" as Zinn did "makes for hopeful literature. It should; it's the old liberal fantasy machine, maybe the best the world has ever known. But it is wrong. Radically wrong." Why? Because "it shows how much the language of radicalism and revolution has become the bauble of liberal fantasies, however 'leftist' they may be." Thus, "The dilemma of Zinn's book is . . . the dilemma of American radicalism as a whole. The radical is sick of the liberal fraud, but his means of opposition to it are . . . puny and have proved . . . ineffectual."[20]

We have already suggested that Zinn got himself into something of a dilemma with his views on prisons as well. His next book, *Justice in Everyday Life: The Way It Really Works*, published in 1974, enables us to explore that issue further, as well as some other important ones in the area of, as Zinn called his course for many years, Law and Justice in America. He has said that the book "came directly out of" that course, and that at least a third of it consisted of his students' reports on their semester projects. "And at the time I did that I was getting more and more interested in prison issues," he remembers. "The Attica massacre," for example, "took place around that time and affected me enormously."[21] (Zinn is referring to events of September 1971, when inmates in the state prison in Attica, New York, rose up against conditions there, took over a part of the prison, and held some forty hostages; eventually negotiations broke down, and authorities moved in with tear gas and automatic weapons, killing some thirty-one prisoners and nine hostages.) But he had already been visiting prisons as well.

Justice in Everyday Life, however, is about far more than just prisons.

There are also sections on police, courts, housing, work, health, schools, and a concluding section entitled "Fighting Back." "*Justice*," Zinn begins his introduction, "is a grand word in the United States." But the justice we read about is very different from the justice we live, and it is the latter that this book looks at, for it is "overlooked and forgotten," yet "by far the most important" aspect of American justice. Many of the contributors to the volume, Zinn notes, have been his students, so they draw their examples from Boston and its environs. But this is more than just convenience, for "we," writes Zinn, obviously including his students, "are sure that what we describe can be found in the other cities of this country." But it is also suggested that Boston is a good choice "because the demand for justice, and the workings of injustice, have so often found expression in this home of the antislavery movement, this birthplace of the American Revolution, this deathplace of Sacco and Vanzetti." Over the past four years, Zinn continued, his students had "discovered for themselves what so many people who live in a city already know but never put on paper," that is, they had "checked formal constitutional rights against the realities of everyday life in the Boston area and found these rights meaningless." If they had just stayed in the classroom, studying such things as Supreme Court decisions about the right to distribute literature to their fellow citizens, they would have assumed they did indeed have that right. "But they soon discovered that, on the street, where literature is actually distributed, it is the police who decide if that right exists. Or the local judge. The Supreme Court is far away and cannot help at that moment when the policeman says, 'Get going!'" In a similar vein, "Money seems crucial for freedom of speech. With it, one can buy prime television time. Without it, one communicates in the streets, subject to police power."[22]

Clearly, one of Zinn's central concerns is the prison system. He is fond of quoting Dostoevski: "The degree of civilization in a society can be judged by entering its prisons" (*The House of the Dead*). If that is true, says Zinn, "then it seems reasonable to say that the degree of justice in a society can be judged the same way." Furthermore, "if prisons are, *in themselves*, monstrously inhuman and cruel (even if not unusual), than as long as we have prisons, we live in an unjust society." Zinn even claimed that the Supreme Court had made a statement which, if carefully observed, would indeed end the practice of imprisonment. He was referring to *Wilkerson* v. *Utah*, an 1879 decision in which the Court, interpreting the Eighth Amendment, said it was "safe to affirm that punishment of torture, . . . and all others in the same line of unnecessary cruelty, are forbidden by that

Amendment." Concluded Zinn: "All we need then, is general recognition that to imprison a person inside a cage, to deprive that person of human companionship, of mother and father and wife and children and friends, to treat that person as a subordinate creature, to subject that person to daily humiliation and reminders of his or her own powerlessness in the face of authority, to put that person's daily wants in the hands of others who have total control over his life, is indeed *torture*, and thus falls within the decision of the Supreme Court a hundred years ago." Finally, to decide if a practice is torture, who do we ask, the torturer or the tortured? Obviously, the tortured. "Are not certain conditions, by their nature, definable only by the people who suffer them?" For example, "Who but a black person can decide if he is being humiliated? Who but a woman can decide if she has been sexually abused?" So, "we will have to listen to the prisoners to decide if what they are living with is torture, and if therefore, not just because the Supreme Court once said it, but because human compassion demands it, the practice of imprisoning people to punish them for past actions must end." Zinn then proceeds to quote several prisoners who do indeed consider imprisonment torture, including one who says, "If we are what we are being treated as, then we should be shot."[23]

At the end of the section on prisons, there is a brief essay in which Zinn suggests "solutions." Referring to "the crime of punishment," and quoting from George Bernard Shaw's *The Crime of Imprisonment*, Zinn concludes that the only real solution is abolition of prisons. "Prisons cannot be reformed, any more than slavery can be reformed. They have to be abolished." But he knows that this will not happen "until people *think* differently about punishment, about law, about crime, about violence, about property, about human beings." Furthermore, he knows it will not happen "until our society works differently: until wealth is equally distributed, and people don't live in slums, and the motivations for crime and punishment become very weak, and the desire to live cooperatively with other people becomes very strong." We have to begin, says Zinn, and, consistent with his views elsewhere, "the only way to begin is from below, with the prisoners themselves, with their families, their friends, people in the community who begin to care. It is they—we—who need to organize, to resist, to pressure, to demand, to persuade, to jolt people into new ways of thinking by confronting them with the horror and unworkability of prisons, the need to abolish them, and what that means for changing so much else." Finally, he acknowledges that immediate reforms are needed, "even while we refuse to fool ourselves about how reforms are not enough, how fundamental change is needed." He sees hope in some men who emerge from prison rehabilitated. "But not in the way the government talks of rehabilitation, not obsequiously taking their place in the accepted, legal criminal order of things. Rather as rebels and organizers, as thoughtful, militant men ready to devote their lives to abolishing prisons along with that complexity of conditions that makes prisons seem logical."[24]

The other areas explored in *Justice in Everyday Life* need not detain us as long here. Suffice it to say that Zinn and his former students give effective examples of the absence of justice in everyday life, and that a central theme for change is the same one presented above for prisons, that is, that the people directly affected are the ones who can and must be instrumental in bringing it about.

There is a powerful essay included by Jonathan Kozol called "Two-Class Health Care in the Boston Ghetto." "Justice must begin with one's body, one's mind," Zinn begins his introduction to that essay. "If we all do not have an equal chance to stay healthy, to be cured if we become sick, then injustice exists at the most fundamental level of human existence." Furthermore, "if a country has great resources for health, and those resources are available according to one's wealth, if lack of money means that you and your children will die sooner, get sicker quicker, get cured later or never, then we cannot talk of justice at all."[25] Kozol's essay about Boston City Hospital provides an example of the reality of this problem.

Zinn presented a strong case for change in educational areas, at all levels. "All Schools Are Prep Schools," he titled one section, emphasizing that sex, race, and class are fundamental divisions in our society, and that most schools do a "good" job of preparing us early for that reality by starting those divisions early. He obviously felt strongest about universities. The university "may *teach* Locke and Jefferson, even Marx and Kropotkin," he noted. "But it *shows* that ultimately, in this microcosm of our social structure, there is very little democracy, that money and power rule." Not surprisingly, Boston University served as an illustration of all this. And though he avoided mentioning John Silber by name, Zinn did manage to lash out. "In the United States, democracy seemed to exist more on paper than in reality," said Zinn. "The situation at Boston University was a good preparation for students going out into this world."[26]

Zinn wrote a lengthy conclusion for *Justice in Everyday Life* called "Fighting Back." He felt the collection of materials in the book had "illustrated what we believe is the most serious injustice in American society— the injustice of everyday life, where we work, study, and live, deep-rooted in the institutions, and human relations, and ways of thinking right around us." Also, he said, "We have just given a few modest examples of people fighting back against such injustice: the tenants of Boston against greedy landlords, the residents of Dorchester against a corrupt judge, the students and faculty of Boston State College against the unfair firing of teachers." Impressive as all this was, it was not enough, not without fundamental changes. "All through American history people have fought back when they felt aggrieved," said Zinn, including farmers, workingmen, black people. And the system responded with reforms. "But these reforms—subsidies for farmers, union recognition for laboring men, civil rights laws for blacks—took the edge off the discontent, helped a little to make life better, yet left the basic structure of injustice intact." Indeed, the United States "has been the most effective [country] in the world in granting reforms in the face of protest," yet "through all these reforms, the arrangements of who owns what, who keeps what, who works for whom, and who has power over whom in the society—all this has remained the same." Relating all this to the book and specifically to Boston, Zinn concluded: "On the only level where reform can be truly evaluated— in our day-to-day lives, we see, in one of the best of American cities, that it has failed to bring about a just society."[27]

Zinn speculated at some length about revolution versus reform as the best way to proceed, and seemed to suggest that even if revolution is the answer, we must start with reform. What we most need before us is a clear vision, "not of some overall utopia, but of how everyday life would be different." Such a vision would involve "a life in which we all woke up in clean, healthful surroundings, went to a job in which we had a voice in what was produced and how and what we would do in that process, studied in a situation jointly worked out by students and teachers without absentee administrators, and came home to be among friends and family and neighbors who were free from any notion that one race or one sex or people of one age group or profession or physical appearance or educational attainment were superior to anyone else." To be believable, that vision would have to start coming into effect at once; thus the necessity of concentrating on "small places we already occupy," and therefore can begin to make changes in, such as students in classrooms, workers in their workplaces, and tenants in their homes. We know that determined people working hard together "can force even giant constellations of power to give in." We have seen blacks, students, employees, tenants, and other groups do this. And we do know that "what seems central in all this is that people must organize themselves to change their own lives." Finally: "Whether these efforts will move beyond traditional reform to deep changes, at first locally, and then in the society at large, no one knows yet. And we will not know unless we begin."[28]

Stuart A. Scheingold reviewed *Justice in Everyday Life* thoughtfully in the *Chronicle of Higher Education*. As one might expect in that publication, Scheingold focused partially on the educational nature of Zinn's book. It was, he said, "the product of an educational experience in which Professor Zinn obviously and understandably takes some pride." But Scheingold also found it "a profoundly disturbing book: first, for the shocking tales of manifest injustice it presents, and second, for my own difficulties in coming to terms with its message despite my sympathy for its values." Other research of a more standard social science variety had already exposed and measured the gap between "the law on the books and the law in action," Scheingold noted, which he described as "part of Zinn's problem." If the book had appeared a decade earlier, it would have been more impressive, indeed "something of an event—more or less on a par with Zinn's cogent and fiery rejoinder to then Justice Fortas on the matter of civil disobedience." But unfortunately, Zinn here "provides very little that could be considered at all new. Only the names and the places have changed." Finally, Scheingold did give Zinn credit in his "fighting back" section for going beyond similar arguments proposed by the likes of Saul Alinsky. That was "the sense in which *Justice in Everyday Life* conveys a feeling for the basic similarities of deprivation in the variety of social settings considered," including school, workplace, and criminal justice system, in all of which "authority relationships breed abuse. While the detached observer may be struck by the differences between the courtroom and the workplace, Zinn suggests that it is the commonality of superordination and subordination that may constitute the essential reality for the participants."[29]

Brief reviews appeared in the *Library Journal* and *Publishers Weekly*, the former critical (a "weak analysis"), the latter quite positive ("sobering and effective," Zinn's students "a perceptive, at times brilliant lot").[30]

Zinn dedicated *Justice* to Peter Irons, a young man who was serving prison time for draft resistance. The story behind that is an interesting one. Irons went on to become a professor of political science and a civil liberties lawyer. He wrote a book entitled *The Courage of Their Convictions* in 1988; as its subtitle, *Sixteen Americans Who Fought Their Way to the Supreme Court*, suggests, it was a "people's history" approach to famous Supreme Court decisions. The dedication was to Howard Zinn, and the dedication page carried Zinn's words from *The Politics of History*, "Are we historians not humans first, and scholars because of that?" Irons explained that he had never met Zinn at the time Zinn dedicated the book to him, but struck up a correspondence with him while in prison and went on to become one of his graduate assistants in the Justice course at BU where Zinn became "mentor, friend, and model of the engaged scholar."[31]

After *Justice in Everyday Life* in 1974, it was to be six years before Howard Zinn published another book. When he did, it was his magnum opus, *A People's History of the United States*. Asked about that longer-than-usual gap between books, Zinn responded first with humor: "I am embarrassed when I think of those long gaps in my writing! What in the world could I have been doing? Having fun? Never." Then he explained that he spent a semester, with Herbert Marcuse, teaching in France in 1974. It was at the University of Paris, specifically, says Zinn, "at the Vincennes Campus—Paris VIII, set up after the 1968 uprisings as a kind of haven for left-wing faculty and open-admissions students." He taught there a second time in 1978, and yet again in 1980. In 1975 the Vietnam War came to an end, for Zinn closing out "a period of intense speaking, writing, demonstrating on the war." He now felt free "to pursue a long-felt desire to write for the theater." His wife, daughter, and son had all been involved in theater. He became interested in Emma Goldman after meeting the historian Richard Drinnon and then reading his biography of her, *Rebel in Paradise*, and her autobiography, *Living My Life*. He even assigned the latter to his students, "thinking it might inspire them as it inspired me." So he wrote a play on Goldman, entitled simply *Emma*. His son, he thought, had probably never read any of his historical writings, but he did read the play, and chose to direct it in a small theater in Greenwich Village in New York, where he was living and doing some acting. It ran for several weeks, which was, for Zinn, "exciting . . . after the solitary experience of writing, to become part of an ensemble of director, actors, lighting person, set designer, a living audience—really exhilarating."[32] Not surprisingly, with those feelings, Zinn would later do more work with the theater.

Also in 1975–1976, Zinn wrote what he called "a biweekly op-ed column" for the *Boston Globe*.[33] He chose to reproduce several of them in his 1997 collection, *The Zinn Reader: Writings on Disobedience and Democracy*. Reading them, it is easy to see why Zinn says he has always enjoyed writing shorter pieces, for they are remarkably effective.

In "When Will the Long Feud End?" on September 19, 1975, Zinn harked back to his argument in *The Southern Mystique* that racism was a national phenomenon rather than a southern one. When the first shipload of

Africans arrived in Virginia, wrote Zinn, "race prejudice began." One fact hard to ignore, he contended, was that it had always been the economically harassed whites who turned in anger against blacks, somehow holding them responsible. Zinn admitted that his own father was "a slum-dwelling immigrant, and prejudiced against Negroes." He concluded by questioning whether white-black hostility would ever end. "Not until black and white people discover together, the source of their long feud," he answered. That source: "an economic system which has deprived them and their children for centuries, to the benefit of, first, the Founding Fathers, and lately, the hundred or so giant corporations that hog the resources of this bountiful country."[34]

On February 28, 1975, Zinn's subject was energy. Problems of class, poverty, deprivation, he suggested in his 1997 introduction, were as true in the 1970s, a decade often seen as prosperous, as any other time. In the column itself, Zinn recalls his own youthful poverty, including coming home to find his family sitting in the dark because the utility company had canceled their electricity because of nonpayment of the bill. "When I learned that Boston Edison had shut off the electricity in over 1,200 homes last month because people did not pay their bills," wrote Zinn, "an old anger returned." He seriously questioned whether "rich corporations" should have the right "to deprive families of electricity, of gas to cook with, of fuel to heat their homes." These things were "life's necessities," claimed Zinn, "like food, air, water. They should not be the private property of corporations, which use them to hold us hostage to the dark, to the cold, until we pay their price." As usual with Zinn, he was not content just to theorize; one thing he advocated was that people file an appeal with the state's department of public utilities claiming that their bill was too high and demanding a hearing, resting comfortably in the knowledge that their power could not be turned off as long as that process was going on.[35]

"The Secret Word," published in the *Globe* on January 24, 1976, was socialism. Introducing the column in 1997, Zinn noted that "the Soviet Union and other countries in Eastern Europe which called themselves 'socialist' have overturned their governments and do not call themselves that any more." This was "just as well," he said, "for those of us who think socialism is an honorable idea, and that it was badly tainted by those ugly dictatorships." Once again, he concluded, with "those governments fallen, and capitalism failing to solve basic problems of human rights (an equal right to life, liberty and the pursuit of happiness, as stated in the Declaration of Independence) this may be a good time to revive the word and the idea." The column itself he had concluded with a reference to Thomas

Paine. "In 1776, the time was right for Tom Paine to speak 'Common Sense' about Independence, and the idea spread through the country. . . . Isn't the time right, in 1976, for us to begin discussing the idea of socialism?" Then, making clear his definition of the much-avoided secret word: "To break the hold of corporations over our food, our rent, our work, our lives—to produce things people need, and give everyone useful work to do and distribute the wealth of the country with approximate equality—whether you call it socialism or not, isn't it common sense?"[36]

On June 2, 1976, Zinn's column was entitled "Whom Will We Honor Memorial Day?" It was one of his most passionate. Memorial Day, he expected, would be celebrated "by the usual betrayal of the dead, by the hypocritical patriotism of the politicians and contractors preparing for more wars, more graves to receive more flowers on future Memorial Days." But Zinn felt that "the memory of the dead deserves a different dedication. To peace, to defiance of governments." Several of those he wished to honor had opposed past wars, including Henry David Thoreau (Mexican War), Mark Twain (Spanish-American War), John Dos Passos (World War I), I. F. Stone (Korean War), and Martin Luther King (Vietnam War). But others were lesser known, including the young woman in New Hampshire who refused to allow her husband, killed in Vietnam, to be given a military burial, and "the B52 pilots who refused to fly those last vicious raids of Nixon's and Kissinger's war." "In the end," concluded Zinn, "it is living people, not corpses, creative energy, not destructive rage, which are our only real defense, not just against other governments trying to kill us, but against our own, also trying to kill us." Whether one agrees or disagrees with Zinn's sentiments in that column, perhaps the aftermath is not surprising. "After it appeared," says Zinn, "my column was canceled."[37]

Vietnam may have been over, but for Zinn, obviously, the issues of war and peace were still very much alive. Indeed, it seems to have been a sense of some of the movements of the 1960s and following years having come to a close that led Zinn to write a general view of U.S. history that reflected those movements and the impact they had had, not only on American society but also on our understanding of our history. Just before going to Paris in 1978, he remembers, he came up with the idea. Cambridge University Press sent two editors to Boston to persuade Zinn to sign on with them to publish such a work. But he went with Harper and Row instead, he says, significantly, "because I thought they would better distribute the book to a popular audience." He went to France thinking he would start the book there, but "didn't write a word." Instead, after his return to the United

States, he "went to work very intensely and probably wrote the book in eight or nine months in 1978–79."[38]

But to say that makes it sound easier than it actually was. As with many things, Zinn credits his wife, Roslyn, with, in this case, pressuring him to get it done. "I must say that I despaired much at the beginning, I despaired doing it," he has said. "It was a big job, and my wife urged me to do it. I think she's more far-sighted than me. . . . I would say to her, 'You know, I think I'm going to give this up, it's just too much. You know, I ought to have some fun, I want to watch a baseball game.' [Zinn is a fan of the Boston Red Sox, a typical one in the sense that he is both loyal and skeptical of any chance of long-range success.] And she'd say, 'No, no, you can finish this. It's something you should do.'"[39]

So he did. And even those who do not share Howard Zinn's radical vision of the American past, present, and future should be glad that he did. For *A People's History of the United States* is crucial not only for understanding Howard Zinn and his work, it is also crucial for understanding all those movements of the 1960s—civil rights, anti–Vietnam War, women's, environmental—and the impact they had on American society, for understanding the whole concept of a "New Left," for understanding also the concept of a "people's history," and, arguably and most importantly, for understanding U.S. history itself.

Perhaps it is important to acknowledge at the outset that not all would agree with that assertion. Indeed, not all agreed with it at the time the *People's History* was published in 1980. Highly respected senior historian Oscar Handlin, of Harvard University, for example, just across the river from Zinn's Boston University, was much further away in his view of U.S. history. He did not review the book in the pages of the *American Scholar* so much as he trashed it. These words and phrases appear: "deranged . . . fairy tale . . . patched together from secondary sources, many used uncritically . . . others ravaged for material torn out of context . . . Zinn is a stranger to evidence. . . . complex array of devices that pervert his pages . . . pays only casual regard to factual accuracy . . . Zinn does not comprehend the simple meaning of words. . . . Zinn does not scruple to use insidious rhetorical questions to convey affirmations he is too shy to make openly. . . . Biased selections falsify events. . . . Conveniently omits whatever does not fit its overriding thesis . . . tears evidence out of context and distorts it . . . pure invention . . . anti-American . . . lavishes indiscriminate condemnation upon all the works of man—that is, upon civilization, a word he usually encloses in quotation marks. . . . The American people of actuality . . . Zinn does not discuss."[40] Enough?

Yet, another distinguished historian, Eric Foner—of a later generation than Handlin, and that may be significant—praised Zinn's work strongly in the *New York Times Book Review*, saying Zinn wrote with "an enthusiasm rarely encountered in the leaden prose of academic history," and even suggesting that some portions of the *People's History* "should be required reading for a new generation of students." Indeed, said Foner, "historians may well view it as a step toward a coherent new version of American history." And at least one person has already referred to it as "a modern classic." (Of course, it may be significant that that label came from an employee of the company that published it.)[41]

What is going on here? What kind of book could produce such incredibly polar responses? (It is hoped that these are not the kind of rhetorical questions Professor Handlin would consider "insidious.") To answer these questions, of course, it is necessary to let Zinn speak for himself. Indeed, one of the things he shows remarkable skill at in the *People's History* is the fine art of quotation, of letting "the people" speak for themselves. It seems to be a product of his philosophical position, that is, if the people *make* their own history, they should also be allowed to *tell* it. In an absolutely crucial passage early in the book, Zinn writes:

> In that inevitable taking of sides which comes from selection and emphasis in history, I prefer to try to tell the story of the discovery of America from the viewpoint of the Arawaks, of the Constitution from the standpoint of the slaves, of Andrew Jackson as seen by the Cherokees, of the Civil War as seen by the New York Irish, of the Mexican war as seen by the deserting soldiers of Scott's army, of the rise of industrialism as seen by the young women in the Lowell textile mills, of the Spanish-American war as seen by the Cubans, the conquest of the Philippines as seen by black soldiers on Luzon, the Gilded Age as seen by southern farmers, the First World War as seen by socialists, the Second World War as seen by pacifists, the New Deal as seen by peons in Latin America. And so on, to the limited extent that any one person, however he or she strains, can "see" history from the standpoint of others.[42]

Read that again, for it is central. Taking sides is inevitable in the writing of history. Zinn chooses to take the side not of the insiders (the presidents and kings and queens and generals, the rich, the powerful, the few), as so much history traditionally has done (but without being honest enough to say so, probably sometimes without even being aware of it), but of the outsiders (the minorities, the poor, the working people, the women, the dissenters and protestors, the many). He knows a historian can do that to only a "limited extent." Extensive quotation helps; it is difficult to thumb through *A People's History of the United States* and find a page that does not include a quotation.

Reading that paragraph again, it is also easy to see why Foner said that "those accustomed to the texts of an earlier generation, in which the rise of American democracy and the growth of national power were the embodiment of Progress, may be startled by Professor Zinn's narrative." Perhaps that was part of Handlin's problem with the book—he was startled. Continued Foner: "From the opening pages, an account of 'the European invasion of the Indian settlements in the Americas,' there is a reversal of perspective, a reshuffling of heroes and villains." In a helpful image, Foner suggested that "the book bears the same relation to traditional texts as a photographic negative does to a print: the areas of darkness and light have been reversed." *A People's History of the United States* is truly a history of most of the American people. It is also, in the phrase that became famous in the 1960s, history from the bottom up. But it is also history from the outside in. That is to say, a concern with social history might not necessarily imply any ideological position on the political spectrum, left or right, on the part of the historian, but rather simply a belief that it is important to look at these long-neglected aspects of our history. With Zinn, there is more than that. His work is also openly radical, considerably to the left on any conceptualized political spectrum. Much of what we have in the *People's History* is a critique, a powerful one, of American racism, imperialism, sexism, class structure, violence, environmental destruction. But, stated positively, what we also have here is a celebration of those who have struggled against these negative forces in the American past.

Zinn's first chapter is called "Columbus, the Indians, and Human Progress," but it deals with far more than that title suggests, including more of Zinn's fundamental philosophy of history. "My point is not that we must, in telling history, accuse, judge, condemn Columbus *in absentia*," he writes. "It is too late for that; it would be a useless scholarly exercise in morality. But the easy acceptance of atrocities as a deplorable but necessary price to pay for progress"—Zinn's examples include Hiroshima and Vietnam "to save Western civilization," Kronstadt and Hungary "to save socialism," nuclear proliferation "to save us all"—"that is still with us."[43] As always with Zinn, it is the present that is the most important thing about our study of the past.

"History is the memory of states." Zinn would never say that, but he does quote Henry Kissinger saying it. "My viewpoint, in telling the history of the United States," says Zinn, is different: that we must not accept the memory of states as our own. Nations are not communities and never have been." If the history of a country, any country, is presented as the history of a family, it is fundamentally misleading, for it conceals "fierce conflicts of interest," between the conquerors and the conquered, for example, and between "masters and slaves, capitalists and workers, dominators and dominated in race and sex. And in such a world of conflict, a world of victims and executioners, it is the job of thinking people, as Albert Camus suggested, not to be on the side of the executioners." Zinn's point "is not to grieve for the victims and denounce the executioners. Those tears, that anger, cast into the past, deplete our moral energy for the present." Again: the present. Besides, admits Zinn, "the lines are not always clear. In the long run, the oppressor is also a victim." And in the short run, "the victims, themselves desperate and tainted with the culture that oppresses them, turn on other victims." Still, he concludes, "Understanding the complexities, this book will be skeptical of governments and their attempts, through politics and culture, to ensnare ordinary people in a giant web of nationhood pretending to a common interest."[44]

Moving from the role of the state to the role of the people, Zinn writes: "I don't want to invent victories for people's movements. But to think that history-writing must aim simply to recapitulate the failures that dominate the past is to make historians collaborators in an endless cycle of defeat." Thus, "if history is to be creative, to anticipate a possible future without denying the past, it should, I believe, emphasize new possibilities by disclosing those hidden episodes of the past when, even if in brief flashes, people showed their ability to resist, to join together, occasionally to win." Zinn is "supposing," he says, "or perhaps only hoping, that our future may be found in the past's fugitive moments of compassion rather than in its solid centuries of warfare." There again, that note of optimism, or at least hope. "That, being as blunt as I can," Zinn concludes this philosophical section, "is my approach to the history of the United States. The reader may as well know that before going on."[45] The reader knows! And after Zinn's survey of American history from this perspective, covering more than six hundred pages, the reader *really* knows.

Zinn is excellent at transitions; he moves very smoothly from Columbus and the "Indians" into a chapter entitled "Drawing the Color Line." The concern, of course, is with racism, and the phrase comes from W. E. B. Du Bois. Racism, in Zinn's words, is "that combination of inferior status and derogatory thought" that African Americans especially have been victimized by from the beginning of their history in America almost at the beginning of American history itself. Zinn insists, "There is not a country in world history in which racism has been more important, for so long a time, as the United States." Therefore, "it is more than a purely historical question to ask: How does it start?—and an even more urgent question: How might it end? Or, to put it differently: Is it possible for whites and blacks to live together without hatred?" Not surprisingly, Zinn places a great deal of emphasis in this chapter on black resistance to slavery, and also on the evidence that "where whites and blacks found themselves with common problems, common work, common enemy in their master, they behaved toward one another as equals." Thus, after referring to "a complex web of historical threads to ensnare blacks for slavery in America," he is still able to conclude that "the elements of this web are historical, not 'natural.' This does not mean that they are easily disentangled, dismantled. It means only that there is a possibility for something else, under historical conditions not yet realized." One of those conditions, thinks Zinn, "would be the elimination of that class exploitation which has made poor whites desperate for small gifts of status, and has prevented that unity of black and white necessary for joint rebellion and reconstruction."[46]

Thus Zinn makes the transition to a chapter entitled "Persons of Mean and Vile Condition," primarily concerned with issues of class. The colonies, he insists, "were societies of contending classes—a fact obscured by the emphasis, in traditional histories, on the external struggle against England, the unity of colonists in the Revolution." The potential combination of poor whites and poor blacks caused great fear among wealthy white planters, Zinn notes. He focuses some attention on "controls" the upper class developed for the lower. One of these was racism. Another was the development of "a white middle class of small planters, independent farmers, city artisans, who, given small rewards for joining forces with merchants and planters, would be a solid buffer against black slaves, frontier Indians, and very poor whites." Zinn quotes Richard Hofstadter effectively to make the point that it was "a middle-class society [but] governed for the most part by its upper classes." Finally, in still another superb transition, Zinn notes that the upper class, in order to rule, needed to make some concessions to the middle class, but without damage to their own wealth or power, and at the expense of slaves, Indians, and poor whites. "This," he suggested, "bought loyalty." And, "to bind that loyalty with something more powerful even than material advantage, the ruling group found, in the 1760s and 1770s, a wonderfully useful device . . . the language of liberty and equality, which could unite just enough whites to fight a Revolution against England, without ending either slavery or inequality."[47]

That sets the stage for Zinn's fundamental perspective on the American Revolution, dealt with in a chapter carrying the title "Tyranny Is Tyranny." Suffice it here to say that in the ongoing debate among American historians about how to answer the question "How revolutionary was the American Revolution?" Zinn's answer would be somewhere between "not very" and "not at all." Indeed, the well-known series of volumes Opposing Viewpoints included one on the American Revolution, and the final chapter, "The Meaning of the American Revolution: Historians' Debate," set Zinn against Gordon S. Wood (author of *The Radicalism of the American Revolution*). Zinn's essay, consisting of substantial excerpts from the *People's History*, appeared under the heading "The American Revolution Was Not a Social Revolution," and the editor summarizes Zinn's interpretation thus: "Zinn argues that the American Revolution had little positive impact on the everyday lives of most Americans. . . . most of the leaders of the Revolution were members of the colonial elite who wished to preserve their wealth and power. They used the war . . . to prevent large-scale internal changes in America's society. In this sense, . . . the American Revolution was really a successful effort to preserve America's status quo."[48] Pretty accurate summary.

Perhaps only one corrective is needed—to Zinn's view, that is, not to the editor of the Opposing Viewpoints volume. That is to say, if we are going to emphasize the minimal change resulting directly from the American Revolution, should we not also emphasize the *potential* for change that it presented? Indeed, some of those changes have occurred: slavery ended, women vote, and so on. But then perhaps Zinn does not need even that corrective, for, as we have seen, he has made one of the central themes of his work the continuing effort of the United States over the course of its history to live up to the ideals of the Declaration of Independence.

In reality, "Tyranny Is Tyranny" carries the story of the Revolutionary era only through the Declaration of Independence, while the chapter significantly entitled "A Kind of Revolution" carries on through the Constitution. True to form, noting that poor whites sometimes saw the military as a route for improving their condition, Zinn observes, "Here was the traditional device by which those in charge of any social order mobilize and discipline a recalcitrant population—offering the adventure and rewards of military service to get poor people to fight for a cause they may not see clearly as their own." The Revolution did not mean much for Native Americans and

African Americans, notes Zinn. Indeed, he suggests that the inferior position of blacks and the exclusion of Indians from the new society was
already settled by the time of the Revolution. "With the English out of the
way, it could now be put on paper, solidified, regularized, made legitimate,
by the Constitution." It is no surprise that one historian whose work Zinn
utilizes positively is Charles Beard, particularly his 1913 book, *An Economic Interpretation of the Constitution*. Zinn asserts that the Constitution
"illustrates the complexity of the American system: it serves the interests of
a wealthy elite, but also does enough for small property owners, for middle-
income mechanics and farmers, to build a broad base of support." In addition, "The slightly prosperous people who make up this base of support are
buffers against the blacks, the Indians, the very poor whites. They enable
the elite to keep control with a minimum of coercion, a maximum of law—
all made palatable by the fanfare of patriotism and unity." Finally, Zinn
notes that approximately half the American people were not even considered by the Founding Fathers: "not mentioned in the Declaration of Independence, . . . absent in the Constitution, . . . invisible in the new political
democracy. They were the women of early America."[49]

Zinn then proceeds to devote a substantial chapter to the history of
women in America through the all-important Seneca Falls Convention of
1848. A central theme is suggested by the title, "The Intimately Oppressed," and is expressed numerous times, as here: "Women rebels have
always faced special disabilities: they live under the daily eye of their
master; and they are isolated one from the other in households, thus
missing the daily camaraderie which has given heart to rebels of other
oppressed groups." Zinn even suggested, in a passage which bothered
Oscar Handlin a great deal, that the condition of women was "something
akin to a house slave."[50]

"As Long as Grass Grows or Water Runs," Zinn calls his chapter on
Native Americans, the conflict between them and the American people (and
government) over their lands, and the ultimate reality of "Indian removal."
Prominent in this chapter is Zinn's emphasis on "the competition and con-
niving that marked the spirit of Western capitalism." Zinn relies rather
extensively on Dale Van Every's *The Disinherited*, quoting him, for
example, saying, "The interminable history of diplomatic relations between
Indians and white men had before 1832 recorded no single instance of a
treaty which had not been presently broken by the white parties to it." Paraphrasing Van Every, Zinn insists that the forces that led to removal did not
come primarily from the poor white frontiersmen who were neighbors to

the Indians, but from "industrialization and commerce, the growth of populations, of railroads and cities, the rise in value of land, and the greed of businessmen." Still, he is also willing to personalize it, and insists rightly that Andrew Jackson was "the most aggressive enemy of the Indians in early American history."[51]

Quoting the *Whig Intelligencer*, Zinn calls his chapter on Texas, Manifest Destiny, and the Mexican War "We Take Nothing by Conquest, Thank God." He refers to the Mexican War as "the war that [President James K.] Polk wanted," praises such individuals as Abraham Lincoln and Henry David Thoreau for their opposition to it, indeed insists there was more opposition to it than usually recognized, including in the army (where desertions were a constant problem, and some even fought for the Mexicans), but he also recognizes the complexity of American motivation. Accompanying all the "aggressiveness," he writes, "was the idea that the United States would be giving the blessings of liberty and democracy to more people." This was also "intermingled with ideas of racial superiority, longings for the beautiful lands of New Mexico and California, and thoughts of commercial enterprise across the Pacific."[52]

Much of Zinn's interpretation of the Civil War and Reconstruction era is made clear by the title of his chapter, "Slavery without Submission, Emancipation without Freedom." As always, Zinn's views strike the reader with remarkable dissonance from the standard view of American history. This is true at the level of personalities: "In 1859, John Brown was hanged, with federal complicity, for attempting to do by small-scale violence what Lincoln would do by large-scale violence several years later—end slavery." It is also true at the level of overall interpretation of the era:

> With slavery abolished by order of the government—true, a government pushed hard to do so, by blacks, free and slave, and by white abolitionists—its end could be orchestrated so as to set limits to emancipation. Liberation from the top would go only so far as the interests of the dominant groups permitted. If carried further by the momentum of war, the rhetoric of a crusade, it could be pulled back to a safer position. Thus, while the ending of slavery led to a reconstruction of national politics and economics, it was not a radical reconstruction, but a safe one—in fact, a profitable one.[53]

"How can slavery be described?" asks Zinn. (An insidious rhetorical question?) "Perhaps not at all by those who have not experienced it," he answers; thus, he relies extensively and effectively on firsthand accounts.

"They say slaves are happy," said a former slave named John Little, "because they laugh, and are merry. I myself and three or four others, have received two hundred lashes in the day, and had our feet in fetters; yet, at night, we would sing and dance, and make others laugh at the rattling of our chains." Why? "We did it to keep down trouble, and to keep our hearts from being completely broken." Interestingly, one of the historians Zinn relies on at some length on the "Peculiar Institution" is Eugene Genovese, in particular his important book on slavery, *Roll, Jordan, Roll: The World the Slaves Made*. As we shall see, Zinn and Genovese by no means always agreed. But Zinn was impressed by Genovese's emphasis on class in his analysis of slavery.[54]

Zinn expresses admiration for the abolitionists, of course, especially the more "radical" ones, but he also insists that "black abolitionists, less publicized, were the backbone of the antislavery movement," and he tells at length of the contributions of such individuals as Frederick Douglass (as well as quoting from him at length). Lincoln, of course, receives some credit for ending slavery, but Zinn is realistic. Lincoln, he says, "combined perfectly the needs of business, the political ambition of the new Republican party, and the rhetoric of humanitarianism." Thus, he "would keep the abolition of slavery not at the top of his list of priorities, but close enough to the top so it could be pushed there temporarily by abolitionist pressures and by practical political advantage." Or, as abolitionist Wendell Phillips put it, if Lincoln was able to grow, "it is because we have watered him."[55]

As for Reconstruction, Zinn notes that there was "that brief period after the Civil War in which southern Negroes voted, elected blacks to state legislatures and to Congress, introduced free and racially mixed public education to the South." But absent a sincere and continuing commitment to black equality, the key word was indeed "brief." An illiterate African American veteran of the Union army, asked why he had left the South, in his case specifically Louisiana, answered: "We seed that the whole South—every state in the South—had got into the hands of the very men that held us slaves."[56]

Handlin singled out Zinn's chapter "The Other Civil War" for some of his harshest criticism. "Biased selections falsify events," he asserted, using this chapter as his primary example. "It includes anti-rent riots in New York State, the Astor Place riot in New York City, Dorr's War in Rhode Island, and the railroad strikes of 1877," complained Handlin, "thus bracketing quite dissimilar and unrelated outbreaks of violence to give the impression of a country torn by ceaseless civil conflict." He is correct that it is a diverse chapter (and long), including for example far more than his list suggests, but he is incorrect in saying the events in it are "unrelated." He either missed, or, more likely, rejected Zinn's rationale. The stories of many of the events in the chapter, notes Zinn, "are not usually found in textbooks on United States history," for "there is little on class struggle in the nineteenth century." Instead, "the period before and after the Civil War is filled with politics, elections, slavery, and the race question." Even some specialized books, for example on the Jacksonian era, that do deal with labor and economic issues, "center on the presidency, and thus perpetuate the traditional dependency on heroic leaders rather than people's struggles."[57] Thus, Zinn here attempts to provide a corrective to standard, traditional textbooks; indeed, that is much of what he is trying to do for the entirety of *A People's History of the United States*.

"In the year 1877," Zinn opens his chapter "Robber Barons and Rebels," "the signals were given for the rest of the century: the black would be put back; the strikes of white workers would not be tolerated; the industrial and political elites of North and South would take hold of the country and organize the greatest march of economic growth in human history." They would do all this "with the aid of, and at the expense of, black labor, white labor, Chinese labor, European immigrant labor, female labor, rewarding them differently by race, sex, national origin, and social class, in such a way as to create separate levels of oppression—a skillful terracing to stabilize the pyramid of wealth." Well, yes; the only possible objection one might make is that Zinn makes it sound more carefully planned than it probably was. He is skeptical of the "reforms" made by the federal government, including the Interstate Commerce Act of 1887, which was "supposed" to regulate railroads on behalf of the consumers, and the Sherman Anti-Trust Act of 1890, which "called itself" an act "to protect trade and commerce against unlawful restraints." In this entire era of industrialization and urbanization, insists Zinn, "the government of the United States was behaving almost exactly as Karl Marx described a capitalist state: pretending neutrality to maintain order, but serving the interests of the rich." He does seem to exaggerate a bit when he writes that 1893 saw "the biggest economic crisis in the country's history." Bigger than 1929? But he is certainly correct in referring to the Populist movement (and its predecessors such as the Farmers Alliances) as "the greatest movement of agrarian rebellion the country had ever seen."[58]

Zinn relies extensively and effectively upon the work of pioneer revisionist diplomatic historian William Appleman Williams in his treatment of "The Empire and the People." But he begins the chapter effectively with a quotation from Theodore Roosevelt: "I should welcome almost any war, for I think this country needs one." Roosevelt wrote those words to a friend in 1897, the year before the Spanish-American War, the war which most agree marks the beginning of "great power" status for the United States—but also, of course, of modern American imperialism. Zinn may be guilty in his treatment of this subject of the "insidious rhetorical questions" that bothered Handlin so much. "And would not a foreign adventure deflect some of the rebellious energy that went into strikes and protest movements toward an external enemy?" he asks at one point. And at another: "Was that taste [the taste of empire] in the mouth of the people through some instinctive lust for aggression or some urgent self-interest? Or was it a taste (if indeed it existed) created, encouraged, advertised, and exaggerated by the millionaire press, the military, the government, the eager-to-please scholars of the time?" But he is not guilty of assigning a degree of intentionality which is not present. After asking still another question—"Would it [a foreign adventure] not unite people with government, with the armed forces, instead of against them?"—Zinn suggests that "this was probably not a conscious plan among most of the elite—but a natural development from the twin drives of capitalism and nationalism."[59]

A chapter entitled "The Socialist Challenge" actually deals with far more than the socialists. "War and jingoism might postpone, but could not fully suppress, the class anger that came from the realities of ordinary life," Zinn begins. Socialism he does indeed cover, and in quite a positive light. "There was an idea in the air," he says, "becoming clearer and stronger, an idea not just in the theories of Karl Marx but in the dreams of writers and artists through the ages: that people might cooperatively use the treasures of the earth to make life better for everyone, not just a few." But the chapter also deals with the continuing struggles of women, blacks, and others. And with the reforms of the so-called Progressive period. Any changes were "reluctant," insists Zinn, "aimed at quieting the popular risings, not making fundamental changes."[60]

By calling his chapter on World War I "War Is the Health of the State," Zinn is quoting radical writer Randolph Bourne. Noting the millions who died in that conflict, Zinn concludes that "no one since that day has been able to show that the war brought any gain for humanity that would be worth one human life." The rhetoric of the socialists and others that it was an "imperialist war," he says, "now seems moderate and hardly arguable." The chapter provides Zinn the opportunity to treat positively some people he admires, such as socialist Eugene V. Debs, anarchist Emma Goldman, and author Dalton Trumbo (*Johnny Got His Gun*), all of whom opposed the war. He also notes with delicious irony the wartime legal case officially listed as *U.S.* v. *Spirit of '76*, a case which came about when the maker of a film on the American Revolution entitled *The Spirit of '76* was prosecuted and convicted (sentenced to ten years in prison) for violation of the Espionage Act because his film depicted British atrocities against the colonists and therefore, in the words of the judge, tended "to question the good faith of our ally, Great Britain."[61]

"Self-help in Hard Times," Zinn calls his chapter on the 1920s and 1930s, to make the point that even before the New Deal, people were helping themselves, because they had no other choice. Zinn's treatment of this era reminds one of two of his early books, since it specifically provides him an opportunity to praise Fiorello LaGuardia as one of the few political figures to speak out for the poor in the 1920s, and an opportunity to critique the somewhat-liberal New Deal from a radical perspective again. When the New Deal was over, he asserted, "capitalism remained intact. The rich still controlled the nation's wealth, as well as its laws, courts, police, newspapers, churches, colleges." Enough help might have been given to enough people to make Roosevelt a hero to millions, "but the same system that had brought depression and crisis—the system of waste, of inequality, of concern for profit over human need—remained."[62]

With more than a touch of irony, Zinn had called his chapter on World War II in *Postwar America* "The Best of Wars." With a similar touch, the one in the *People's History* carries the title "A People's War?" But early on in the chapter, Zinn asks, "Was it?" It was a war against an enemy of "unspeakable evil," and it is true that certain evidence suggests that it was the most popular war the country ever fought, he acknowledges. But then—insidiously?—he questions: "But could this be considered a manufactured support, since all the power of the nation—not only of the government, but the press, the church, and even the chief radical organizations—was behind the calls for all-out war? Was there an undercurrent of reluctance; were there unpublicized signs of resistance?" But for the United States to step forward as a defender of helpless countries, while matching the image in high school history textbooks, did not match up with our actual record in world affairs. We were hardly free of racism ourselves. Troops were segregated, the Red Cross separated "black" and "white" blood. In a powerful historical image, Zinn notes that "when troops were jammed onto the *Queen Mary* in early 1945 to go to combat duty in the European theater, the blacks were stowed down in the depths of the ship near the engine room, as far as possible from the fresh air of the deck, in a bizarre reminder of the slave voyages of old." And in its treatment of Japanese Americans, says Zinn, "the United States came close to direct duplication of Fascism." It was a war "waged by a government whose chief beneficiary—despite volumes of reforms—was a wealthy elite," and thus, not surprisingly, "quietly, behind the headlines in battles and bombings, American diplomats and businessmen worked hard to make sure that when the war ended, American economic power would be second to none in the world."[63]

Looking further at the concept of a "people's war," Zinn acknowledges that "there was a mass base of support for what became the heaviest bombardment of civilians ever undertaken in any war: the aerial attacks on German and Japanese cities." But, "if 'people's war' means a war of people against attack, a defensive war—if it means a war fought for humane reasons instead of for the privileges of an elite, a war against the few, not the many—then the tactics of all-out aerial assault against the populations of Germany and Japan destroy that notion." (We have seen Zinn's participation in those efforts, and the impact they had, among other things, on his view of war.) So German and Japananese fascism were destroyed. But were the essential elements of fascism destroyed, including militarism, racism, imperialism? Zinn quotes revolutionary pacifist A. J. Muste: "The problem after a war is with the victor. He thinks he has just proved that war and violence pay. Who will now teach him a lesson?" Sure enough, says Zinn, "the war not only put the United States in a position to dominate much of the world; it created conditions for effective control at home." Right after the war, the government "worked to create an atmosphere of crisis and cold war."[64]

> What happens to a dream deferred?
>> Does it dry up
>> like a raisin in the sun?
>> Or fester like a sore—
>> And then run?
> Does it stink like rotten meat?
> Or crust and sugar over—
> like a syrupy sweet?
>
> Maybe it just sags like a heavy load.
>
> Or does it explode?[65]

Zinn takes the title of his chapter on the civil rights movement from the last line of that famous poem by Langston Hughes. Explode it did. But we have perhaps seen enough of Zinn's coverage of that movement, a movement he was so much involved in himself. The greatest contribution here is perhaps his extensive and effective use of quotation. But also impressive is his personal perspective on the movement, especially when dealing with the role of an organization such as the Student Nonviolent Coordinating Committee (SNCC).

Perhaps not much further need be said of Zinn's analysis of Vietnam, either. He does summarize it succinctly here. "From 1964 to 1972," he says, "the wealthiest and most powerful nation in the history of the world made a maximum military effort, with everything short of atomic bombs, to defeat a nationalist revolutionary movement in a tiny, peasant country— and failed." When the United States fought in Vietnam, Zinn added, "it was organized modern technology versus organized human beings, and the human beings won." Vietnam also saw "the greatest antiwar movement the nation had ever experienced, a movement that played a critical part in bringing the war to an end." If we had been honest, the talk would have been of rice and rubber, but instead it was of Communism and freedom. The Gulf of Tonkin "incident" was, quite simply, "a fake." In the end, the whole thing marked "the first clear defeat to the global American empire formed after World War II."[66]

The women's movement, prison rebellions, and the new militancy within the American Indian community are the subjects of Zinn's chapter entitled "Surprises." "The Seventies: Under Control?" he questions in the next. He felt that "the system was acting to purge the country of its rascals and restore it to a healthy, or at least to an acceptable, state," in the mid-1970s after Watergate. However, he still saw many signs, including remarkable drops in the approval ratings Americans gave business, the military, and politicians, that things indeed were not "under control." Zinn suggested that much of the dissatisfaction was due to the state of the economy, in particular unemployment and inflation. This helps to explain also that "when the 200th anniversary of the Boston Tea Party was celebrated in Boston, an enormous crowd turned out, not for the official celebration, but for the 'People's Bi-Centennial' countercelebration, where packages marked 'Gulf Oil' and 'Exxon' were dumped into the Boston Harbor, to symbolize opposition to corporate power in America."[67]

Interestingly, as his coverage approaches the present, Zinn focuses more and more on presidents—numerous earlier ones were not even mentioned in his narrative. "Carter-Reagan-Bush: The Bipartisan Consensus," he calls one chapter. Insightfully, it harks back to Richard Hofstadter's contention in *The American Political Tradition* that "the range of vision embraced by the primary contestants in the major parties has always been bounded by the horizons of property and enterprise," intensely capitalistic and nationalistic. Jimmy Carter, "despite a few gestures toward black people and the poor, despite talk of 'human rights' abroad, remained within the historic political boundaries of the American system, protecting corporate wealth and power, maintaining a huge military machine that drained the national wealth, allying the United States with right-wing tyrannies abroad." And the dozen years of the Ronald Reagan–George Bush era, of course, lacked "even the faint liberalism of the Carter presidency." The policies, therefore, "would be more crass—cutting benefits to poor people, lowering taxes for the wealthy, increasing the military budget, filling the federal court system with conservative judges, actively working to destroy revolutionary movements in the Caribbean." Thus, "corporate America became the greatest beneficiary of the Reagan-Bush years," and by the end of that era, "the gap between rich and poor in the United States had grown dramatically." Zinn bemoans the failure of the government to substantially reduce the military budget after the end of the Cold War, and is especially hard on the tendency to confuse "national interest" with "special interests." Politics, for example, specifically the upcoming presidential election of 1992, and the continuing desire to control Middle Eastern oil, clearly determined American action in the Gulf War, but the American people were continuously told that our goal was to "liberate Kuwait."[68]

Typically, in "The Unreported Resistance," Zinn finds hope. After all, he notes, only 27 percent of the people of the United States who were eligible to vote in 1980 voted for Reagan, and when the people did speak about issues, in public opinion surveys, "they expressed beliefs to which neither the Republican nor Democratic parties paid attention." After reporting numerous specific incidents, Zinn concludes that "there was, unquestionably, though largely unreported, what a worried mainstream journalist had called 'a permanent adversarial culture' which refused to surrender the possibility of a more equal, more humane society. If there was hope for the future of America, it lay in the promise of that refusal."[69]

Zinn called his final chapter "The Coming Revolt of the Guards." The title, he said, was "not a prediction, but a hope." In this closing portion of the book, Zinn returns to some of the themes about U.S. history, and history in general, that he had set out in the beginning. The title of his book, he admitted, *A People's History of the United States*, was "not quite accurate," for "a 'people's history' promises more than any one person can fulfill, and it is the most difficult kind of history to recapture." Still, he calls it

that "because, with all its limitations, it is a history disrespectful of governments and respectful of people's movements of resistance." Zinn knows
that makes his "a biased account, one that leans in a certain direction." But
he is not troubled by that, he says, "because the mountain of history books
under which we all stand leans so heavily in the other direction—so trem-
blingly respectful of states and statesmen and so disrespectful, by inatten-
tion, to people's movements." Thus, "we need some counterforce to avoid
being crushed into submission."[70] Then, one of those essential passages for
understanding Zinn which bears quoting at length:

> All those histories of this country centered on the Founding Fathers and
> the Presidents weigh oppressively on the capacity of the ordinary citizen
> to act. They suggest that in times of crisis we must look to someone to save
> us: in the Revolutionary crisis, the Founding Fathers; in the slavery crisis,
> Lincoln; in the Depression, Roosevelt; in the Vietnam-Watergate crisis,
> Carter. And that between occasional crises everything is all right, and it is
> sufficient for us to be restored to that normal state. They teach us that the
> supreme act of citizenship is to choose among saviors, by going into a
> voting booth every four years to choose between two white and well-off
> Anglo-Saxon males of inoffensive personality and orthodox opinions.
>   The idea of saviors has been built into the entire culture, beyond pol-
> itics. We have learned to look to stars, leaders, experts in every field, thus
> surrendering our own strength, demeaning our own ability, obliterating our
> own selves. But from time to time, Americans reject that idea and rebel.[71]

It is, obviously, in that rebellion that Zinn finds his hope. He knows, of
course, that so far the rebellions have been contained, for "the American
system is the most ingenious system of control in world history." Just
enough wealth, just enough freedom exists "to limit discontent to a trouble-
some minority." But look at our history, says Zinn, the history he has been
unfolding for us here at great length. The secret "the Establishment" would
like for us to forget is "the enormous capacity of apparently helpless people
to resist, of apparently contented people to demand change."[72]

But who are the "guards" of his title? The Establishment knows it
"cannot survive without the obedience and loyalty of millions of people who
are given small rewards to keep the system going," so it is these people, "the
employed, the somewhat privileged," who are in effect drawn into an
alliance with the elite. "They become the guards of the system, buffers
between the upper and lower classes." And "if they stop obeying, the system
fails." Zinn thinks that will happen, but "only when all of us who are slightly

privileged and slightly uneasy begin to see that we are like the guards in the prison uprising at Attica—expendable; that the Establishment, whatever rewards it gives us, will also, if necessary to maintain its control, kill us." Strong stuff. And Zinn thinks there is indeed evidence of "growing dissatisfaction among the guards." Capitalism, he insists, "has always been a failure for the lower classes. It is now beginning to fail for the middle classes." Building toward his conclusion, Zinn says, "Let us imagine the prospect— for the first time in the nation's history—of a population united for fundamental change. Would the elite turn as so often before, to its ultimate weapon—foreign intervention—to unite the people with the Establishment, in war?" But the most recent time they tried that, he notes, was in 1991 with the war against Iraq, and it did not seem to work as well or as completely as they hoped, or as it had in the past. "With the Establishment's inability either to solve severe economic problems at home or to manufacture abroad a safety valve for domestic discontent, Americans might be ready to demand not just more tinkering, more reform laws, another reshuffling of the same deck, another New Deal, but radical change."[73]

Zinn is aware that he is being "utopian" here, but insists that we should be, "so that when we get realistic again it is not that 'realism' so useful to the Establishment in its discouragement of action, that 'realism' anchored to a certain kind of history empty of surprise." At some length, then, he describes his vision of a new cooperative economic and social order with power in the hands of the masses of the people rather than in the hands of "the giant corporations, the military, and their politician collaborators." Food, housing, health care, education, and transportation would be available equally, and free, to all. To bring this about "would require combining the energy of all previous movements in American history—of labor insurgents, black rebels, Native Americans, women, young people—along with the new energy of an angry middle class." People would begin by taking control of their immediate environments, including the school, workplace, community. The tactics would include all the ones previously used by people's movements: "demonstrations, marches, civil disobedience; strikes and boycotts and general strikes; direct action to redistribute wealth, to reconstruct institutions, to revamp relationships; creating—in music, literature, drama, all the arts, and all the areas of work and play in everyday life—a new culture of sharing, of respect, a new joy in the collaboration of people to help themselves and one another." Zinn knows there would be "many defeats." But he also believes that "when such a movement took hold in hundreds of thousands of places all over the country it would be impossible to suppress, because the very guards the system depends on to crush such a movement would be among the rebels."[74]

Finally, Zinn also knows that all this "takes us far from American history, into the realm of imagination." But he insists it is "not totally removed from history." For "there are at least glimpses in the past of such a possibility." He has in mind especially the 1960s and 1970s, when "for the first time, the Establishment failed to produce national unity and patriotic fervor in a war," and there was "a flood of cultural changes such as the country had never seen—in sex, family, personal relations—exactly those situations most difficult to control from the ordinary centers of power." So, "The prisoners of the system will continue to rebel, as before, in ways that cannot be foreseen, at times that cannot be predicted," asserts Zinn. But "the new fact of our era is the chance that they may be joined by the guards. We readers and writers of books have been, for the most part, among the guards," Zinn notes, bringing it all close to home. "If we understand that, and act on it, not only will life be more satisfying, right off, but our grandchildren, or our great grandchildren, might possibly see a different and marvelous world."[75] Howard Zinn's radical American vision—perhaps nowhere else has he spelled it out so succinctly, passionately.

The 1995 edition of *A People's History of the United States* did give Zinn the opportunity to add a brief afterword on the Clinton presidency. Not surprisingly, he is unimpressed, and places Clinton squarely in the consensus with Reagan and others, noting, for example, his support from the centrist Democratic Leadership Council, and his admiration for Nixon. To bring about "even a rough equality of opportunity," suggested Zinn, "would require a drastic redistribution of wealth, a huge expenditure of money for job creation, health, education, the environment." There were two possible sources to pay for all this—the military budget and the wealth of the super-rich—and "the Clinton administration was not inclined to use either one."[76]

Zinn responded to the critical review by Oscar Handlin, a rare act for him. Some of his response, and some of his other comments about his book, are worthy of consideration. The first sentence of his response to Handlin was clever and hard-hitting; to understand it, one needs to know that Handlin was a rather hefty man. "In reviewing my book, *A People's History of the United States*, in your fall issue," he wrote to the editors of the *American Scholar*, "Oscar Handlin is beside himself—a formidable juxtaposition." Zinn refers to Handlin's "rage," then says it "recalls his famous vituperations against other historians," such as Carl Degler and William Appleman Williams, "who simply differed with his interpretations of

American history." Noting that Handlin supported the Vietnam War and Nixon, Zinn suggests, "We might not be surprised if a reviewer with such beliefs were very critical of a book like mine." But we should also be able to expect him to be honest, and Handlin is not; he "tampers with the truth, repeatedly misleading readers about what my book says."

One example of what Zinn had in mind must suffice here. Quoting Handlin that Zinn had condemned American imperialism, but had "not a word about the Soviet Union of course," Zinn reminds the reader that he had condemned Soviet action in Hungary in 1956, that he had noted the Soviets, "under the cover of 'socialism,'" had set out after World War II to carve out their empire, and that he had written, "The Soviet Union, like the United States, did not seem to be willing to help revolutions it could not control." Then he asks, effectively, "Not a word?" Responding specifically to Handlin's claim that Zinn paid "only casual regard to factual accuracy," Zinn presents documentary evidence to support his position on several of the issues Handlin had raised. In conclusion, Zinn says he cannot comment on all of Handlin's "distortions." "Behind them, I suspect, is a fundamental difference in our viewpoints which drives Handlin to fury." Handlin's logic, thinks Zinn, is that "humanity consists of states; Zinn does not speak well of any state; therefore Zinn hates humanity." But "I do speak well of lots of people," insists Zinn, "and of many movements of dissent and protest; indeed, that's what most of the book is about. But it is *states* Handlin cares about. And I seem to think there is a humanity beyond states; indeed, that states have generally acted against humanity. Well, that's worth an argument," concludes Zinn with a clever barb, "but not a fit."[77]

A rough draft of *A People's History of the United States* reveals that Zinn initially called it "Struggle for Democracy."[78] Significant, obviously, for that was indeed one of the major themes of his work, here and elsewhere. But it is probably best that the title was changed to the broader one the book finally carried. In response to the question about which of his books he was proudest of, that he thought might have made the greatest impact, Zinn began with the *People's History*. Sales figures alone, he thought, suggested it "has undoubtedly had the greatest effect of all my books." He said he also knew this from the mail he received and the fact that people all over the country tell him about the impact it has had for them. He looks at the book, he says, as "sort of a straightforward account, at least not complicated." He is speaking primarily about the writing style. "The thing that I always felt good about in my writing style was that I never had to struggle to write clearly and understandably," he says, and people who read the *People's History* "would tell me that again and again. 'I can give your book to my grandmother,' or 'I can give your book to my fifteen-year-old kid.'"

That raised a question about Zinn's writing: "What would you say briefly about your writing methods; how do you write a book?" He responded primarily by talking about the *People's History*. He started out with "a fairly orthodox outline—the Revolution, the Jacksonian period, the Civil War, the Reconstruction, and so on." But then, "once I had a chapter that I knew I was going to write about, I would collect whatever books I thought were relevant . . . and bring them into my study and pile them up, read them, put slips in them to the pages that I would want to refer to." Also, "I would go to my files, because, after all, with twenty years of teaching, collecting files on the American Revolution and the Civil War and the industrial development of the United States, etc." So "I would pile up the books and the slips and would pile up my folders, my file folders, and I would sit down at the typewriter; you know, I wrote the *People's History* on my Royal typewriter, manual Royal typewriter." He says he considers himself a pretty fast writer, and that his writing does not seem to require a great deal of revision after he writes it. "I'll type a first draft, consulting these books and these files. I will type out a first draft, go over it with pen and ink to make changes, and so on, and then type up the final copy. And that's it."

Zinn has clearly been surprised by the book's success. "Neither I nor the publisher knew it would take off the way it did," he says. Seeking to explain it, he says, "Obviously it came at just the right time, served a need." Further, "It came out just at the time we had just gone through all these movements. And all those generations of people who had been affected by the civil rights and anti–Vietnam War movements were looking for a new history." There were, of course, "partial histories, in fact that I depended on a great deal while writing about specific periods and specific issues, [but] there was no overall view, from a radical point of view."[79]

In *A People's History of the United States*, Howard Zinn did indeed provide an "overall view, from a radical point of view" of U.S. history. Oscar Handlin to the contrary notwithstanding, most reviewers recognized that. (Or perhaps Handlin recognized it as well, recognized it as that "step toward a coherent new version of American history" that Eric Foner considered it, and that was what had him so uptight?) It was reviewed more widely than most of Zinn's books, including in some perhaps surprising places. The *Christchurch Press*, for example, a New Zealand newspaper, reviewed it, under the headline "American History Seen from Below," and the *Journal of*

Education gave it a lengthy "Review Essay," which concluded that it might help move us "one step closer, as a society, to being prepared to use *all* voices from the past in our efforts to confront the issues that face us."[80]

The *Library Journal*'s reviewer considered Zinn's volume "a brilliant and moving history of the American people from the point of view of those who have been exploited politically and economically and whose plight has been largely omitted from most histories," and thus "an excellent antidote to establishment history." He also noted that "seldom have quotations been so effectively used; the stories of blacks, women, Indians, and poor laborers of all nationalities are told in their own words."[81]

Bruce Kuklick in the *Nation* referred to the *People's History* specifically as "a radical textbook history of the United States." His review was not without its criticisms, perhaps most effective when he said he "was struck by the brevity" of Zinn's treatment of the subjugation of women, "as if he were a relative latecomer to feminism who hadn't fully integrated its views into his own."[82] Zinn himself has admitted elsewhere that he "can't really claim to be involved in the women's movements."[83]

A strange little review appeared in the *Kliatt Young Adult Paperback Book Guide*. The reviewer actually considered it "boring" that Zinn spent so much time "compiling" specific incidents to support his chapter theses, but then went on to recommend the book for high school libraries "because the general texts now available need the counter-balance of this different viewpoint."[84]

One of the more interesting devices reviewers chose was to link the *People's History* with other books. David O'Brien, for example, in *Commonweal*, reviewed Zinn along with the third volume of Page Smith's (eventual) eight-volume people's history, *The Shaping of America: A People's History of the Young Republic*. Though he insisted that both Smith and Zinn "believe that their colleagues among professional historians have contributed to [the] debasement of American historical scholarship," O'Brien fortunately realized that Smith is "less directly political than Zinn, more inclined to 'tell the story of our past as fairly and accurately as possible.'" O'Brien obviously knew Zinn and his work. "Everyone who has observed Zinn's long struggle for justice from a distance," he said, "and follows his current battle with Boston University President John Silber, knows that his tie is never straight, his voice is always ruffled, and he seldom keeps his emotions to himself." Thus, the *People's History* "is a fitting expression of its author: committed, angry, one-sided, polemical, and profoundly true."[85]

In the *New Statesman*, Charles Glass chose to review Zinn along with Sandy Vogelgesang's *American Dream, Global Nightmare* and Daniel Patrick Moynihan's *Counting Our Blessings: Reflections on the Future of America*. Though he considered Zinn's book the best of the three, Glass did have some criticism, including the book's "undramatic" nature, and that it lacked adequate primary sources and "sufficient evidence" to support its contentions.[86]

In the *Newton Teachers Quarterly*, it was the important 1979 critique of American history textbooks *America Revised*, by Frances FitzGerald, that was reviewed jointly with the *People's History*. The reviewer felt Zinn had "written the fluent counter-textbook to answer her [i.e., FitzGerald's] concerns about bland, packaged history." There was even the interesting suggestion that Zinn had "accomplished a true patriot's task. By going . . . to the very roots of the American people, by giving us stories of that people in all their variety and contradition [sic], he has provided us with a firm ground on which to erect the kind of society Thomas Jefferson might have been dreaming of when he wrote" the Declaration of Independence.[87]

Murray Rosenblith, in the pages of *WIN*, reviewed Zinn jointly with David Armstrong's *A Trumpet to Arms: Alternative Media in America*. Noting that the United States has a rich history of dissent, radical politics, and alternative movements, but that it is usually left out of the textbooks, so that every new generation has to rediscover it, Rosenblith says he has "had this fantasy of sneaking into every secondary school in the country and substituting copies of this book for all those dreary tomes in the closets of history teachers."[88]

Students have indeed been known to respond with interest to Zinn. The only item worthy of note from the review in the *English Journal* is the quotation from a student after reading *A People's History*: "The reader becomes more sensitive, more aware. It's like wearing a new pair of glasses for the first time."[89]

Commentary presented one of the most important reviews. It was actually an essay entitled "Radical Historians," written by James Nuechterlein, but it dealt extensively with Zinn's *People's History*. Nuechterlein suggested that the "extensive common ground between the New Left and the radical fringes of the new social history becomes clear in . . . [Zinn's] recent left-wing survey of American history," and also that through Zinn, "Jesse Lemisch's dream of seeing things from the bottom up has found expression," for Zinn is "the ultimate populist historian."

But it should by no means be assumed that Nuechterlein's analysis is without criticism. He thinks Zinn operates, for example, "on the apparent assumption that, biases once confessed, anything goes," and that even though Zinn "denies that it is his intention to romanticize the victims or vilify the executioners, . . . that is the way the book turns out." He does credit Zinn with "lively prose" and "extensive, and often effective, use of quotations." But his analysis turns especially harsh when he quotes at length Zinn's vision of the future and then says, "In the end, we either believe in that sort of thing or we do not, but even those who believe ought to understand that they must find support for their vision in eschatological hope and not, Zinn's willed illusions to the contrary notwithstanding, in the record of the past." On a roll, Nuechterlein refers to Zinn's "utopian projections, . . . populist romanticism, . . . [and] selective sorting of the past for present purposes." He suspects that more "tough-minded radicals . . . would resist any notion that *A People's History of the United States* represents the state of the radical historian's art." Yet he also acknowledges that "the problems exemplified in Zinn's book plague other, more subtle, left-wing historians as well, and they do so because they are inherent in the nature of American history." Explaining that, Nuechterlein writes, "The problem for Zinn and for radical historians generally is that while they imagine the people existing in a state of perpetual protest, the people seem, in the end, to have so little to show for it." In short, "Things change, but—from the radical perspective—nothing changes. The system remains securely in place, the establishment firmly in control."

Moving away from Zinn specifically, Nuechterlein concludes his essay by insisting that "most American radicals know that for their hopes to be realized the past must be transcended, not recaptured."[90]

Nuechterlein's claim that Zinn's book should not really be regarded as a radical American history textbook is an interesting one, for that is indeed what many have considered it. Perhaps it can prove insightful to see how an editor of the *Radical History Review* dealt with Zinn's work—though he did so in the pages of the *Monthly Review*. Mike Wallace began by bemoaning America's "historicidal culture," then said Zinn's *People's History* "seeks to sum up the body of critical scholarship developed in the 1960s and 1970s, and present it in an accessible way to a general public." Clearly, he noted, Zinn "hopes that such a book will help to counteract the anti-historical tendencies of the dominant culture." As for himself, Wallace considered Zinn's work "one of the best popular introductions to the history of the United States now available," though he did go on to delineate some methodological problems. He felt Zinn "repeatedly overstates the capacity of elites to control events," "unwittingly undermines our respect for the autonomy of popular cultures," "tends to overdramatize history as a record of purposive action," and is inattentive "to structures and processes in history." Perhaps more important, he felt the *People's History* "subtly encourages—despite all Zinn's calls to revolutionary action—a quiet fatalism."[91]

This point leads, finally, to the review by Eric Foner quoted extensively on the back cover of Zinn's book. The portions used to promote the book are, of course, the most positive passages. But Foner also concluded that the *People's History* "reflects a deeply pessimistic vision of the American experience." It is tempting to simply say that Foner is wrong, for has not Zinn himself emphasized repeatedly his optimism? (Later, he would entitle a book *Failure to Quit: Reflections of an Optimistic Historian.*) But it should be noted, with all due respect, that Foner is making essentially the same point Wallace made. The book's "salutary emphasis on 'the enormous capacity of apparently helpless people to resist' is tempered by an underlying frustration at the meager results produced by this history of resistance," states Foner. Also, "The stirring protests, strikes, and rebellions never appear to accomplish anything. Uprisings are either crushed, deflected, or co-opted. Apparent victories, such as the emancipation of the slaves, simply serve the interests of businessmen; incremental gains, such as those of the 1930s, merely stabilize the system."

Foner also insists that "history from the bottom up, though necessary as a corrective, is as limited in its own way as history from the top down." To illustrate, he points to Zinn's treatment of the Jacksonian era. Instead of portraying it, traditionally, as a time of democracy and reform, and ignoring Indian removal, Zinn makes Indian removal "virtually the only aspect of the period that warrants attention." Says Foner, "The result is still a partial view of Jacksonian America." What is really needed, he insists effectively, is "an integrated account incorporating both Thomas Jefferson and his slaves, Andrew Jackson and the Indians, Woodrow Wilson and the Wobblies, in a continuing historical process, in which each group's experience is shaped in large measure by its relation to others." Still, Foner clearly recognizes the value of Zinn's work, and on the issue of whether Zinn's is a radical textbook of American history, says Zinn is indeed "the first historian to attempt to survey all of American history from the perspective of the new scholarship."[92]

Reviews are important, indeed a necessary part of the effort to place a book in historical context, summarize it, and evaluate it. But there are other ways of doing that as well, some of them perhaps even more revealing and important, especially in the case of a work such as Zinn's. The *Daily Free Press* reported on March 30, 1981, that *A People's History of the United States* had been nominated for a prestigious American Book Award. It also reported that both the hardback edition, released in January 1980, and the first paperback printing, released in September of the same year, had sold out, and that new printings in both English and Japanese were on the way. Zinn was quoted as saying he did not think all this success was likely to change his standing with the administration at Boston University, "with which he has long been at odds."[93]

In Zinn's home he has boxes with folders of materials related to each of his books; the folders include reviews, letters, and other items. The most impressive folders are those on the *People's History*, three of them, literally bulging with hundreds of items. Only a few can be mentioned here. A community college instructor wrote to say that he had found the book "absolutely invaluable in my entire conception of U.S. History"—but also to ask for advice about graduate schools. A prisoner wrote from Maryland to say he thought it was "the most important book I ever read"—and to ask for a free copy of Zinn's latest at that time, *Declarations of Independence*. A Unitarian Universalist minister wrote to request an autographed copy of the *People's History* to sell in his church's fund-raising auction—and to sweeten the pot informed Zinn that it was "one of the most highly quoted books among our members" and that the church was a sanctuary for war resisters. A graduate student wrote to say that it was "thanks to historians like you, who have a passion for the truth and a willingness to rock the boat of 'official' history, that teachers like me have the resources from which to learn and to teach"—and to thank Zinn for replying to an earlier query. A law school student, a former student of Zinn's, wrote to say she was in a law school (CUNY Law School at Queens College) which had as its motto "Law in the Service of Human Needs"; she thought Zinn would like that—and the fact that his *People's History* had been used in a class. ("You took a Jewish girl from Long Island and opened up a world of information to her," she said of Zinn's teaching.) Two attorneys with the Institute for the Practice of Nonviolence wrote to say that they used the *People's History* "with great frequency"—and to thank Zinn for being an expert witness in one of their cases.[94] Such letters go on and on and on; clearly there is an impact here that goes far beyond the confines of book reviewing, beyond the scholarly world as usually defined.

There was an even longer gap in Zinn's book-publishing record after *A People's History of the United States* in 1980 than there had been before; his next book did not appear until 1990, two years after his retirement. "I don't know where those years went," he has said. But it seems obvious that the success of the *People's History* helps to account for the hiatus. Quite simply, Howard Zinn was a name known to many more people now, and there were many more demands on his time, including increasingly large numbers of speaking engagements around the country. In addition, Zinn says there were several more productions of his play, *Emma*, in London and New York in 1986 and 1987; each new production entailed some rewriting.[95]

When he did finally publish that next book, *Declarations of Independence*, he based it, he said, on "the two big lecture courses I had taught over the years: 'Law and Justice in America' and 'Introduction to Political Theory.'"[96] It is possible to see what those courses were like in the closing years of Zinn's teaching career by looking at course syllabi. The syllabus for Introduction to Political Theory, for example, for the spring semester of 1986, included Emma Goldman and Dalton Trumbo among the required books, but there were briefer portions of many other works to be read also, by such authors as Staughton Lynd, Stephen Gould, George Orwell, Plato, Thucydides, Machiavelli, Noam Chomsky, Karl Marx, and Reinhold Niebuhr. Topics covered included "Ideology and Commitment: Objectivity and Neutrality in Social Science, and History," "Human Nature and Violence: Evidence from the Sciences and History," "Obedience and Resistance: The Law and the Citizen," "War: Means and Ends," and some more specific ones such as "Accident and Structure: Vietnam and U.S. Foreign Policy" and "American Capitalism: A Marxist Critique." Assignments were a journal, a letter to the editor of a newspaper, and class participation. How Zinn kept a record of the latter is not at all clear, but taped class sessions reveal that he was indeed remarkably successful at getting students involved.

For Law and Justice in America in the fall of 1986, Zinn required Richard Wright's *Black Boy* and Ron Kovic's *Born on the Fourth of July*, among other things. But once again the actual reading was far more extensive than that, and included court cases, the Federalist Papers, and Plato's "Crito." Assignments were, again, a journal, and a "project," which was to be done in groups and to involve work "on some problem of *justice*, or *human rights*, or *freedom of expression*." Topics included the First Amendment, free speech, the Fourteenth Amendment, "The Government as Lawbreaker: The FBI and Martin Luther King," "The Supreme Court and the Vietnam War," and "Women's Rights and the Law." Zinn said on an earlier syllabus (1970) for this course that topics were "subject to abrupt change on short notice;" certainly the course appears to have changed with the times also, for the 1970 syllabus and the 1986 one reveal minimal overlap.

Tapes are also available for a limited number of Zinn's classroom sessions. They reveal an informal approach, with effective use of humor, quotes from original sources, and, again, extensive student participation. In terms of content, one thing Zinn did repeatedly, whether the subject was Bacon's Rebellion, the Constitution, or Emma Goldman and anarchism, was to draw contemporary parallels. Occasionally, he utilized a historiographical approach, as when he talked about Beard versus Robert Brown and Forrest McDonald on the Constitution. One example of Zinn's humor will suffice. Beginning to discuss Emma Goldman's *Living My Life*, Zinn felt he was not getting much response from the students. In a series of questions, each eliciting a little more laughter than the previous one, Zinn asked, "Have you read it? Have you *started* reading it? Have you *looked* at it? Have you held it in your hands?" But the response was not only laughter; students began to speak up about the book as well.[97]

After more than thirty years of eliciting student response, Zinn decided in 1988 to retire. The decision was sudden, he says. "I surprised myself by this, because I love teaching, but I wanted more freedom, to write, to speak to people around the country, to have more time with family and friends." Specifically, his wife, Roslyn, had stopped doing social work and was playing music and painting; he wanted to do more with her. Their daughter, Myla, and her husband lived in the Boston area, and had given the Zinns three grandchildren; he wanted to spend more time with them as well. And their son, Jeff, and his wife lived on Cape Cod, where Jeff was involved in theater; the Zinns shared a beach house on the Cape with some old friends from their Spelman College days, so it would be easy to spend time with their son and his family.

News of Zinn's pending retirement "seemed to spread," he says. He recalls that his last class was "especially crowded, with people there who were not my students, standing against the wall, sitting in the aisles. I answered questions about my decision, and we had a final discussion about justice, the role of the university, the future of the world."[98] Appropriate. But there is more:

> Then I told them that I was ending the class a half-hour early and explained why. There was a struggle going on between the faculty at the B.U. School of Nursing and the administration, which had decided to close the school down because it was not making enough money, in effect firing the nursing faculty. The nurses were picketing that very day in

protest. I was going to join them and I invited my students to come along (Roz had given me that idea the evening before). When I left the class, about a hundred students walked with me. The nurses, desperately needing support, greeted us happily, and we marched up and down together.

It seemed a fitting way to end my teaching career. I had always insisted that a good education was a synthesis of book learning and involvement in social action, that each enriched the other. I wanted my students to know that the accumulation of knowledge, while fascinating in itself, is not sufficient as long as so many people in the world have no opportunity to experience that fascination.[99]

NOTES

1. Howard Zinn, e-mail message to the author, March 7, 1997.

2. Howard Zinn, *Postwar America: 1945–1971* (Indianapolis: Bobbs-Merrill, 1973), pp. x–xi.

3. Ibid., pp. xiii–xvii.

4. Ibid., pp. xiii, xviii.

5. Ibid., p. xix.

6. Ibid.

7. Ibid., pp 7, 9–10, 16.

8. Ibid., pp. 20, 22, 26.

9. Ibid., p. 77.

10. Ibid., pp. 89–90, 102.

11. Ibid., pp. 148, 149.

12. Ibid., p. 178.

13. Ibid., p. 103.

14. Howard Zinn, *Declarations of Independence: Cross-Examining American Ideology* (New York: HarperCollins, 1990), pp. 147–49.

15. Ibid., pp. 183–85.

16. Ibid., pp. 196–197.

17. Ibid., pp. 198–199, 201, 215, 231, 244.

18. James T. Patterson, review of *Postwar America* by Howard Zinn, *Journal of American History* 60 (September 1973): 513–14.

19. Review of *Postwar America* by Howard Zinn, *Choice* 10 (October 1973): 1274.

20. Peter Michelson, review of *Postwar America* by Howard Zinn, *New Republic* 169 (July 28 & August 4, 1973): 24–26.

21. Howard Zinn, e-mail message to the author, March 29, 1997.

22. Howard Zinn, ed., *Justice in Everyday Life: The Way It Really Works* (New York: William Morrow, 1974), pp. ix–xii.

23. Ibid., pp. 143–44.

24. Ibid., pp. 190–192.

25. Ibid., p. 233.

26. Ibid., pp. 275, 281–82.

27. Ibid., pp. 353–54.

28. Ibid., pp. 354, 356–57, 361, 366–67.

29. Stuart A. Scheingold, review of *Justice in Everyday Life: The Way It Really Works* by Howard Zinn, *Chronicle of Higher Education* 10 (April 7, 1975): 15.

30. Steven Puro, review of *Justice in Everyday Life* by Howard Zinn, *Library Journal* 99 (November 1, 1974): 2864; review of *Justice in Everyday Life* by Howard Zinn, *Publishers Weekly* 206 (August 12, 1974): 54–55.

31. Peter Irons, *The Courage of Their Convictions: Sixteen Americans Who Fought Their Way to the Supreme Court* (New York: Penguin Books, 1988), dedication and p. xiii.

32. Howard Zinn, e-mail messages to the author, June 9, 1997, and June 21, 1998.

33. Howard Zinn, e-mail message to the author, June 9, 1997.

34. Howard Zinn, *The Zinn Reader: Writings on Disobedience and Democracy* (New York: Seven Stories Press, 1997), pp. 139–41.

35. Ibid., pp. 220–22.

36. Ibid., pp. 223–25.

37. Ibid., pp. 328–30.

38. Howard Zinn, e-mail message to the author, June 9, 1997.

39. Howard Zinn, interview, Boston, Mass., March 14, 1997.

40. Oscar Handlin, review of *A People's History of the United States* by Howard Zinn, *American Scholar* 49 (autumn 1980): 546–50.

41. Foner's review is conveniently, and not surprisingly, quoted on the back cover of *A People's History*; the "modern classic" label is quoted in J. Max Robins, "The Robins Report: Damon and Affleck to Make *History*?" *TV Guide*, June 20–26, 1998, p. 37.

42. Howard Zinn, *A People's History of the United States*, revised and updated ed. (New York: HarperPerennial, 1995), p. 10. (All references here are to this edition.)

43. Ibid., pp. 8–9.

44. Ibid., pp. 9–10.

45. Ibid., pp. 10–11.

46. Ibid. pp. 23, 31, 32, 37–38.

47. Ibid., pp. 50, 55, 56–57, 58.

48. William Dudley, ed., *The American Revolution: Opposing Viewpoints* (San Diego, Calif.: Greenhaven Press, 1992), pp. 242–43.

49. Zinn, *People's History*, pp. 77, 88–89, 98–99, 101.

50. Ibid., pp. 107, 102.

51. Ibid., pp. 127, 140, 135, 125.

52. Ibid., pp. 166, 152.

53. Ibid., p. 167.

54. Ibid., pp. 168, 180.

55. Ibid., pp. 180, 182, 185.

56. Ibid., pp. 193, 204.

57. Handlin, review, *American Scholar*, p. 548; Zinn, *People's History*, p. 211.

58. Zinn, *People's History*, pp. 247, 253, 252, 271, 276.

59. Ibid., pp. 290–92.

60. Ibid., pp. 314, 331, 341.

61. Ibid., pp. 350, 362.

62. Ibid., pp. 375, 394.

63. Ibid., pp. 398–404.

64. Ibid., pp. 412, 416.

65. Ibid., p. 435.

66. Ibid., pp. 460, 466, 492.

67. Ibid., pp. 544–45, 550.

68. Ibid., pp. 551, 553, 561–62, 569, 572, 580–81, 583.

69. Ibid., pp. 598–99, 617.

70. Ibid., p. 618.

71. Ibid.

72. Ibid., pp. 618–19, 621.

73. Ibid., pp. 622–25.

74. Ibid., pp. 625–27.

75. Ibid., pp. 627–28.

76. Ibid., pp. 629–34.

77. Howard Zinn, letter to the editors of *American Scholar*, undated copy supplied to the author by Howard Zinn.

78. A rough draft of this and several other Zinn books is located in the Boston University Archives, Mugar Library, Boston University, Boston, Massachusetts.

79. Howard Zinn, interview, Boston, Mass., March 14, 1997.

80. John Wilson, review of *A People's History of the United States* by Howard Zinn, *Christchurch Press*, November 18, 1980; Jean Anyon, review of *A People's History of the United States* by Howard Zinn, *Journal of Education* (summer 1980): 67–73.

81. James Levin, review of *A People's History of the United States* by Howard Zinn, *Library Journal* 105 (January 1, 1980): 101.

82. Bruce Kuklick, review of *A People's History of the United States* by Howard Zinn, *Nation* 230 (May 24, 1980): 634–36.

83. Howard Zinn, e-mail message to the author, June 21, 1998.

84. Review of *A People's History of the United States* by Howard Zinn, *Kliatt Young Adult Paperback Book Guide* 15 (winter 1981): 44.

85. David O'Brien, review of *A People's History of the United States* by Howard Zinn, *Commonweal* 108 (January 16, 1981): 24–26.

86. Charles Glass, review of *A People's History of the United States* by Howard Zinn, *New Statesman* 100 (October 24, 1980): 27.

87. Review of *A People's History of the United States* by Howard Zinn, *Newton Teachers Quarterly* (winter 1980): 4.

88. Murray Rosenblith, review of *A People's History of the United States* by Howard Zinn, *WIN*, April 15, 1982, pp. 29–30.

89. Review of *A People's History of the United States* by Howard Zinn, *English Journal* 82 (April, 1993): 33.

90. James Nuechterlein, review of *A People's History of the United States* by Howard Zinn, *Commentary* 70 (October 1980): 56–64.

91. Mike Wallace, review of *A People's History of the United States* by Howard Zinn, *Monthly Review* (December 1980): 27–38.

92. Eric Foner, review of *A People's History of the United States* by Howard Zinn, *New York Times Book Review*, March 2, 1980, pp. 10, 31.

93. Ami Finkelthal, "Zinn Book Nominated for Paperback Award," *Daily Free Press*, March 30, 1981, p. 9.

94. Letters to Howard Zinn from Joseph A. Palermo, January 7, 1991; Kenneth Williams, March 31, 1991; Donald H. Wheat, February 28, 1991; Anne Fairbrother, January 16, 1997; Suzan Glickman, October 22, 1985; and S. Brian Willson and Holley Rauen, September 25, 1990. All documents are from the Howard Zinn Papers.

95. Howard Zinn, e-mail message to the author, June 9, 1997.

96. Ibid.

97. Syllabi and tapes are all in the Howard Zinn Papers.

98. Howard Zinn, *You Can't Be Neutral on a Moving Train* (Boston: Beacon Press, 1994), pp. 201–202.

99. Ibid., pp. 202–203.

FIVE

FAILURE TO QUIT
1988-PRESENT

oward Zinn has been arrested, he recalls, nine times for participating in various protests and demonstrations. Most have had to do
with the civil rights movement and the Vietnam War. Others
involved protesting against police brutality, against U.S. "support of death
squads in El Salvador," against "Reagan's blockade of Nicaragua," and still
another "in Everett, Massachusetts, for refusing, with twelve others, to
leave a factory which refused to rehire immigrant women workers fired for
union organizing." (Not to mention his first arrest, in Atlanta, simply for
being in a car with one of his students.)[1]

One of those arrests explains the title for this chapter. Zinn was one of
a group of over five hundred individuals who were arrested for sitting in at
the John F. Kennedy Federal Building in Boston as a protest against the
Reagan administration's Nicaragua policies. The "official charge against
us," says Zinn, "used the language of the old trespass law: failure to quit
the premises." But on the letter he received informing him the case was
being dropped, apparently because "there were too many of us to deal
with," the charge was shortened to "failure to quit." Zinn loved it. "I think

that sums up what it is that has kept the Bill of Rights alive," he said in a 1992 celebration of the Bill of Rights at historic Faneuil Hall in Boston. "Not the President or Congress, or the Supreme Court, or the wealthy media. But all those people who have refused to quit, who have insisted on their rights and the rights of others, the rights of all human beings everywhere . . . to equality, to life, liberty, and the pursuit of happiness." That, he concluded, "is the spirit of the Bill of Rights, and beyond that, the spirit of the Declaration of Independence, yes the spirit of '76: refusal to quit."[2]

Failure to quit. It seems an apt metaphor for Howard Zinn in retirement. Since 1988, for example, he has published nine additional books (not counting plays and reissues of earlier books), served as Fulbright Distinguished Professor at the University of Bologna, Italy (in 1995, at age seventy-three), written more plays, and done an amount of speaking that would be unimaginable even for many younger people.

Most of Zinn's books published since his retirement have had a sort of anthological and/or retrospective quality. In 1990, for example, *Declarations of Independence: Cross-Examining American Ideology* grew out of Zinn's teaching of Introduction to Political Theory and Law and Justice in America. If one is familiar with Zinn's work to this point, the volume includes little that is new; some portions had previously been published. Zinn himself has said he considers *Declarations of Independence* one of his least satisfactory books. He describes it, accurately, as a "varied set of essays on all sorts of topics—war, law, and representative government, human nature—it's sort of a potpourri." But then he follows with, "In that sense, it's not successful. I would've done better taking any one of those topics and writing a short book on that topic. In retrospect, that's how I feel about it." It was too much of a "jumble," he felt, and "while the individual elements of a jumble may be good, if you put them all together, it's indigestible." He concluded that if he had a chance to do it over again, he would do it differently.[3]

But Zinn is too hard on himself. It is revealing to look at a few of the many letters in his files on *Declarations of Independence*. A lawyer from Los Angeles wrote to say he had recently read both *A People's History of the United States* and *Declarations of Independence*; he considered them both "excellent," but actually preferred *Declarations*. A self-proclaimed anarchist who identified himself only as "Squirrel" printed a five-page letter by hand; he said, "Seeing mainstream American thinking taken apart so systematically and with such a strong historical foundation articulated a lot of things clearly that I understood on an intuitive level but could not put into words." One resident of Boston felt so strongly that he quoted Kafka saying, "A book should be an axe to crack the frozen sea within us," and then said, "I think yours is such a book. It is one of those rare books that can change the reader's life." An actress in New York City wrote to thank Zinn, and to compare a production she was in called "Democracy in America" with Zinn's book. A high school sophomore from Windsor, Connecticut, said he thought *Declarations* was one of the finest books that he had ever read; he also admitted it was "one of the only books that I have ever read that was not assigned to me." His last sentence read: "If you do not feel that you have the time or the desire to respond to this letter, I can understand completely and I am sure that I will get over it in a couple of years." His signature was followed by a postscript: "The last part was obviously a feeble attempt at a guilt trip. I hope it worked." There is no record indicating whether Zinn replied, but he frequently does reply to such letters. He replied to the L.A. lawyer, for example, and to a letter from a New York City father who said he was giving *Declarations* to his daughter, who was in her first year of law school, in hopes that it would "help her save her soul before she loses it." The father's major concern was the Gulf War then going on. "Unfortunately, this is our war," he wrote. "We the People" elect our Congress, our president, and "'We the People' are sending our agents to bomb Iraq." His faith in the democratic process, he said, had been "badly shaken." Another person wrote from Daly City, California, making the Gulf War connection. "Just as Twain's words in *The Mysterious Stranger* were tested and proven with World War I, so too were your words from *Declarations of Independence* tested and proven with the current American involvement in the Persian Gulf." Still another individual, from New Hampshire, wrote to thank Zinn for his book, to share a *New Yorker* cartoon (in which an irate father enters the living room where his son is reading and says, "Look, son, if you don't watch TV you won't know what's going on!")—and to say "do not bother to answer this letter."[4]

Some of the reviewers of *Declarations of Independence* also thought more highly of the volume than Zinn did. And several of them seem worthy of serious attention here, since they reveal much about not only *Declarations*, but Zinn's work in general. Erwin Knoll, for example, editor of the *Progressive*, felt that *Declarations* was "a worthy successor" to Zinn's "splendid . . . modern classic," *A People's History of the United States*. Helpfully, he wrote that Zinn was "a radical in the true sense of that much-abused word," meaning that he discusses the most important issues of public policy and in doing so "gets down to the roots, deep down to the bedrock questions: Why do we believe what we believe? How much of what we believe is true? Why are things the way they are? Whose interests are served? How should things be changed to serve the common interests of suffering humanity?"[5]

H. Bruce Franklin agreed with Knoll about Zinn's radicalism. But he went further. Zinn's *arguments*, he said, were "truly radical," in that they "burrow right to the roots of the unexamined assumptions essential to this ideology, allowing him to expose the delusions about 'human nature,' race, class, socialism, and capitalism that feed the power and wealth of a few at tremendous cost to the human needs of the many." Also, Zinn's "unwavering commitment to nonviolent direct action radically contradicts what he defines as the central precept of 'modern political thought,' that 'a worthwhile end could justify any means.'" Yet Zinn's *ends*, said Franklin, were "not especially radical." Zinn proposes, felt Franklin, "merely a reform of capitalism through greater equalization of wealth, more decentralization of power, and some shift away from market toward moral values—while studiously avoiding any fundamental challenge to the nation-state." Similarly, while Zinn "does present an eloquent defense of the liberating powers of Marxism, especially in its motivating quest to escape from alienation to human freedom," his own analysis of ideology is "notably un-Marxist, for he almost invariably locates the causes of historical movements in ideas, while eschewing efforts to discover the material forces that might have generated these ideas."

Even more insightful than Franklin's emphasis on Zinn's radicalism, or absence thereof, is the opening of his review. "If there was such a thing as a just war, this was it," he begins, quoting a truism about World War II. By "digging ever deeper" into this truism, says Franklin, Zinn "exposes the taproot not just of his latest book, but evidently of the life work of this remarkable scholar, teacher, and activist." *Declarations of Independence*, he suggests, is "both an inquiry by a major historian and political scientist and a meditation by a moral philosopher and activist who has inspired countless students and others." What this book displays, with Zinn's "customary clarity and concision," is Zinn's "characteristic integration of scholarship, analysis, morality, and activism." But finally, what Franklin found "especially illuminating—and moving—about *Declarations of Independence* is his revelation of how this integration flowed from his personal experience."[6] Obviously, Franklin is onto something. As we have seen, Zinn's writings frequently flowed out of and related directly to things that he was concerned about and involved in at the moment. And, of course, he was never willing to do the kind of compartmentalizing modern life seems to expect: professional versus personal, personal versus political, and so on.

Major professional organizations, in both history and political science, were paying attention to Zinn's books now. Both the *Political Science Quarterly* and the *Journal of American History* reviewed *Declarations of Independence*. The reviewer for the *Political Science Quarterly* was Mark A. Graber, of the University of Texas. He felt Zinn's work was indeed "a successful cross-examination of American ideology," and that it would "enliven any introduction to American government or history." Speaking of Zinn's readability, Graber said the book "demonstrates that radicals need not speak fluent post-structualism [*sic*] to critique the influence of class, race, and (with much less emphasis) gender in the United States." While he felt that few students or professors would agree with Zinn's conclusions, he also felt that "if they learn that 'it is a crucial act of independent thinking to be skeptical of someone else's thinking' [quoting Zinn], their undergraduate education will not have been in vain." But Graber threw one barb that must have disturbed Zinn as much as almost anything ever said in a review, feeling the way he did about Boston University president John Silber. Graber said that "for a scholar devoted to the power of ideas, Zinn seems surprisingly contemptuous of everyone who disagrees with him. . . . In this respect, Zinn seems quite similar to his nemesis, John Silber."[7]

The Organization of American Historians' *Journal of American History* assigned Michael Kazin, of American University, to review Zinn. Howard Zinn, he begins, "writes the type of history scholars are supposed to disdain." Right away, one gets the impression Kazin himself does not "disdain" it. He extracts a crucial quote from Zinn: "For me, history could only be a way of understanding and helping to change (yes, an extravagant ambition!) what was wrong in the world." Then he notes that this book is "the committed radical's latest attempt to scour the past for lessons to instruct those who might transform American society." Many traditionalists, he states accurately, charge left-wing academics with writing "polemical" history: "Zinn never pretends to be doing anything else." Then to the task of criticism. To "strip away from rulers their mask of legitimacy," says Kazin, "a polemicist must understand why they continue to rule. And Zinn is quite unequal to that admittedly complex task." Kazin insists that Zinn has a "single-minded emphasis on self-interest," and thus "betrays the sensibility of a muckraker with a fistful of grievances instead of a radical armed with a sophisticated theory of history." This, says Kazin, is Zinn's "major weakness": "Because he gives his antagonists no credit for having a world view of their own, he cannot convincingly explain why a majority of Americans have usually agreed with the ideas put forth by members of ruling elites (or their publicists)." Despite this weakness, *Declarations of Independence* was "a work that should be taught," concludes Kazin. "In a clear style and compassionate voice, it challenges the political preconceptions most undergraduates bring to survey classes." Furthermore, it "keeps alive a tradition, more than two centuries old, that currently has few serious practitioners." While Kazin insists that Zinn is no Tom Paine or Henry George, he, "like those visionaries, . . . believes historical interpretation should liberate Americans and not merely inform them."[8]

Though *Declarations of Independence* covered some ground Zinn had already been over, in some cases numerous times, it did so quite well, in some cases even powerfully. Certainly his introduction bears looking at closely. "Because force is held in reserve and the control is not complete, we can call ourselves a 'democracy,'" Zinn asserts. And it is true, he acknowledges, that "the openings and the flexibility make such a society a more desirable place to live. But," he warns, "they also create a more effective form of control." For we are "less likely to object if we can feel that we have a 'pluralist' society, with two parties instead of one, three branches of government instead of one-man rule, and various opinions in the press instead of one official line." But this is a "very limited" pluralism. Certain ideas dominate. We hear them from parents, school, church, newspapers, radio, television. "They constitute an American *ideology*—that is, a dominant pattern of ideas. Most people accept them, and if we do, too, we are less likely to get into trouble." What are some of those ideas? Here is Zinn's list:

> Be realistic; this is the way things *are*; there's no point thinking about how things *should be*.

> People who teach or write or report the news should be *objective*; they should not try to advance their own opinions.

> There are unjust wars, but also just wars.

> If you disobey the law, even for a good cause, you should accept your punishment.

> If you work hard enough, you'll make a good living. If you are poor, you have only yourself to blame.

> Freedom of speech is desirable, but not when it threatens national security.

> Racial equality is desirable, but we've gone far enough in that direction.

Our Constitution is our greatest guarantee of liberty and justice.

The United States must intervene from time to time in various parts of the world with military power to stop communism and promote democracy.

If you want to get things changed, the only way is to go through the proper channels.

We need nuclear weapons to prevent war.

There is much injustice in the world but there is nothing that ordinary people, without wealth or power, can do about it.

If we accept all that, what we have is "an obedient, acquiescent, passive citizenry," says Zinn. But that is "a situation that is deadly to democracy." If, on the other hand, at some point in time "we decide to reexamine these beliefs and realize they do not come naturally out of our innermost feelings or our spontaneous desires, are not the result of independent thought on our part, and, indeed, do not match the real world as we experience it, then we have come to an important turning point in life. Then we find ourselves examining, and confronting, American ideology." In brief, continues Zinn, "that is what I want to do in this book."[9] One might say that is what Zinn has done for his entire career.

Typically Zinnian, after noting the "endless arguments that go on in academic circles about what Plato or Machiavelli or Rousseau or Marx *really* meant," Zinn says, "Although I taught political theory for twenty years, I don't really care about that. I am interested in these thinkers when it seems to me their ideas are still alive in our time and can be used to illuminate a problem." Similarly, on teaching, Zinn says, "I never listened to the advice of people who said that a teacher should be objective, neutral, and professional." All the experiences of his life, he insists, including growing up on the streets of New York, working in the shipyards as a teenager, service in the Air Force, and participating in the civil rights movement, "cried out against that." Why should we cherish "objectivity," he asks, "as if ideas were innocent, as if they don't serve one interest or another?" Of course, objectivity is desirable "if that means telling the truth as we see it, not concealing information that may be embarrassing to our point of view," but not "if it means pretending that ideas don't play a part in the social struggles of our time, that we don't take sides in those struggles." Hinting at the title of a later book, Zinn argues that "it is impossible to be neutral. In a world already moving in certain directions, where wealth and power are already distributed in certain ways, neutrality means accepting the way things are now." The world we live in is "a world of clashing interests—war against peace, nationalism against internationalism, equality against greed, and democracy against elitism." Given that situation, "it seems to me both impossible and undesirable to be neutral."[10] You can't be neutral on a moving train.

Emphasizing the importance of participatory democracy, Zinn insists that to depend on "great thinkers, authorities, and experts is . . . a violation of the spirit of democracy." For democracy "rests on the idea that, except for technical details for which experts may be useful, the important decisions of society are within the capability of ordinary citizens." Then, in an important philosophical statement for Zinn, similar to his argument that ordinary people make and should be allowed to tell their own history: "Not only *can* ordinary people make decisions about these issues, but they *ought* to, because citizens understand their own interests more clearly than any experts." On a typical note of hope, Zinn suggests that the new ideas that result from times of social change such as the 1960s "live on through quieter times, waiting for another opportunity to ignite into action and change the world around us." Finally, in a passage that explains the title of this book, Zinn says he is aware that dissenters "can create their own orthodoxy. So we need a constant reexamination of our thinking, using the evidence of our eyes and ears and the realities of our experience to think freshly." In short: "We need declarations of independence from all nations, parties, and programs—all rigid dogmas."[11]

For some three hundred pages, Zinn proceeds to follow up on the ideas expressed in his introduction, applying them to such areas as foreign policy, violence, history, war, law, justice, free speech, representative government (focusing on the African American experience), and "Communism and Anti-Communism." As the reader will have noted by now, Zinn is sometimes remarkably effective in presenting his case, sometimes carrying one along against one's will; thus, it is tempting to work through *Declarations of Independence* in detail. However, as noted, there is little new here. In "Machiavellian Realism and U.S. Foreign Policy: Means and Ends," Zinn insists that while the Declaration of Independence hangs on schoolroom walls, our foreign policy follows Machiavelli. In "Violence and Human Nature," he attempts to make the case that nowhere—not in genetics, psychology, anthropology, zoology, or history—is there evidence for a human instinct for the kind of aggressive violence that characterizes war. In "The Use and Abuse of History," we get his philosophy of history again. (By leaving out people's movements, he says, most history creates "a passive and subordinate citizenry." This is not the deliberate intention of the historian, "but it comes from a desire to avoid controversy, to go along with what has always been done, to stress what has always been stressed, to keep one's job, to stay out of trouble, and to get published.")[12] By the time he wrote the chapter "Just and Unjust War" here, Zinn was convinced that "there is no such thing as a just war"; thus "the great challenge of our time" is "how to achieve justice, with struggle, but without war."[13] In "Law and Justice," he emphasizes the difference between the two. In "Economic Justice: The American Class System," he argues that there is and always has been a class structure in America, along with more class consciousness than usually admitted and a system of laissez faire for the poor and government intervention for the rich; he concludes that only when wealth is equalized (at least roughly) will liberty be equalized, and that only then will true justice be possible. In "Representative Government: The Black Experience," he concludes that the history of African Americans makes clear that our much-celebrated democratic institutions (representative government, voting, constitutional law) have never proved adequate for solving the basic problems of human rights.

Perhaps we can justify taking a bit of a closer look at just two subjects. In "Communism and Anti-Communism," Zinn is at his best, his humorous best. Referring to a 1948 pamphlet distributed by the House Committee on Un-American Activities entitled "One Hundred Things You Should Know about Communism," which utilized a question-and-answer approach, Zinn quoted the first question, "What Is Communism?" And the answer, "A system by which one small group seeks to rule the world." "When I came across this in my files (the committee probably had files on me, so it seemed to me I should have files on them)," he continues, "I thought these men had taken an advanced course in political theory, also in expository writing, to be able to sum up such a complicated theory in so few words." Noting that one question was "Where can a Communist be found in everyday life?" Zinn says, "This question interested me because there had been times when I was in need of a Communist, and didn't know where to find one."[14] More seriously, Zinn asserts that the hysterical anti-Communism of the McCarthy era actually continued throughout the Cold War and was used to justify all sorts of terrible things in Vietnam and elsewhere. He also thinks it is very important to distinguish between the communist *ideal* of a classless society with plenty for all and the ugly betrayal of that ideal by the Soviet Union.

The other subject requiring a closer look is found in Zinn's chapter entitled "Free Speech: Second Thoughts on the First Amendment." Several times in earlier works Zinn had hinted at his analysis here. In 1967, for example, in *Disobedience and Democracy*, he had said: "We forget that the information on which the public depends for judging public issues is in the hands of the wealthiest sections of the community (true, we have freedom to speak, but how *much* of an audience we can speak to depends on how much money we have)."[15] And in *Justice in Everyday Life*, in 1974, he had insisted that the Supreme Court is not a dependable protector of free expression, that most issues in this area were settled by the policeman on the street or by the lower courts, and that these authorities "pay little attention to the Constitution, or to Supreme Court decisions."[16] Zinn's chapter on the subject here allows him much more opportunity to expand his views, covering as it does almost fifty pages. He argues that "to depend on the simple existence of the First Amendment to guarantee our freedom of expression is a serious mistake, one that can cost us not only our liberties but, under certain circumstances, our lives." Explaining the "ingenious" doctrine of "no prior restraint," Zinn writes: "You can say whatever you want, print whatever you want. The government cannot stop you in advance. But once you speak or write it, if the government decides to make certain statements 'illegal,' or to define them as 'mischievous' or even just 'improper,' you can be put in prison." He shows how freedom of expression has been seriously curtailed in every war in U.S. history, though arguably it is more important then than at any other time. He notes that *state* laws have often curbed freedom of expression. The basic lesson: "Our right to free expression is not determined by the words of the Constitution or the decisions of the Supreme Court, but by who has the *power* in the immediate situation where we want to exercise our rights." Free speech on the street? It's up to the police. Free speech on the job? It's up to the boss, or the company. In this country, says Zinn, "so proud of its democratic institutions," we even have our own "national secret police," the FBI and the CIA.[17]

Still, says Zinn, we have not yet come to "perhaps the most serious issue of all in regard to freedom of speech and press in the United States." Suppose we could indeed say anything we want, without fear, he imagines. Two problems would still remain, and they are both "enormous." First, how many people could we reach with our message? The answer, he says, is clear: "It depends on how much money we have." More specifically, "A poor person, however smart, however eloquent, truly has very limited freedom of speech. A rich corporation has a great deal of it." The second problem: "Suppose no one—not government, not the police, not our employer—stops us from speaking our mind, *but we have nothing to say.*" At first, one wonders where Zinn is going with this. "In other words," he explains, "what if we do not have sufficient information about what is happening in the country or in the world and do not know what our government is doing at home and abroad? Without such information, having the freedom to express ourselves does not mean much." Basically, then, Zinn's concern here is that, frequently in the name of "national security," much information is withheld from the average citizen. Clearly, Zinn finds this an intolerable situation in a so-called democracy. The answer? If the government and the press keep information from us, even deceive us, the First Amendment will not help us much. And since we cannot count on the courts, the Congress, the presidency, to protect our freedom to speak or write or assemble or petition; since we cannot count on the government or the mainstream press to give us the information we need to be well-informed, active citizens; since we cannot count on those who own and control the media to give us the opportunity to reach large numbers of people; there seems only one choice. Zinn quotes British novelist Aldous Huxley: "Liberties are not given; they are taken." That is what we will have to do, says Zinn. "Historically, that has always been the case."[18]

Zinn is hesitant to call his next book, *Failure to Quit: Reflections of an Optimistic Historian*, an anthology, noting in his introduction that the word originally meant "a collection of flowers," and would therefore "be going too far." But truly, *Failure to Quit* is just that—a collection, and therefore an anthology in the common usage, if not a collection of flowers. Virtually every piece here had seen print before, several as articles in the radical Z magazine. Zinn admits it is a challenge to find a common thread; the closest he could come, he says, "is that all the pieces represent the thinking of someone who wants to address urgent issues of peace and justice with the perspective (presumably long-range and very wise) of a historian."[19] The topics are standard fare for Howard Zinn: optimism, objectivity ("Objections to Objectivity," he called that essay), civil disobedience ("Our problem is civil *obedience*," he states in one essay),[20] the Bill of Rights (especially the First Amendment again), war, Columbus.

Two pieces deserve further notice. David Barsamian interviewed Zinn in Boulder, Colorado, in 1992, and was able to get Zinn to talk freely about his early life and his philosophy. As Zinn put it, "He drew from me things about my life which I was saving for my own slightly shorter version of *Remembrance of Things Past*." (Zinn was surely referring to *You Can't Be Neutral on a Moving Train*, his next book.) The interview appears here under the title "Who Controls the Past Controls the Future," part of George Orwell's dictum. (The other part, of course, is "Who controls the present controls the past.") Zinn reveals that Orwell is one of his favorite writers, and explains: "What the . . . quote means to me is a very important observation that if you can control history, what people know about history, if you can decide what's in people's history and what's left out, you can order their thinking. You can order their values." Obviously, he feels it has traditionally been mostly rich white males who have exercised that kind of control. Later in the interview, Barsamian says, "In the popular culture, ideology and propaganda are attributes of our adversaries. It's not something that we have here in our democracy." In case the tongue in cheek is not evident, here is his question of Zinn: "How do you persuade people in your talks and writings that in fact there is a good deal of propaganda and a great amount of ideology right here in the United States?" Zinn said the best way was "to give them examples from history and to show how the government has manipulated our information."[21] He could also have said that *Declarations of Independence*, published not that long before this interview, was an effort, sometimes a very effective one, to do just that.

The other striking piece is a brief one that appears under the title "Je Ne Suis Pas un Marxiste." Says Zinn, "I never expected to have a fancy title for a piece of mine." In fact, the essay had appeared earlier in *Z* magazine under the title "Nothing Human Is Alien to Me"— perhaps just as fancy a title. The quotation, of course, is from Marx himself, turning down an invitation to speak to a Karl Marx Club; he had been irritated to excess by a German refugee in London, where Marx was then living, who seemed to think Marx's every word was holy. Zinn uses the quote to discuss his own relationship with Marxist thought. Again in a humorous mood, Zinn notes that not long before he had twice been referred to publicly as a "Marxist professor." Once it was a spokesperson for the conservative group Accuracy in Academia, which worried that there were some five thousand Marxist faculty members in the United States. Zinn says that news "diminished my importance, but also my loneliness." More seriously, Zinn says, Marx "had some very useful thoughts," including "that the capitalist system violates whatever it means to be human" and, perhaps "the most precious heritage of Marx's thought," his internationalism.[22]

Zinn has been even more dismissive of *Failure to Quit* than *Declarations of Independence*. *Failure to Quit*, he says, was "not a writing job but a collection of pieces." Somehow that is both true and excessively demeaning. The little volume—Zinn ordinarily likes small books, remember, but this one is not one of his favorites, probably because it does not focus on a single subject—was not as widely reviewed as most of Zinn's books, but some reviewers did see its value. The *Bloomsbury Review*, for example, was brief but full of praise, for both Zinn and the book. "Is it possible for a left-wing activist to have a sense of humor about his work and the world?" the review asked; clearly, in Zinn's case, the answer was yes. "Zinn is a marvel," the review continued, "a man who has dedicated himself to the struggle for justice while still maintaining a sense of perspective about his own humanity." *Failure to Quit* was a "great book for inspiring personal commitment to some kind of purposeful action."[23]

The *Progressive* liked the book as well, especially the final essay, "Failure to Quit," which it considered "vintage Zinn, full of hope, taking a hard look at his students in the late 1980s—without finding the apathy, conservatism, and selfishness that caused others to label them 'the me generation.'"[24]

Do people grow more conservative as they age? In the case of Howard Zinn, apparently not. And his sense of humor seems to improve. In the folder of items in Zinn's papers related to *Failure to Quit*, which of course is not nearly so bulging a folder as the ones about the *People's History*, is a letter he wrote to Greg Bates, the editor/publisher at Common Courage Press, which published the book. The subject is a forthcoming advertisement in the *Nation*. Zinn thinks listing the topics of the book in the ad is a "dull" idea. His wife, Roslyn, he says, suggests printing the picture from the back of the book and letting folks guess about the topics. "She thinks that if an ordinary photo is worth a thousand words, mine is worth at least fifty." He liked using the "Zinn is a marvel" quote from the *Bloomsbury Review*; "How can I quarrel with *that*?" he asked. Also "vintage Zinn" from the *Progressive*; except that "'vintage' has different meanings dependent on the noun it is modifying—take 'vintage vinegar' or 'vintage horse manure,' . . ." The ad, by the way, included both the quotes, as well as both a list of topics and the picture.[25]

That folder also contained a photocopy of an article from the *Baltimore Chronicle*, partly a review, partly an advertisement for a forthcoming Zinn lecture there to help celebrate the twenty-fifth anniversary of the Viva House–Baltimore Catholic Worker. The *Chronicle* said the essays in *Failure to Quit* "give Zinn room to do what he does best: to puncture the myths of ideological power and to try to bring our understanding of the past (and present) more into line with the lived experience of the majority of the people."[26]

Finally, there were the usual letters in the folder. One, for example, signed simply "Ruth," said of *Failure to Quit*, "I have failed to quit reading it, that's for sure." "Thanks for writing it, and thanks for refusing to quit," wrote another.[27]

You Can't Be Neutral on a Moving Train has come up numerous times in these pages—as source, explaining the title. The book itself carried the full title *You Can't Be Neutral on a Moving Train: A Personal History of Our Times*, and was published in 1994. It is a bit difficult to know exactly what Zinn had in mind with this one. Notice the words "personal history" in the subtitle: it is tempting to call it an autobiography, for much of it is autobiographical; Zinn himself prefers to call it a memoir. He does explain, in an interesting introduction, called "The Question Period in Kalamazoo," why he wrote it. It was the night of the last televised presidential debate of the 1992 election, and Zinn was speaking, as he has done so often since retirement but especially in the quincentennial year of the Columbus landing in the Western Hemisphere, on the Columbus portion of his *People's History* (the portion that has attracted the most interest, he says). Obviously, he was in Kalamazoo, Michigan. With typical modesty, he wonders why "several hundred" were in the audience—"did they need a break from election madness?" At the end of his talk, someone asked a question which stuck in his mind: "Given the depressing news of what is happening in the world, you seem surprisingly optimistic. What gives you hope?" The question has been put to him many times in many different ways over the years; we have seen some of his answer already, and will again. He attempted an answer that night. But "to really answer," he says, "I would have had to go back over my life. . . . It would take a book. So I decided to write one."[28] The focus in the book is overwhelmingly on the civil rights and anti–Vietnam War movements, Zinn's role in them and the way he sees them. But there is also a chapter on his early life, and chapters on jails and courts and his battles at Boston University.

Roland Wulbert, reviewing *You Can't Be Neutral* in *Booklist*, predicted readers would find Zinn as "engaging, open-minded, informative, politically committed, and attentive to the exigencies of writing as ever." But then the review took a rather strange twist. Wulbert felt Zinn's "uncharacteristic admiration of elites here startles." After all, Zinn knew such individuals as Julian Bond, Stokely Carmichael, John Lewis, Etta Baker, Dick Gregory, Jim Foreman, James Baldwin, says Wulbert, "he knew them all. The 18-year-olds he taught at Spellman [*sic*] all went on to become prominent civil rights lawyers or found the Children's Defense Fund or mother the mayor of Atlanta. They're successful. He's successful. Yet oppression in American is as brutal as ever, he assures us, when he is not recounting his part in the Good Fight that ameliorated it markedly. Aw hell, he's lived a good life. Who can blame him for a little inconsistency?"[29]

Zinn did not like that; he questioned, "Is he arguing that the fact that these people being successful and I've been successful shows that things are not as bad as we radicals claim?" Clearly, that did seem to be part of Wulbert's point. Zinn acknowledged that is "a very common criticism of radicals." But he felt it missed the point. "You know, we will get up and say . . . 'There isn't real freedom of speech in America.' People say, 'Well, look, you have the right to say that. You're living proof.' But what they are missing is that America is a much more complex country than simply an oppressive, totally oppressive country where nobody can rise up from the ranks and become successful." Continuing further in his response to the review, Zinn said that the thing that makes the United States "such a sophisticated country and so complicated in its injustice is that it does have openings and apertures and it does let some people become successful while still maintaining this fundamental structure, class structure, race structure, so in that [review] he is not allowing for that complicatedness of what is wrong with the American system. We are not claiming that everybody fails and that nobody rises." To Zinn, obviously, it did not seem very fair or insightful to criticize him for being celebratory about successes while still pointing to oppression.[30]

Paul Buhle, himself a historian of American radicalism, wrote the longest and most thoughtful review of *You Can't Be Neutral on a Moving Train*, in the *Nation*. First, Buhle allowed his imagination to run free. He had, he admitted, "always imagined that . . . Zinn somehow took part in the multitudinous radical movements of the 1840s–50s, campaigning for abolition, women's rights, dress reform, and nonviolence." Zinn would have been "a rare Jew among Yankees and African-Americans," and would have "commanded the platform with figures like Susan B. Anthony and Frederick Douglass, held his own against hostile audiences and broadcast the prospects for universal freedom." Buhle felt there was something "about Zinn's style and bearing [that suggested] the prophetic profile so common to radicals in those days and so rare in our own." Brilliant. Buhle also gave a good summary of Zinn's entire life and career. Noting that Zinn "modestly takes no credit except for being there" in the civil rights movement, Buhle also notes that Marian Wright Edelman "describes her teacher as totally inspirational, a formidable influence on the movement spreading around him." Buhle felt Zinn's greatest strength was the "popular narrative," and, giving *SNCC: The New Abolitionists* as his example, wrote:

"Hardly a better current history has been written than this instant classic, which combined oral history with a novelistic narrative and a burning sincerity." Buhle also considered Zinn's *People's History* "the standard textbook alternative against the reality of Reagan America," and sided with Zinn in his conflicts with John Silber, the "clown prince of neoconservatism." After all this praise, for Zinn and some of his earlier work, one might be a bit surprised that Buhle did not consider *You Can't Be Neutral* Zinn's best. What he really wrote was: "If *You Can't Be Neutral on a Moving Train* seems sometimes less than Zinn's best, it is because he has too much modesty to construct a world view out of his own experiences."[31]

Presented with that last comment from Buhle, Zinn said, thoughtfully and in a manner that reveals much of his democratic approach, his faith in the ability of people to do their own intellectual work: "Hmm, well, construct a worldview. I remember somebody criticizing *A People's History* for that same reason. I didn't really have an overall analysis, total analysis of America. Let's talk about this, talk about that, talk about that, but not a worldview." Continuing, Zinn admitted he was "suspicious about worldviews, although maybe because I think I want to leave it to the reader to develop a worldview out of the raw material. I think it is a little arrogant to deliver a packaged worldview." He even had some reservations about "giving an analysis," he said, like "now I am handing you an analysis," for he felt that if you give people that raw material, "they can analyze it for themselves." Interesting. But Zinn then concluded that he was confident that people, given the raw material "together with their own input," would come out with an analysis "close to my own." He insisted it was not his modesty, though, that kept him from constructing the world view that Buhle missed, "no, not at all my modesty."[32]

A review in the *Journal of American History* is always important for an American historian. This time, they assigned someone, Maurice Isserman, of Hamilton College, who thought very highly of Zinn and his work. He focused on a key sentence from Zinn: "The events of my life, growing up poor, working in a shipyard, being in a war, had nurtured an indignation against the bullies of the world, those who used wealth or military might or social status to keep others down." This memoir, said Isserman, "like most of Zinn's writings, [was] lucid and unpretentious." More important, he felt it provided "the links between the Old and New Left." Isserman explained that he meant the way Zinn was initiated into radical politics as a "teenage Communist" (though we have seen Zinn take issue with that), then became disillusioned with the Soviet Union during World War II, but remained an "independent-minded socialist" who "found a way to put his radical beliefs into action when new opportunities arose in the 1960s."[33]

Other reviews were less valuable. Patricia O'Connell wrote just a paragraph in the "In Short" review column for the *New York Times Book Review*. She called *You Can't Be Neutral* a "memoir," said it contained some "lively tales," but felt also that it "may leave some readers unsatisfied." Anyone wanting a "full-blown autobiography," she said, would find too little information on Zinn's upbringing and family, as well as his writings.[34] The latter is certainly a valid point, if not necessarily a criticism. Zinn does not mention, for example, any of his other books in this one—while they have provided our primary focus in this narrative.

R. H. Immerman, in *Choice*, began by noting that for three decades Zinn had been "the prototypical scholar-activist." Zinn's "breezy memoir" should attract "an eclectic audience," Immerman predicted, including "several generations of students he taught or who read his works, radicals who either worked with Zinn or were influenced by him, and conservatives seeking to learn more about the enemy in order to destroy him." Interestingly, Immerman also predicted that "none will be disappointed." Still, while there were "many instructive anecdotes," there was not much analysis. "The intellectual roots of Zinn's politics, including but not limited to his education and scholarship, remain obscure. Hence this memoir wets [*sic*] the appetite but does not satisfy."[35]

We have noted before that some of the most interesting and important responses to Zinn's books do not come in the form of reviews. *You Can't Be Neutral on a Moving Train*, for example, elicited a powerful, emotional three-page letter to Zinn from Ron Kovic, of *Born on the Fourth of July* fame. Clearly, Kovic's reading of *You Can't Be Neutral* led to his writing the letter, but it was near the end of the letter before he remembered to mention the book. "I suddenly realize I have written quite a bit to you today and I only wanted to write you a note. You see what your wonderful book has done?" At the beginning, he wrote: "I am writing this note to once again tell you how important and inspirational you have been to me. You are a wonderful person. How can words even begin to express what you have meant to our country and to the millions of people who have been touched by your teachings and your work?" At the end, he came back to inspiration, hope: "I wonder how many other people out there are inspired as much as I have been by you," said Kovic. "You've got me talking about a whole new country. You've got me believing that it can actually become a reality. You've got me thinking about risking again, taking chances again. You've got me feeling confident. Most of all, you've got me believing in my own history."[36]

Colman McCarthy described a moving scene in a Washington, D.C., bookstore, a reception for Zinn on the occasion of the publication of *You Can't Be Neutral*. "Few joys touch a retired teacher's heart more than getting together with former students after the classroom years have long passed," began McCarthy. He continued by referring to the "reminiscent moments, seeing which paths have been taken, what truths have held up. A spell of such amiable retrospection came the other evening in a bookstore reception here for Howard Zinn." Zinn himself was described: "Now 72, Zinn is an erect 6 feet 4 inches [according to Zinn, a three-inch exaggeration], marathon-runner thin, has a thatch of hair and exudes healthiness. He's not in need of a rest. His physical vigor matches his intellectual and spiritual well-being which, if anything, is picking up speed, not losing it."[37]

Greg Sargent reported on a Zinn lecture at Cooper Union in New York in *New York Newsday*; the specific occasion for this lecture was also the release of *You Can't Be Neutral*. Rather strangely, he predicts, six years after Zinn's retirement, that "partial retirement may not come easily to Zinn. His pacifism notwithstanding, Zinn has always thrived in an environment of frequent verbal slugfests." (Sargent's reference to support that is to Zinn's struggles with Silber at BU.) Sargent quotes Zinn: "Today's crises are not as obvious [as civil rights and Vietnam], but are in a way much more deadly. There's an ongoing malaise, represented by economic insecurity, enormous amounts of violence and crime, and alienation from the political process." Then Sargent concludes: "Despite such gloomy assessments, Zinn still lectures around the country, laying out his hope for social upheaval and redistribution of wealth."[38]

Gary Susman reported in a similar vein in the *Boston Phoenix*. He had obviously interviewed Zinn about *You Can't Be Neutral* and many other things. He quoted Zinn as saying his primary reason for writing the memoir was to encourage young readers who were disillusioned by the apparent collapse of 1960s progressivism and the conservative backlash. "There aren't issues today that are as clearly focused and have as obvious solutions as the civil-rights and antiwar movements did," said Zinn. "They require very radical changes and a movement much more powerful than the movements that existed in the 1960s." Yet, of course, Zinn found hope, not only in the "little clusters of people who are politically and socially conscious, who are really interested and active in environmental issues, feminist issues, the military budget, health care," but also in the existence of an infrastructure which exists today in a way that it did not in the 1960s. "We had a superstructure but not an infrastructure," he explained. "We had enormous gatherings of people at huge, nationwide demonstrations. But when people left those demonstrations, they did not go back to local groups that were nuclei of some continuing movement. I believe these little groups can form the basis for some new, important social movement. That's why, in spite of all the terrible things that are happening, I feel somewhat hopeful." Some of these are, of course, things Zinn has said many different times, in many different ways. "Some people want scholars to be pure and apolitical," Susman quotes him as saying. "They even expect political scientists to be apolitical. Sometimes I refer to the field as 'political silence.' I never wanted to be like that."[39] And he never has.

When it was called to Zinn's attention that his postretirement books all had a kind of retrospective quality, especially *Failure to Quit* and *You Can't Be Neutral on a Moving Train*, he noted that he was also working with a publisher to develop a Howard Zinn reader, a collection of writings over the course of his career. Asked, "What does this suggest about where you stand as a writing historian? Do you have other books you're planning or hoping to write still?" he responded, "I guess the fact that I wrote a memoir, and the fact that I'm going to have a collection covering almost forty years of writing, I detect this as a hint in your question, this is just, I'm coming to the end, you know." Then, in response to the comment "This is a winding down," he said, "I'm two days away from an assisted suicide." And laughed. More seriously, he continued, "I don't know if I'm going to write any more history books. I don't want to weigh down the shelves with stuff." Instead, he said, there were two kinds of things he would still like to write, plays and "short journalistic pieces."[40] He has done both, as we shall see.

In addition, *The Zinn Reader: Writings on Disobedience and Democracy* was published in 1997. Notice the subtitle, representing central themes of Zinn's work; the six sections of the book deal with race, class, war, law, history, and means and ends. *Kirkus Reviews* observed correctly that it was a "portly tome" (nearly seven hundred pages)—and also correctly that it was by "the dean of radical American historians." The reviewer also helpfully suggested that Zinn "has a good time arguing for an equitable, just, and division-free America." These comments are from the Internet, a site which obviously allows customer reviews, for there is one by a Charles Drago of Providence, Rhode Island. He raves inarticulately (for this reader) about Josef Goebbels and Kenneth Starr (by implication—"a certain not-so-special prosecutor"), but obviously likes Howard Zinn. "The most common side-effect brought on by reading Howard Zinn," he says, "is a profound, disquieting loss of equilibrium: All these years history has been so . . . unbalanced." True enough. Furthermore, claims Drago: "Without a thorough and, as I'm sure the author would demand, critical reading of the Zinn oeuvre . . . , you simply cannot enjoy a meaningful appreciation of American history in the 20th century. Period."[41] Right again.

In Madison, Wisconsin, the *Capital Times* waxed eloquent about Zinn and his work in general, and *The Zinn Reader* in particular, in connection with Zinn's upcoming free lecture at the state historical society. (He also appeared as the guest of honor at a reception sponsored by the *Progressive*.) "No American historian is more willing to reveal himself—both personally and professionally," said John Nichols in the *Capital Times*, referring specifically to Zinn's "lyrical introduction" to his *Reader*. "Zinn's writings over the past 40 years have provided a powerful antidote to the lies of 'objectivity' and 'neutrality' that warp our national discourse," continued Nichols; thus this collection of over sixty items was a "tremendous resource." Referring back to Zinn's essay "The Uses of Scholarship," which appeared in 1969 in the *Saturday Review* and in 1970 in *The Politics of History* before appearing in the *Reader*, Nichols said: "That essay was a powerful call to action, which begged academics to emerge from the library stacks and enter the discourse of their times. No longer, argued Zinn, should scholars accept a scenario where 'we publish while others perish.'" That was a "necessary statement" in the late 1960s, but "even more necessary" in the late 1990s, according to Nichols, for *The Zinn Reader* "could not have arrived at a better time. More than ever, those of us who are academics and those of us who are not academics need to read with a contemporary eye Zinn's inspired demand for an activist response on the part of those who may be comfortable in a professional or an economic sense, but who know that their circumstance is not shared by the great mass of humanity."[42]

Harvey Wasserman wrote an excellent review of *The Zinn Reader* for the *Progressive*. (Zinn had earlier written an introduction on the concept of people's history for *Harvey Wasserman's History of the United States*.) Wasserman begins by referring to Zinn's "characteristic innocence." "To say that Zinn is unique in the panoply of American writer-teacher-activists is to vastly understate his importance," insists Wasserman. "National treasure" comes closer to the truth, for Zinn's *People's History* "remains the most important leftwing narration of America's story yet published." Wasserman is impressed by Zinn's "gentle style," the way he presents "his case for radical change in terms of self-effacing human decency and understated common sense." "'Isn't it obvious,' he [Zinn] seems to ask, 'that these things are wrong, and that we have to change them?' And isn't it equally obvious, he then adds, that the evils of racism, war, and class injustice will sooner or later fall away under the evolving power of nonviolent action?'"

Wasserman is far from the first to notice Zinn's eternal optimism. "When Zinn describes busting segregation in the Georgia capital, he writes with the wide-eyed tones of an intrigued, eternally optimistic neophyte who just happened upon a struggle for truth and justice and had no choice but to jump in." Zinn was more than just a casual participant in the early civil rights movement: "His skill as a writer with access to key national journals was crucial in helping to spread the word." Next, Zinn took on the role of "author-teacher-activist" in the anti–Vietnam War movement, in which he had a "major impact." His writings, for Wasserman, always showed a unique ability to "balance rational thought with quiet rage."

"Along the way, Zinn helped a new generation of budding historians rethink our national past, especially as illuminated by the social fireworks of the day." Thus, what gives *The Zinn Reader* its "special magic" for Wasserman "is that, taken in concert with his introductions, they [the essays] comprise an autobiography of the man and a chronicle of his time."

Noting Zinn's probing exploration of "Just and Unjust War," Wasserman acknowledges that Zinn "does not have all the answers." He then concludes: "Even without all the answers, this book is a healing read. Take two of these essays each night before bed. Soon, you'll feel restored, even hopeful. Then get everyone you know to repeat the process."[43] Not bad advice.

But let Zinn speak; he always speaks best for himself. He dedicates *The Zinn Reader* to a grandson "and his generation." In the acknowledgments, Zinn's wife, Roslyn, is prominent, as always. In his introduction, Zinn says he knows this is "a big book to swallow." (For this kind of retrospective collection, obviously, he was willing to forget that he preferred small books.) He blames it on Dan Simon, the son of friends, whom he met while teaching in Paris in 1978; Simon went on to become editor and publisher of Seven Stories Press, and suggested the idea of a Zinn reader. Says Zinn, "I delayed my response for two years, to give the appearance of modesty, and then agreed." He wanted "to think of it as a generous act," he says, "giving all those who know my biggest-selling book (*A People's History of the United States*) a chance to sample my other work: books out of print, books still in print, essays, articles, pamphlets, lectures, reviews, newspaper columns, written over the past thirty-five years or so, and often not easy to find. An opportunity, or a punishment? Only the reader can decide."[44]

That is a pretty good description of *The Zinn Reader*, with a little Zinnian humor thrown in. The time span for the collection is actually five decades, from the 1950s (including Zinn's first article, "The Southern Mystique," from *Harper's* magazine, which subsequently became a part of his book by the same title) on through the 1990s. Some important Zinn pieces already considered at length appear again here, including portions of most of his books. But there is also much that, even though in some cases written much earlier, deserves note here, especially some items that had appeared in rather obscure places, or have not been readily available for whatever reason.

"Abolitionists, Freedom Riders, and the Tactics of Agitation," for example, appeared originally in an important 1965 book, *The Anti-Slavery Vanguard*, edited by Martin Duberman. It is even more effective than some of Zinn's other work in dealing with the abolitionists, and with the connections between them and the civil rights movement. Dismissing those scholars who would psychoanalyze the abolitionists as some kind of "emotional deviates," Zinn found it "tempting to join the psychological game and try to understand what it is about the lives of academic scholars which keeps them at arm's length from the moral fervor of one of history's most magnificent crusades." He also found it "paradoxical that the historian, who is presumably blessed with historical perspective, should judge the radical from within the narrow moral base of the radical's period of activity, while the radical assesses his immediate society from the vantage point of some future, better era." And he insisted that throughout history, "it has been first the radical, and only later the moderate, who has held out a hand to men knocked to the ground by the social order." What the abolitionists did was certainly not to cause the war, "but to ensure, by their kind of agitation, that in the course of the war, some social reform would take place." Then, writing in 1965 remember, Zinn insisted hopefully that "progress toward racial equality in the United States is certain," but also insisted that "this is because agitators, radicals and 'extremists'—black and white together—are giving the United States its only living reminder that it was once a revolutionary nation."[45]

Sometimes it is just Zinn's brief introductions to each piece reproduced in the *Reader* that seem especially important, as when, introducing his essay on "Just and Unjust War" from *Declarations of Independence*, he reminds us that he began World War II as "an eager bombardier," but by the end of the war was writing "Never Again" on a folder of war mementos, and then writes: "After my own experience in that war, I had moved away from my own rather orthodox view that there are just wars and unjust wars, to a universal rejection of war as a solution to any human problem. Of all the positions I have taken over the years on questions of history and politics, this has undoubtedly aroused the most controversy."[46]

A little publication called *The New South Student* carried an interesting essay by Zinn in December 1967. Cleverly entitled "Dow Shalt Not Kill," it was originally a speech Zinn gave as a part of a protest against the Dow Chemical Company's manufacture of napalm for use in Vietnam. It was reprinted in several places, including *The Zinn Reader*. Among other things, it illustrates clearly the difference between radicals, such as Zinn, and liberals. Some liberals, he noted, had felt that acts of trespassing, blockading, or obstruction were possible violations of civil liberties. In this piece, Zinn differed strongly. Responding specifically to the suggestion that "physical interposition" against Dow's business activities would constitute "taking the law into your own hands," Zinn said, "That is exactly what civil disobedience is: the temporary taking of the law into one's own hands, in order to declare what the law *should* be. It is a declaration that there is an incongruence between the law and humane values, and that sometimes this can only be publicized by breaking the law." One must not do this for light and transient causes, of course; there are "two essential conditions for the right to civil disobedience." First, "the human value at stake must involve fundamental rights, like life, health, and liberty." Thus, there is no real cause for disobeying a traffic light because it is inconveniently long, but when the napalm being manufactured by Dow was being used in the "saturation bombing" of Vietnam in "one of the cruelest acts perpetrated by any nation in modern history," there was a compelling reason to protest. The second condition for civil disobedience was "the inadequacy of legal channels for redressing the grievance." This was "manifestly true" in the case of Vietnam, Zinn argued, for the war there was "being waged completely outside the American constitutional process, by the President and a handful of advisers."[47]

Zinn reviewed Richard Nixon's memoir, *No More Vietnams*, in the Madison, Wisconsin, *Capital Times* in 1985. He acknowledged in his introduction to the review for the *Reader* that no one American president could be blamed for what had happened in Vietnam, that the "long line of blame" could go back all the way to FDR and come all the way forward to Nixon. But not surprisingly, he was devastatingly critical of Nixon's book, referring to it as "a desperate attempt to make a silk purse out of a sow's behind," and giving a long list of "falsehoods and omissions." "Why is

Nixon writing all this nonsense now?" he questions. "What he seems to want is to persuade us that we didn't kill enough GIs and Vietnamese in Vietnam. If we had killed more, we might have 'won.' Therefore, we must not be so hesitant in Central America." Zinn called his review "What Did Richard Nixon Learn?" His answer was "nothing."[48]

Some of the items Zinn reproduced in the *Reader* were introductions to books he had written over the years; just to see what some of those books were is revealing. In 1978, for example, when Upton Sinclair's *Boston*, a novel about the Sacco and Vanzetti case, was reissued, Zinn wrote a strong introduction, saying that Sinclair "shows us America in the way it does not want to be seen, as a class society, its politics as class politics, its justice as class justice." Though that was "an old-fashioned view," said Zinn, it was "still fundamentally true."[49] Similarly, in 1971, Zinn wrote an introduction for a new edition of socialist Jack London's political novel, *The Iron Heel*. He found the book, written in 1906, still relevant, for "the United States has not changed its basic characteristics: the rule of corporate wealth, the use of the big stick to bludgeon the discontented, both at home and abroad." And again, "London's [basic] point still holds: the profit of corporations, not the needs of people, decides what is done with the country's natural wealth."[50]

In a somewhat different vein, but in the same year, 1971, Zinn wrote an introduction for the first American edition of anarchist Herbert Read's *Anarchy and Order*. Obviously, Zinn has shown considerable interest in and been considerably attracted by anarchist thought over the years; his play on Emma Goldman is just one small example of that. In his 1997 comments presenting his introduction to Read's book, he still felt strongly: "That I could get a Ph.D. from a major American university without knowing anything about anarchism, surely one of the most important political philosophies of modern times, is a commentary on the narrowness of American education." In the 1971 introduction itself, noting that the very word *anarchy* "unsettles most people in the Western world," suggesting "disorder, violence, uncertainty," Zinn concludes: "We have good reason for fearing those conditions, because we have been living with them for a long time, not in anarchist societies (there have never been any) but in exactly those societies most fearful of anarchy—the powerful nation-states of modern times." More specifically, using one of his favorite devices, the insidious question: "Is there anything closer to 'anarchy' (in the common use of the word, meaning confusion) than the incredibly wild and wasteful economic system in America?" Zinn notes the anarchist claim that both capitalist and socialist bureaucracies fail on "their greatest promise: to bring democracy." "The *vote* in modern societies is the currency of politics as *money* is the currency of economics; both mystify what is really taking place—control of the many by the few." Read's "attraction to both art and anarchy," concludes Zinn, "seems a fitting response to the twentieth century," underscoring as it does "the idea that revolution must be cultural as well as political."[51]

It was not a book but a movie that gave Zinn the opportunity to write one piece, "Discovering John Reed." And interestingly, it was the *Boston Globe*, which some years earlier had canceled Zinn's regular column, that invited him to write about what he called "Warren Beatty's grand movie, *Reds*." Zinn considered the appearance, in 1981, of a movie in which the main character was a Communist, and was sympathetically portrayed, "startling." It was, he felt, "one of many pieces of evidence that the nation had moved a critical distance away from the Communist hysteria of the Fifties." Zinn noted that journalist John Reed's body was buried near the Kremlin wall as a hero, but insisted that "his soul does not belong to any Establishment, there or here or anywhere." If, he concluded, even a fraction of the millions who would watch the movie "are led thereby to think about war and injustice, art and commitment, about enlarging friendship beyond national boundaries for the possibility of a better world, that is a huge accomplishment for one brief, intensely lived life."[52]

Zinn's career path has never been an orthodox one. Seldom, for example, has he published in standard history or political science journals. But occasionally he published in places that were unusual even for him. The *American Journal of Orthopsychiatry*, for example, published an essay of Zinn's entitled "Non-Violent Direct Action," in 1966. (Orthopsychiatry involves the study and treatment of incipient and borderline mental disorders, especially in the young.) After dismissing war, revolution, and gradual reform (the "three traditional ways of satisfying the need for institutional change") as inadequate "for the kind of problems we face today in the United States and in the world," Zinn concluded that some technique was needed "which is more energetic than parliamentary reform and yet not subject to the dangers which war and revolution pose in the atomic age." The answer, of course, is nonviolent direct action. It is "up to the citizenry," says Zinn, "those outside of power, to engage in permanent combat with the state, short of violent, escalatory revolution, but beyond the gentility of the ballot-box, to insure justice, freedom and well-being, all those values which virtually the entire world has come to believe in."[53]

Not quite so strange as orthopsychiatry, but still hardly standard fare for historians and political scientists, is publishing in journals read by archivists. Zinn was asked to speak at the annual meeting of the Society of American Archivists in Washington, D.C., in 1970. He called his paper "The Archivist and the New Left," and it was published several years later (in 1977) in the *Midwestern Archivist*; here it is called "Secrecy, Archives, and the Public Interest." It is little short of brilliant, for it shows Zinn applying some of his central notions about openness and democracy in an entirely different area than usual, but a crucial one. At the end, Zinn said he had only two proposals for archivists. First, they should "engage in a campaign to open all government documents to the public." And second, they should "take the trouble to compile a whole new world of documentary material, about the lives, desires, needs, of ordinary people." Zinn concluded by insisting that both of these "are in keeping with the spirit of democracy, which demands that the population know what the government is doing, and that the condition, the grievances, the will of the underclasses become a force in the nation." Further, he said, to "refuse to be instruments of social control in an essentially undemocratic society, to begin to play some small part in the creation of a real democracy: these are worthy jobs for historians, for archivists, for us all." According to the editor of the *Midwestern Archivist*, Zinn "shocked and offended" many in his audience; but a small group of mostly younger archivists were moved to found "an informal caucus dedicated to reform within both the Society of American Archivists and the archival profession."[54]

The Zinn Reader showed, not only by its publication but also by some of the items it included, that Zinn continued to be active in retirement. He was a participant in a symposium on the university, for example, in 1991; his comments were published by the *Gannett Center Journal* under the title "How Free Is Higher Education?" Looking back from the perspective of 1997, Zinn said, "There had been going on for some time a hot national debate on 'multi-culturalism,' on freedom of speech in the university, on 'political correctness.' As a result of the movements of the Sixties, changes had taken place in American education, and some of these changes were causing a kind of hysteria among conservatives. I thought I would add my bit to the debate, based on my own experience in higher education."

"Education has always inspired fear among those who want to keep the existing distributions of power and wealth as they are," Zinn began strongly. The educational environment is unique in our society, he said: "It is the only situation where an adult, looked up to as a mentor, is alone with a group of young people for a protracted and officially sanctioned period of time and can assign whatever reading he or she chooses, and discuss with these young people any subject under the sun." Of course, the subject "may be defined by the curriculum, by the catalog course description," but "this is a minor impediment to a bold and imaginative teacher, especially in literature, philosophy, and the social sciences, where there are unlimited possibilities for free discussion of social and political issues." Early in his own teaching career, Zinn stated unequivocally, he had "decided that I would make the most of the special freedom that is possible in a classroom. I would introduce what I felt to be the most important, and therefore the most controversial, questions in my class." He proceeded to give several examples, from both Spelman College and Boston University, of having done just that. "Was I committing that terrible sin which is arousing the anger of today's fundamentalists: 'politicizing the curriculum'?" Of course, seems to be the answer, for as Zinn asks, in one of his favorite stylistic devices, "Is there any rendition of constitutional law, any recounting of American history that can escape being *political*—that is, expressing a political point of view?" Clearly, he thinks the answer is no; as an example, he insists that it is just as "political" to treat Theodore Roosevelt as a hero as it is to point to "his role as an early imperialist, a forerunner of a long string of crude U.S. interventions in the Caribbean."

Zinn had never concealed his political views, he said; his detestation of war and militarism, his anger at racial inequality, his belief in a democratic socialism, in a rational and just distribution of the world's wealth. "To pretend to an 'objectivity' that was neither possible nor desirable seemed to me dishonest." He always made it clear to students at the beginning of each course that they would be getting his point of view, but that he would try to be fair to other points of view, and that they were completely free to differ with him. "My students had a long experience of political indoctrination before they arrived in my class," he insisted, "in the family, in high school, in movies and television. They would hear viewpoints other than mine in other courses, and for the rest of their lives. I insisted on my right to enter my opinions in the marketplace of ideas, so long dominated by orthodoxy."

The expression of "political views," then, Zinn found inevitable in education. "It may be done overtly, honestly, or it may be there subtly. But it is always there, however the textbook, by its very bulk and dullness, pretends to neutrality, however noncommittal is the teacher." Partly this is inevitable because "all education involves *selection*—of events, of voices, of books— and any insistence on one list of great books or great figures or great events is a partial (in both senses of that term) rendering of our cultural heritage." The "pluralism in thought that is required for truly free expression in higher education," insisted Zinn, "has never been realized." For its "crucial elements—an ideologically diverse faculty, a heterogeneous student body (in class, race, sex—words that bring moans from the keepers of the 'higher culture')—have always been under attack from outside and from inside the colleges and universities." Lashing out specifically at some of the critics of change in higher education, including Roger Kimball, author of *Tenured Radicals*, Zinn said: "Yes, some of us radicals have somehow managed to get tenure. But far from dominating higher education, we remain a carefully watched minority." Zinn drew on his own experience at Boston to make his point. "Did I have freedom of expression in my classroom?" he asked. "I did," was his answer, but only "because I followed Aldous Huxley's advise [*sic*]: 'Liberties are not given; they are taken.'" Building toward his conclusion, Zinn asserted that "the fundamentalists of education fear the possibilities inherent in the unique freedom of discussion that we find in higher education."[55]

> And so, under the guise of defending "the common culture" or "disinterested scholarship" or "Western civilization," they attack that freedom. They fear exactly what some of us hope for, that if students are given wider political choices in the classroom than they get in the polling booth or the workplace, they may become social rebels. They may join movements for racial or sexual equality, or against war, or, even more dangerous, work for what James Madison feared as he argued for a conservative Constitution: "an equal division of property." Let us hope so.[56]

It is, of course, true that "all education involves *selection*." Zinn closed out his *Reader*—many thought it would surely be his last book—with some "Suggestions for Further Reading." Not really intended as a full bibliography, it shows what some of Zinn's selections would be for students, but more, it shows who some of the formative authors have been in his own work. He insists the most useful works to read on race, for example, are "the writings of African Americans themselves," then goes on to discuss Cornel West, Richard Wright, Frederick Douglass, W. E. B. Du Bois, Zora Neale Hurston, Alice Walker (of course), Malcolm X, Toni Morrison, and others. For African American history, Zinn thinks highly of John Hope Franklin, and for multicultural history, Ronald Takaki.

Zinn began his suggestions for reading on class by saying, "Perhaps the first book I read that spoke to my own working-class upbringing was by Upton Sinclair: *The Jungle*." He also mentions John Steinbeck's *The Grapes of Wrath*. Historical works include those by Charles Beard, Gary

Nash, Matthew Josephson, and Richard Hofstadter. ("Without presenting itself explicitly as a class analysis of American history, . . . *The American Political Tradition* made clear how behind the sparring of the major political parties throughout the country's history there was a basic consensus around the capitalist system.") Of course, Zinn also recommends the reading of Karl Marx.

On war, Zinn says that the "first blow" to his "youthful awe of martial heroism" came when he was about eighteen and read Walter Millis's *The Road to War*, "a devastating critique of our nation's entrance into World War I." But "probably the most powerful influences that . . . turned the glamour of war into unmitigated horror were novels" by Henry Barbusse, Erich Maria Remarque, Dalton Trumbo, Joseph Heller, and Kurt Vonnegut. Historians William Appleman Williams on American foreign policy in general and Marilyn Young on Vietnam in particular are also highly recommended, as are the various works of Zinn's friend the radical linguist Noam Chomsky on contemporary U.S. foreign policy. Finally, for alternatives to war, Zinn recommends the writings of Gene Sharp, particularly *The Politics of Non-Violent Direct Action*.

Zinn thinks highly of the work of Morton Hurwitz, Zecchariah Chafee, and David Caute on legal history. But he is more impressed by Clarence Darrow, Henry David Thoreau, Leo Tolstoy, Albert Camus, and Martin Luther King Jr.

"I had not thought much about the social role of the historian," claims Zinn, "until I read Robert Lynd's *Knowledge for What?*" Alfred North Whitehead, E. H. Carr, James Harvey Robinson, and Hans Meyerhoff he also found useful in this area. Peter Novick's *That Noble Dream* he considered "superb." Zinn also recognized fellow radical historian Jesse Lemisch for his "biting critique of the historical profession," *On Active Service in War and Peace*. Finally, Zinn says there are "certain historians who represent for me the ideal joining of impeccable research and social conscience." He gives two examples: E. P. Thompson for *The Making of the English Working Class*, and Richard Drinnon for his "brilliant book about American expansionism, *Facing West*."

Drinnon appears again in the final section of Zinn's suggested readings, "On Means and Ends." This time it is for his biography of Emma Goldman, *Rebel in Paradise*, which, says Zinn, led him to Goldman's autobiography, then her writings and the writings of other anarchists. Also appearing prominently in this section is *Non-Violence in America* by Staughton and Alice Lynd.[57]

All of these are good selections—but the works of Howard Zinn himself should be read along with them! Zinn is probably through writing books. But he is not through writing. And he certainly is not through speaking.

Zinn's play on Emma Goldman has continued to be produced around the country and abroad. He has also written three other plays: *Unsafe Distances*, *Marx in Soho*, and *Daughter of Venus*.

Book reviewing usually seems a thankless task, but Zinn has even taken on that challenge at times in retirement. The *Guardian* of London, for example, asked him to review the massive tome *A History of the American People*, by conservative and somewhat controversial scholar Paul Johnson. Zinn begins by saying the book is "what we have come to expect from this prolific writer—clear, colorful narrative, vivid character sketches, prodigious research, sweeping, confident statements," but also "an insistent conservative viewpoint which tempts him into serious omissions." The first such omission, and Zinn considers it basic, is Columbus. "How you treat that story—what you choose to tell of it—signals your view of the longer American experience, reaching to our time," says Zinn. And Johnson ignores the ugly parts, the way Columbus "encountered native Americans who were peaceful and generous (by his own admission) and tortured them, kidnapped them, enslaved them, murdered them." It is not that Johnson does not have space; he finds plenty of room to cover other clearly more trivial matters, including Ronald Reagan's jokes. Thus what he omits, here and elsewhere, he omits because he "wants us to look benignly on the history of the United States," the "first, best hope for the human race," a "human achievement without parallel."

It is not the fact that Johnson has a bias that bothers Zinn, of course; he could hardly complain about that and be consistent with what he has said repeatedly over the years about everybody having one. "He will not conceal his opinions, he tells us," Zinn writes of Johnson. "Good. Then we can judge his history free of pretenses to objectivity—his or ours." What seems most significant to Zinn is what Johnson chooses to tell us, what to omit, what to downplay. "Johnson's history of 'the American people' pays only passing attention to the great people's movements for social justice," for example, that is, it practically ignores the material which Zinn made central in his *People's History*. Clearly, Zinn does not approve of Johnson's lack of "sympathy for the American people in those instances when they have protested and rebelled, demanding a redress of grievances, as with the Bonus March of World War I veterans in 1932." Zinn seems amazed at Johnson's view of Vietnam: "His criticism of the Vietnam War, in which the

United States dropped three times as many bombs as it did in World War II and was responsible for the deaths of several million people, was that it did not use enough force!" Nor does Zinn approve of Johnson's view of the 1960s, saying it is "that of the American Establishment, frightened by the challenge to its authority." Indeed, Zinn feels that Johnson's treatment of the sit-ins and Freedom Rides is "malicious," since it accuses the participants of those "classic instances of non-violent protest" (Zinn's words) of using or threatening or provoking violence.

So, Zinn is somewhat severe in his criticism of Johnson throughout the chronological span of American history, including "rather astounding blindness to the long history of America's military interventionism" when he refers to the Spanish-American War as the nation's "one imperialist adventure." But he becomes more severe as Johnson approaches the present. "As he moves into the last decades," suggests Zinn, "Johnson becomes a bit hysterical," seeing the congressional investigation of President Reagan's illegal activities to arm Nicaraguan counterrevolutionaries as a "witch-hunt," for example, and resenting the demands of blacks, Latinos, and women (citing a report by the right-wing American Enterprise Institute that "women had effectively achieved equality"). Zinn concludes his review with strong words, words which show what a fundamental difference there is between his concept of a "people's history" of the United States and Johnson's concept of a history of the "American people." "Since Johnson has decided that the United States is 'the first, best hope for the human race,' he has shaped its history accordingly," says Zinn. But "if we prefer to see that history as a complex and unfinished struggle of Americans for justice, against militarism, for economic, racial, and sexual equality, we are badly served by a fawning admiration of those in power, pretending to be a history of 'the people.'"[58]

For several months in late 1997 and early 1998, Zinn wrote a column for a site called Tripod on the Internet. This was consistent with his desire to write "short journalistic pieces, op-ed pieces on current events, you know, when something strikes me." Seven such pieces appeared. The first, close to Columbus Day, concluded that "we should welcome the crumbling of the Columbus myth, welcome the new skepticism about the glories of 'Westward Expansion.'" The second argued that while we might vote, the candidates and parties available to us are really so limited that we need to move "Beyond Voting" to "build a new national citizens movement dedicated to political and economic democracy—a force so widespread, so powerful, that whoever is in office, attention will have to be paid." "A Tale of Two Cities" Zinn called his column in December 1997, drawing on his longtime love of Charles Dickens to raise skepticism about whether the excellent performance of the stock market really meant anything for most Americans.

Zinn began 1998 with a series of columns on some of the hot topics in higher education (and beyond) in recent years: multiculturalism, political correctness, and women's history. He drew on his own experience to show the need for exposing students to diversity, finding it absolutely "shocking" that he had studied the Reconstruction era without reading W. E. B. Du Bois. And he drew from American history to show the need for correctives to traditional views; his example was the much-vaunted "reform" era of Progressivism—during which, according to African American historian Rayford Logan, more black people were lynched than in any other period of American history. The "cry goes up," he concludes, that the multiculturalists who want to change the teaching of history and literature have a "'political agenda.' (As if the old teaching is innocently 'objective!')" Indeed, says Zinn, "there is such an agenda. It is to begin dismantling the walls that separate us from one another: white from black, men from women, Americans from other people of the world. The agenda is to stop the escalation, from ignorance to distrust to hatred of other people, that makes it possible for political leaders to plan wars and carry out genocides." Of course, Zinn acknowledges, education should prepare the young to be "successful." But it also needs to do something more: "to bring up a new generation, humane and cosmopolitan, that will try to free the next century of the narrowness, the hostility, that has plagued the history of our time."

Moving from that powerful case for multicultural education to the thorny issue of "political correctness," Zinn begins bluntly by calling pc "the latest example in American culture of linguistic intimidation." It is like "witch" or "Communist," but with a "peculiar twist, that its use constricts discussion while pretending to defend freedom of expression." He acknowledges "there are some on the left who appoint themselves political commissars," but insists the problem is greatly exaggerated by those on the right who are alarmed by the changes in education and society that came out of the movements of the 1960s. The alarm over political correctness, suggests Zinn pungently, is "the cultural counterpart of the cries of pain when corporate multi-millionaires face a slight increase in their taxes." Those who decided for so long what is "politically correct"—"that Columbus was a hero, that 'Western Civilization' is the summit of human achievement, that fighting for 'your country' is noble, that slavery and racism were minor blots in a society fundamentally free and democratic, that health, jobs, care of children should be left to 'private enterprise'"—they "now complain bitterly that these beliefs are being challenged. They shout 'political correctness,' as a way of avoiding a rational reexamination of the old, dominant ideology." In short, political correctness "is a phrase that obscures rather than enlightens, and should be used, I am suggesting, with great caution."

Zinn has said himself that he was not much involved with the women's movement. His February 1998 Tripod column, "Women's History Month," shows, however, great sensitivity to women's issues, in both the past and the present. The thing that set him off was the new welfare law recently passed by Congress. "I can think of no better way to celebrate Women's History Month than to think about the women and their children affected by the new law," he writes; but, typically, not just "think": "Treated cruelly by our government, they need our attention, our support, our protests." There are, notes Zinn, "safe" ways and "troubling" ways to celebrate holidays. We always play Martin Luther King's "I Have A Dream" speech for his holiday, but how often do we hear that he denounced the war in Vietnam, criticized the FBI, and expressed doubts about the morality of the capitalist system itself? So for Women's History Month we need to honor Abigail Adams ("Do not put such unlimited power in the hands of husbands," she said) and other great women, but also the unknown masses. And, of course, we need to apply the same principle to the unknown women of *today*; Zinn tells of a Portuguese immigrant woman living in New Bedford, Massachusetts, threatened by loss of food stamps by the new welfare law who cried out to a reporter, "What will I do? I have no one. I don't want to starve. Oh, my God." Perhaps some of these immigrant women, Zinn suggests caustically, were deceived by the words on the Statue of Liberty: "Give me your tired, your poor, your huddled masses yearning to breathe free, the wretched refuse of your teeming shore. Send these, the homeless, tempest-tossed to me. I lift my lamp beside the golden door." And he follows this with a suggestion "that the Statue of Liberty, a woman with perhaps a woman's special compassion for the poor, should be removed from its moorings in New York Harbor and put on Pennsylvania Avenue in Washington, to remind members of Congress and the President of its message."

Zinn used his last column for Tripod, in March 1998, to praise peace activists, those "Christian pacifists who have been acting in the spirit of the Hebrew prophet Isaiah: 'They will beat their swords into plowshares.'" Recently six Roman Catholic pacifists had entered the Bath Iron Works in

Maine and poured their own blood on the missile launchers of a billion-dollar destroyer under construction there. Said Zinn: "Just as we take heart when we learn of those Germans who resisted Hitler, so we must take heart from the actions of these Americans who, without national publicity or fanfare, have been carrying on for at least seventeen years a campaign to rid the world of nuclear weapons. And their immediate target is the nation with the greatest stockpile of nuclear bombs—our own." Among the contemporary peace activists who drew Zinn's praise was Freda Berrigan, daughter of Phil and niece of Daniel, who had both been prominent in the protest movement against the Vietnam War. "The Soviet Union has fallen apart," notes Zinn, "yet the United States continues to maintain an enormous military machine, spending as much money on this as the combined military budgets of all possible enemies," billions of dollars which "could be better used for housing, jobs, education, health."[59]

These Tripod essays show some of Zinn's continuing concerns; more, they show that his concerns do indeed continue. Asked if he is happy with what he is doing at this stage of his life, including writing shorter pieces such as columns, plays, and book reviews, spending more time with family, and also traveling and lecturing a great deal, he says yes. But he also emphasizes that many of the speaking opportunities come to him, in a sense. "I get a lot of requests to lecture. Most of the requests come on the basis of *A People's History*. People here and there are, have been reading my *People's History*, so they invite me to come and speak," and he is "happy, especially since I'm not teaching anymore, happy to have an opportunity to do a kind of teaching without having to grade papers and deal with college administrations." No surprise there. Zinn is also pleased that he gets "very heterogeneous audiences as opposed to, let's say, Boston University students." At BU, his students were "fairly homogeneous. They were mostly upper-middle-class students," though "fortunately" there was "a sprinkling of foreign students and scholarship working-class students." But going around the country, "I speak to community colleges, I speak to high schools, I speak to state colleges." Recently, he had spoken at Sacramento City College, "to an audience of students who were Indian, black, Hispanic, Asian, wonderful." The other thing he likes about such speaking is that "it's always a revelation to just speak in places you've never heard of. And to find in these places, wonderful people. And . . . it encourages you about what's possible in this country." He had spoken, for example, in Texas City, Texas, during the Gulf War, and found "an audience of four hundred people who were totally with me in my criticism of the Gulf War.

So, it gives me a sense of what's out there." He even likes to speak to "captive audiences" sometimes, he says, like "high school students, who don't know who I am, who have been forcibly assembled to hear me." That kind of coercion, he says, he does not mind. "They're not being imprisoned for life. So it's, I think, it's satisfying to do that."[60]

One inescapable conclusion is that Howard Zinn is what is usually called a people person; whether he needs "frequent verbal slugfests" might be debated, but there is no doubt that he needs interaction with people. He is so amiable, and so good at expressing his radical views in his understated way, that people find themselves being carried along by him, having that head-nodding effect—then suddenly realizing that they have been conditioned, in many cases all their lives, *not* to agree with the stuff he is saying. Remember the secretary in the political science department at Boston University, where Zinn occasionally still shows up, who said, "Everybody likes him." Obviously, she was not necessarily saying everybody agrees with him, just that everybody likes him.

So Zinn has not quit. He has not even really quit teaching, but simply takes an approach to it now that enables him to avoid some of the marginalia of it that he did not like. In the first six months of 1998, Zinn's calendar shows that he had thirty talks scheduled! A few had to be canceled because of the flu, and one because of a minor swimming accident his wife had on a vacation trip to Florida; still, quite a schedule. It included bookstores, colleges and universities, high schools, and other venues; it included a "conversation with Studs Terkel" at Berkeley, the "Annual Most Censored Stories Awards" at Fordham University, a fundraiser for a documentary on activists in Northampton, Massachusetts, a teachers conference on nonviolence at Lesley College in Cambridge, Massachusetts—and a commencement address for the graduating class of his granddaughter at Middlesex Academy in Concord, Massachusetts.[61]

Zinn's name appeared on another book in 1999; he was not, however, the author in the usual sense. Entitled *The Future of History*, the volume was really a collection of interviews of Zinn by the prominent leftist journalist, founder and director of Alternative Radio, David Barsamian. While it might be argued that the little book broke no new ground, that would miss the point; it is a fun read, and could even serve as an introduction to some of the major themes of Zinn's work. Barsamian is an excellent interviewer, and obviously had an excellent rapport with Zinn. "Some humor is lost in transcription," writes Barsamian in the introduction, "but I hope enough survives to give you a chuckle or two." It does. Barsamian again: "It is inspiring to work with a mensch like Howard Zinn, even if he does like the coffee at Dunkin' Donuts!" All the interviews in *The Future of History*, as well as some others, are available on audiotape from Alternative Radio.[62]

After the unprecedented September 11, 2001, terrorist attack on New York City's World Trade Center and the Pentagon in Washington, D.C., Zinn, now seventy-nine years of age, spoke and wrote vigorously; it might be said that an already unusually busy retiree stepped up his level of activity another notch. Not surprisingly to those who know his life and writings, the central thrust of what he had to say was made clear by the title of an essay he wrote for the *Chronicle of Higher Education*: "Compassion, Not Vengeance." The images on television, he said, have been "heart-breaking." But "then our political leaders came on television, and I was horrified and sickened again." For they spoke of retaliation, vengeance, punishment, war. "And I thought: They have learned nothing, absolutely nothing, from the history of the 20th century. . . . We need to think about the resentment all over the world felt by people who have been the victims of American military action. . . . We need to decide that we will not go to war, whatever reason is conjured up by the politicians, because war in our time is always indiscriminate, a war against innocents, a war against children. War is terrorism, magnified a hundred times." Zinn concluded: "Our security can only come by using our national wealth, not for guns, planes, and bombs, but for the health and welfare of our people, and for people suffering in other countries. Our first thoughts should be not of vengeance, but of compassion, not of violence, but of healing."[63] On September 18, Zinn was interviewed on MSNBC and conveyed essentially the same message.

In 2001 Howard Zinn's name appeared as author or coauthor on three more books. For *Three Strikes: Miners, Musicians, Salesgirls, and the Fighting Spirit of Labor's Last Century*,[64] Zinn contributed an essay on the 1913–1914 Colorado Fuel and Iron strike, while Dana Frank wrote on the Woolworth girls' sit-down strike of 1937 and Robin D. G. Kelley on a musicians' strike in the 1930s.

Howard Zinn on History and *Howard Zinn on War* were both collections of previously published material on those topics. Despite the claim on the back of each that they consist of "new and selected writings," the only thing new is Zinn's introduction to each piece, usually a paragraph. Still, these are clever, insightful, and revealing of Zinn's own view of the importance of some of his smaller writings. Also, some of these items are a bit hard to find otherwise. Thus, the collections do have value.

Zinn notes in *Howard Zinn on History* that his essay from the *Progres-*

sive, reproduced here, elicited considerable response, some positive, some critical. His point, he says, is "not to diminish the experience of the Jewish Holocaust, but to enlarge it," that is: "to remember what happened to Jews served no important purpose unless it aroused indignation, anger, action against all atrocities, anywhere in the world."[65] Considering the sensitivity around the Holocaust, it is possible to see why some would find those words upsetting. But remember that to Zinn our only concern with the past is to see how it speaks to the present.

Two frequently overlooked but interesting Zinn pieces appear here: his account of the Freedom Schools from the *Nation* (November 23, 1964); and his contribution, "Marxism and the New Left," to the 1969 collection of essays edited by Priscilla Long on *The New Left*. There are also two pieces that remind us of the tension between Zinn and John Silber—and Zinn's willingness to go public with it: "Silber, the University, and the Marines," from the alternative newspaper the *Boston Phoenix* in 1972, in which Zinn is devastatingly critical of Silber's bringing the Marines on campus at Boston University to recruit and then arresting students who protested; and the more general description of BU under Silber from the *Progressive* in 1980 entitled, revealingly, "A Showcase of Repression."

Howard Zinn on War is a similar collection. It includes his comments on contemporary events in Kosovo and Yugoslavia, Libya, Iraq, as well as historical materials on Vietnam and World War II; in all of these, Zinn is concerned with the problem of war in general. Most of the pieces here are taken from earlier books such as *Failure to Quit, Vietnam: The Logic of Withdrawal, The Politics of History*, and *Declarations of Independence*, some also from the *Progressive*, the *Boston Globe*, and other sources. Of special interest is Zinn's essay on the popular movie *Saving Private Ryan*, taken from the *Progressive*, "Respecting the Holocaust." Admitting that he was "taken in" when he saw it, he came away angry just for that reason. The basic problem, he felt, was that it was a war movie, not an antiwar movie. All the effusive critics failed to ask the most important question: "Will this film help persuade the next generation that such scenes must never occur again?" And in conclusion: "Our culture is in deep trouble when a film like *Saving Private Ryan* can pass by, like a military parade, with nothing but a shower of confetti and hurrahs for its color and grandeur." But then, "it is nothing new that people with moral sensibility must create their own culture."[66]

We have noted that America's "war on terrorism" caused Zinn to step up his level of activity; though almost unimaginable, the increasing possibility of war on Iraq in late 2002 seems to have caused him to step it up still further. For the first time, he had difficulty finding time to respond to e-mail queries. "I hope that you're less busy than this retired person has been," he wrote on September 20. "I have been doing a lot of traveling and speaking, much of it about the 'war on terrorism.'" "I think my answers to these questions will have to wait until I'm finished with this flurry of traveling and speaking which is taking up my life right now," he said on October 7. Still, on October 15: "I haven't responded to your questions. . . . I've been traveling a lot, and haven't had the time. Just back from Maine, and last week Wisconsin."[67]

The speaking Zinn was doing impacted even more people than attended his talks. For example, in Tulsa, Oklahoma, on November 3, twenty people gathered under the auspices of the Tulsa Peace Fellowship to view a videotape of a Zinn lecture, "War, Terrorism, and the Media." Apparently filmed at Massachusetts Institute of Technology in March (Zinn was introduced by Noam Chomsky of MIT), it provided the basis for a spirited discussion of how government and media have been known to misinform, and how the group might spread the word and become involved with others in promoting peaceful alternatives.

Zinn finally did find time to answer the questions; he also found time, in 2002, to write forewords for two books, and to come out with still another book of his own. (His last? One wonders.) The two books for which he wrote forewords are obviously on subjects about which he cares deeply. Daniel M. Friedenberg's *Sold to the Highest Bidder* is about the power of big money to determine who lives in the White House. Zinn's foreword reminds us that the Founding Fathers intended the Constitution to maintain the dominant position of the wealthy in society—and it has. Noting the "simplistic test of democracy which asserts that the more people vote, in what is called a 'free election,' the more democratic the society is likely to be," Zinn concludes: "But when huge sums of money enter the electoral process, determine who are to be the candidates, and create a dependency of those elected on the wealthy interests who made their election possible, democracy has been corrupted." Friedenberg, he feels, establishes that this has indeed been the case, focusing on the last ten presidents, from Eisenhower to the current Bush; he also suggests solutions. Zinn feels this to be a valuable, even patriotic, service for democracy in America.[68]

The second foreword was for Nancy Chang's *Silencing Political Dissent*. The central concern, of the book and of Zinn's foreword, is how the Bush administration is using the current terrorist crisis to erode civil liberties, especially with the incredibly named USA PATRIOT Act. (One wonders how many of those who unquestioningly support it even know its full name: the Uniting and Strengthening America by Providing Appropriate Tools Required to Intercept and Obstruct Terrorism Act.) Zinn calls it a "draconian law, worthy of a police state," and continues:

> It is ironic, but a historic truth, repeated again and again, that at exactly those moments when citizens need the greatest freedom to speak their minds, exactly when life and death issues are involved, that is, when the question is war or peace, it is then that our liberties are taken away. The juggernaut of war crushes democracy, just when the nation claims it is fighting for democracy.

And once again, patriotism is a central concern; the so-called PATRIOT Act, he insists, "is the opposite of patriotism, if patriotism means love of your country and not the government, love of the principles of democracy and not the edicts of authority."[69]

Entitled *Terrorism and War*, Zinn's own book represents his effort specifically to address the events of September 11, 2001, and since. Edited by Anthony Arnove, socialist editor/publisher/writer, the little volume is based on interviews he conducted with Zinn between September 2001 and January 2002, as well as some of the talks Zinn has been giving. While consistent with Zinn's earlier writings, this one includes enough new material to warrant some attention.

Asked how he responds to those who favor a military solution to terrorism, Zinn insists that the continued expenditure of more than $300 billion every year has "absolutely no effect" on terrorism. Rather, "if we want real security, we will have to change our posture in the world—to stop being an intervening military power and to stop dominating the economies of other countries." Furthermore, "the horror of the terrorist attacks we experienced on September 11 is something that people in other parts of the world"—Southeast Asia, Iraq, and Yugoslavia are his examples—"have experienced as a result of our bombings, of terrorism carried out by people we have backed and armed." And "knowing this should have a sobering effect on any desire to continue with military solutions."

Reminded that President George W. Bush had claimed the United States had become a target of terrorists because they oppose our freedom and democracy, Zinn becomes intense. He thinks there are many people in the Middle East who would like more freedom and democracy themselves, he says; what "seems clear" is that what bothers people who want to strike at the United States is not what we do internally, but what we do externally.

"What angers them are the troops we've stationed in Saudi Arabia, the enormous economic and military support we give Israel, our maintenance of sanctions against Iraq, which have devastated the country and hurt so many people. They have made it very clear what troubles them." Asked why the United States has such an interest in Iraq and such a massive presence in the Middle East, Zinn insists that the answer is a single word—oil. "You can trace everything that the United States has done in the Middle East to the concern for oil—and the profits from oil."

"Can we learn anything from 9-11?" Arnove asks Zinn. His response is that we need to realize that our image is *not* that of a peaceful nation. "We have our troops everywhere in the world. We have military bases all over the world. We have naval bases in every sea in the world." Surely 9-11 teaches us that we must change that. Citing as examples Sweden, Denmark, Holland, and New Zealand, Zinn insists that there are places in the world that are not worried about terrorists; what we have to do to join them is to "be a more modest nation." Then, "all sorts of possibilities open up":

> Imagine what that $350 billion that we spend every year on being a military superpower could do to help people, to combat AIDS, to feed people, to immunize people. We could use the great wealth that would be freed up by no longer being a military power to pay for free health care for all, affordable housing for all, and helping people in other parts of the world.

This kind of thing, Zinn believes, could help make us more secure. He insists again that "bombing is not making us more secure."[70]

As usual, Zinn moves from concern with a specific war—or, in this case, a specific impending war—to concern with war in general. When he does so, one is reminded of his earlier thinking about just and unjust wars. Though perhaps he has developed that thinking a bit further. His central point: "In war, the evil of the means is certain and the achievement of the end, however important, is always uncertain." Admitting that World War II was "the closest you could come to a just war," Zinn acknowledges it is not easy to answer the question "What would you have done?" But the answer, he insists, must begin "I would not accept a solution that involves mass killing. I would try to find some other way." That "other way," he continues, is not passivity or acceptance—"the other way is resistance without war." He is referring to underground movements, strikes, general strikes, noncompliance. "War is inherently unjust," he concludes, "and the great challenge of our time is to how to [*sic*] deal with evil, tyranny, and oppression without killing huge numbers of people." Yet pushed one step further by Arnove, asked if he considered himself a pacifist, Zinn stopped just short of doing so. "I have never used the word 'pacifist' to describe myself because it suggests something absolute, and I am suspicious of absolutes," he begins, then continues: "I think there might be situations where a small, focused act of violence against a monstrous evil would be justified. Even such committed pacifists as Gandhi and Martin Luther King believed this."[71]

Zinn may be cautious of absolutes, but these words sound pretty absolute to some: "To me, those liberals, even radicals, who have to some degree supported the war have made a pact with the devil, which they themselves do not understand."[72] A pact with the devil? Strong words. One example of the people Zinn had in mind when he made that statement is surely Charles E. Angeletti, a history professor at Metropolitan State College in Denver, Colorado. He is a self-proclaimed leftist, is quoted elsewhere in these pages with high praise for Zinn and his work, but differs emphatically with Zinn in this area. Zinn "has no clue about American foreign policy today—which is why he is a great 'historian,'" said Angeletti recently.[73] What he meant, he has explained, is that he feels Zinn's approach is indeed absolute, a closed system, so to speak, which precludes consideration of other options, including the possibility of limited force.[74] One might lament such division within the left, but then the left has always struggled with fragmentation. And these are indeed complex and important issues.

Perhaps Edward S. Herman helps to clarify this split in the November 2002 issue of Z magazine. He writes of those "claiming to speak from the left [who] have aligned themselves with the national leadership in support of an aggressive military interventionism and projection of power abroad"—in other words, those who differ with Zinn—as the "cruise missile left [CML]." In case that does not make it clear, Herman does indeed take sides: These "CMLs," he says, are "by no means a genuine left—that is, one that opposes the powerful in the interest of the nonelite majority." The CMLs seem to think that the use of force is good when it is "decimating the forces of evil," as in Afghanistan—and Iraq? The problem, of course, is that once started down that road, it is hard to stop. CMLs think of the "Chomsky-left" (and Zinn left?) as "extremist, angry, reflexively anti-American, etc." Helpfully, Herman compares the CMLs to those in the 1850s who were critical of the radical abolitionists, telling them to "tone down their message and alter or even drop their antiracist and antislavery message given the 'political realities' and public sentiment."[75]

Zinn explains further what he meant. "You see this again and again in the liberal press," he says. "They support the war, and yet they think that

Attorney General John Ashcroft ordering the detention of people and secret evidence hearings is wrong. They don't seem to understand that you can't have one without the other. That's the devil's pact liberals and people on the left have signed and they don't want to acknowledge."[76]

Still, ever the optimist, Zinn sees the possibility of common ground not only among those on the left, but with all Americans. There is common ground, he believes, in "a universal instinct for compassion"; in having the same objective, that is, "to do away with terrorism"; in a concern with the way the Bush administration is using the "war on terror" to take people's attention away from the economic and social problems that concern us all; and finally common ground in the concern that all people ultimately have about the restriction of freedom.[77]

When Arnove quotes President Bush to Zinn, "We are a peaceful nation," Zinn responds vigorously that "obviously Bush hasn't read any history;" and when Arnove reminds him that Bush also "speaks as if war is the main way in which people in this country have won their freedoms and expanded their rights," Zinn insists that "war has always diminished our freedom." Emphasizing a central theme of his *People's History*, Zinn says that "when our freedom has expanded, it has not come as a result of war or of anything the government has done but as a result of what citizens have done."[78]

Zinn reviews the history of American wars and interventions—and the history of antiwar activism and pacifism—to support his position. He draws also on his own experience as a bombardier in World War II to make a point about the nature of a bombing campaign, that is, that it is inevitably a war on civilians. "The people prosecuting this war are committing murder," he argues, referring to the then-current bombing campaign in Afghanistan. "They are engaging in terrorism."[79]

At the end of his review of our history, Zinn is nothing if not passionate. He wants desperately to believe, as historians at all points on the political spectrum surely do, that knowledge of history will help us make more intelligent decisions in the present and future. Reminded by Arnove of a September 23, 2001, *New York Times* headline, "Forget the Past: It's a War Unlike Any Other," Zinn raged, "They want us to forget the history of our government. Because if you forget history, if you were born yesterday, then you'll believe anything. . . . If people knew some history, if teachers gave them history, if the media gave people history, if anyone with power over communication networks gave them some history, they might recognize in this rush of Congress to war the same subservience as we have seen in the past."[80]

Similarly, but this time perhaps more typical of leftists than historians, Zinn quotes famous journalist I. F. Stone: "Among all the things I'm going to tell you today about being a journalist, all you have to remember is two words: governments lie." Zinn follows with:

> If more people knew something about the history of government deception, of the lies that were told getting us into the Mexican War, the lies that were told getting us into the Spanish-American War, the lies that were told getting us into the war in the Philippines, the lies that were told getting us into World War I, the lies that were told again and again in Vietnam, the lies on the eve of the Gulf War, they would have questions about what they are hearing from the government and the media to justify this war.[81]

Finally, on history, Zinn says that the time we are living in now reminds him very much of the Cold War era: "Terrorism has replaced Communism as the rationale for the militarization of the country, for military adventures abroad, and for the suppression of civil liberties at home."[82]

Zinn was concerned specifically with the possibility of the war on terror being expanded from Afghanistan into Iraq. When this did indeed occur in early 2003, Zinn continued to speak out. These events, he believes, "will have a disastrous effect on American relations with the Arab world and with Muslims." He thinks the American public "has not yet absorbed the statements that the Bush administration is making about this being a war that will go on and on." The American people need to ask themselves, "Do we want our children and our grandchildren to be living in a state of perpetual warfare, with more and more of the world becoming hostile to us, and with the United States responsible for more and more human casualties in the world?"[83]

Clearly, Howard Zinn's answer to that question is a resounding "no!" He feels it so strongly that he is devoting incredible energy, at a point in life when many rest and observe, to trying to keep it from happening. Zinn turned eighty on August 24, 2002, and as he approached eighty-one, was still guilty of failure to quit.

NOTES

1. Howard Zinn, e-mail message to the author, June 21, 1998.
2. Howard Zinn, *Failure to Quit: Reflections of an Optimistic Historian* (Monroe, Maine: Common Courage Press, 1993), p. 67.

3. Howard Zinn, interview, Boston, Mass., March 14, 1997.

4. Letters to Howard Zinn from Abraham C. Meltzer, February 16, 1993; "Squirrel," February 18, 1993; John O'Brien, January 18, 1994; Francine Zerfus, January 29, 1992; Daniel Gertsacov, April 11, 1991; John Rudden, January 21, 1991; Thad N. Leach, February 1, 1991; and Paul deN. Burrowes Sr., May 23, 1991. All documents are from the Howard Zinn Papers.

5. Erwin Knoll, review of *Declarations of Independence* by Howard Zinn, *Progressive* 55 (February 1991): 40–41.

6. H. Bruce Franklin, review of *Declarations of Independence* by Howard Zinn, *Bulletin of the Atomic Scientists* 47 (September 1991): 43–44.

7. Mark A. Graber, review of *Declarations of Independence* by Howard Zinn, *Political Science Quarterly* 107 (spring 1992): 187–89.

8. Michael Kazin, review of *Declarations of Independence* by Howard Zinn, *Journal of American History* 78 (December 1991): 1034–35. Brief reviews also appeared in the *New York Times* (by Herbert Metgang, January 5, 1991, p. 10), and *Choice* (by P. J. Galie, vol. 28, March 1991, p. 1230).

9. Howard Zinn, *Declarations of Independence: Cross-Examining American Ideology* (New York: HarperCollins, 1990), pp. 2–5.

10. Ibid., pp. 5–7.

11. Ibid., pp. 6, 8.

12. Ibid., p. 62.

13. Ibid., pp. 80, 105.

14. Ibid., p. 259.

15. Howard Zinn, *Disobedience and Democracy: Nine Fallacies on Law and Order* (New York: Random House, 1968), p. 65.

16. Howard Zinn, ed., *Justice in Everyday Life: The Way It Really Works* (New York: William Morrow, 1974), pp. 126–27.

17. Zinn, *Declarations of Independence*, pp. 183, 186, 199, 205.

18. Ibid., pp. 210–13, 226–27.

19. Zinn, *Failure to Quit*, p. 1.

20. Ibid., p. 45.

21. Ibid., pp. 10, 15.

22. Ibid., pp. 145–50.

23. Review of *Failure to Quit* by Howard Zinn, *Bloomsbury Review* 13 (May 1993): 22.

24. Review of *Failure to Quit* by Howard Zinn, *Progressive* 57 (September 1993): 42.

25. Letter from Howard Zinn to Greg Bates, September 2, 1993, Howard Zinn Papers; *Nation* (October 18, 1993): 421.

26. Bill Harvey, "Howard Zinn Reflects on His 'Failure to Quit,'" *Baltimore Chronicle*, October 1993. Photocopy from Howard Zinn Papers.

27. Letters to Howard Zinn from "Ruth," September 5, 1993; and Vic Walter, Labor Day, 1993. Howard Zinn Papers.

28. Howard Zinn, *You Can't Be Neutral on a Moving Train: A Personal History of Our Times* (Boston: Beacon Press, 1994), pp. 1, 4, 6, 12.

29. Roland Wulbert, review of *You Can't Be Neutral on a Moving Train* by Howard Zinn, *Booklist* 91 (September 1, 1994): 22.

30. Zinn, interview, March 14, 1997.

31. Paul Buhle, review of *You Can't Be Neutral on a Moving Train* by Howard Zinn, *Nation* 259 (November 21, 1994): 623–25.

32. Zinn, interview, March 14, 1997.

33. Maurice Isserman, review of *You Can't Be Neutral on a Moving Train* by Howard Zinn, *Journal of American History* 82 (September 1995): 834–35.

34. Patricia O'Connell, review of *You Can't Be Neutral on a Moving Train* by Howard Zinn, *New York Times Book Review*, October 9, 1994, p. 22.

35. R. H. Immerman, review of *You Can't Be Neutral on a Moving Train* by Howard Zinn, *Choice* 32 (June 1995): 1674.

36. Letter from Ron Kovic to Howard Zinn, October 28, 1994. Howard Zinn Papers.

37. Colman McCarthy, "Master of Education," *Washington Post*, October 1, 1994.

38. Greg Sargent, "Never in Neutral: The Life of a True Believer," *New York Newsday*, October 20, 1994.

39. Gary Susman, "Loud and Clear: Zinn Is One Academic Who Never Taught 'Political Silence,'" *Boston Phoenix Literary Supplement*, October 1994. Photocopies of the McCarthy, Sargent, and Susman pieces are found in the Howard Zinn Papers.

40. Zinn, interview, March 14, 1997.

41. Information on *The Zinn Reader* from amazon.com, including review from *Kirkus Reviews*, October 1, 1997.

42. John Nichols, "Author Profile: Howard Zinn—Historian Makes Point by Avoiding Objectivity," *Capital Times*, November 14, 1997, http://www.thecapitaltimes.com/zinn.htm.

43. Harvey Wasserman, review of *The Zinn Reader* by Howard Zinn, *Progressive* (March 1998): 43–44.

44. Howard Zinn, *The Zinn Reader: Writings on Disobedience and Democracy* (New York: Seven Stories Press, 1997), p. 15.

45. Ibid., pp. 112–38.

46. Ibid., p. 229.

47. Ibid., pp. 302–308.

48. Ibid., pp. 331–35.

49. Ibid., pp. 462, 472.

50. Ibid., pp. 579, 581, 583.

51. Ibid., pp. 644–55.

52. Ibid., pp. 586, 592.

53. Ibid., pp. 612–19.

54. Ibid., pp. 516, 528.

55. Ibid., pp. 567–73.

56. Ibid., p. 573.

57. Ibid., pp. 663–68.

58. A copy of this review was supplied to the author by Howard Zinn via e-mail, July 19, 1998.

59. Copies of these seven essays for Tripod were supplied to the author by Howard Zinn.

60. Zinn, interview, March 14, 1997.

61. Howard Zinn, e-mail message to the author, June 21, 1998.

62. Howard Zinn, *The Future of History: Interviews with David Barsamian* (Monroe, Maine: Common Courage Press, 1999).

63. Howard Zinn, "Compassion, Not Vengeance," *Chronicle of Higher Education,* September 28, 2001, http://chronicle.com/free/v48/i05/05b00801.htm.

64. Howard Zinn, Dana Frank, and Robin D. G. Kelley, *Three Strikes: Miners, Musicians, Salesgirls, and the Fighting Spirit of Labor's Last Century* (Boston: Beacon Press, 2001).

65. Howard Zinn, *Howard Zinn on History* (New York: Seven Stories Press, 2001), pp. 69, 66.

66. Howard Zinn, *Howard Zinn on War* (New York: Seven Stories Press, 2001), pp. 101–104.

67. Howard Zinn, e-mail messages to the author, September 20, October 7, and October 15, 2002.

68. Daniel M. Friedenberg, *Sold to the Highest Bidder: The Presidency from Dwight D. Eisenhower to George W. Bush* (Amherst, N.Y.: Prometheus Books, 2002), pp. 11–14.

69. Nancy Chang, *Silencing Political Dissent* (New York: Seven Stories Press, 2002), pp. 11–12.

70. Howard Zinn, *Terrorism and War*, ed. Anthony Arnove (New York: Seven Stories Press, 2002), pp. 9–18.

71. Ibid., pp. 22–25.

72. Ibid., p. 44.

73. Charles E. Angeletti, postcard to the author, October 19, 2002.

74. Charles E. Angeletti, phone interview, November 1, 2002.

75. Edward S. Herman, "The Cruise Missile Left," Z (November 2002): 46–50.

76. Zinn, *Terrorism and War*, p. 45.

77. Ibid., pp. 32, 34, 39.

78. Ibid., pp. 50, 114.

79. Ibid., p. 88.

80. Ibid., pp. 52–53.

81. Ibid., pp. 62–63.

82. Ibid., pp. 47–48.

83. Ibid., p. 29.

SIX

HOWARD ZINN'S RADICAL AMERICAN VISION

A PRELIMINARY ASSESSMENT

Howard Zinn has commonly been linked with the New Left or radical or revisionist or neo-Progressive or conflict historians of the 1960s (and after). In some ways, that is perfectly valid, but in others it is overly simplistic, obfuscating, even misleading. On the one hand, as we have seen, Zinn has shared the concern with minorities, women, working people, with the lives of the masses of people, which is usually associated with that group of historians. History from the bottom up, it has often been called, or simply people's history. He has also been devastatingly critical of American imperialism and interventionism, a stance also associated with the conflict school. On the other hand, as we have also seen, Zinn has long been an admirer of Richard Hofstadter and his work, in particular *The American Political Tradition*, the 1948 book which is sometimes considered as the opening installment in the consensus school of American historiography, in part a conservative reaction against the old Progressive historians. Perhaps, as Zinn himself has suggested, the whole conflict/consensus dichotomy is obfuscating.

The New Left school is certainly an interesting group if we consider

Zinn one of the most important members along with William Appleman Williams, Staughton Lynd, and Eugene Genovese.[1] Zinn admired the work of William Appleman Williams, who began a New Left–style critique of U.S. foreign policy before anyone thought of calling it New Left. And he not only admired Staughton Lynd's work, including his model of the historian as activist and his idea that one important task of the historian was the chronicling in depth of our own time, but came to consider him a close friend. Grouping Zinn and Genovese in the same school of thought, however, is in some ways like the proverbial effort to mix oil and water, and may suggest the need for a reconceptualization of the school of thought itself.

Asked a question about the relationship between Lynd and Genovese, a question which suggested specifically that they had become "rather nasty with each other in print," Zinn responded quickly: "When you say Lynd and Genovese became nasty with one another in print, let me amend that by saying Genovese became very nasty and Lynd fought back, but he is not a nasty person. He just doesn't have nastiness in him." Of course, continued Zinn, up front as ever about his biases, Lynd "is my friend, my colleague at Spelman and we've been friends ever since." One of the reasons Zinn likes Lynd "is that he is a very gentle person, although very strong in his views." Genovese, on the other hand, "is a very admirable historian, and he has written some fine books, and his book on slavery, *Roll, Jordan, Roll*, is a wonderful book. But Genovese is one of those people, you say, well, his book would be very useful for the revolution, but I don't want to be alongside of Genovese for the revolution, and if he takes power, I might be shot." Zinn's response in this area is not only humorous, but revealing, enough so that it deserves to be quoted further at some length:

> The difference, one difference, between Genovese and Lynd . . . after all, Genovese got angry at Lynd because Lynd dared to take a view of history that Genovese disagreed with, and that is not something that should lead to vituperation, but should lead to good critical discussion, but instead it got denunciation, and denunciation was partly the result of an actual difference of opinion, but when something gets that heated up, you always suspect that there is something more to it, and there was something more to it there, it was a personal thing, when Genovese saw Lynd as a, he sees Lynd as a self righteous person, because Lynd is a very Quaker type, even his life is hard to emulate, I can't emulate it, I can't be as dedicated as he is, because I want to go to the movies, I want to take time off, but Lynd is a totally dedicated guy, something else, enormously admirable for that reason, but you can't emulate that, but I think, Genovese saw that as a

rebuke to him because he has not been an activist, in fact, he believes, he wrote an essay in *In Red and Black* [subtitled "Marxian Explorations in Southern and Afro-American History"] . . . he thought, if you'll just be a scholar, be a scholar, yes, and neither Lynd nor I believe it is enough to be a radical scholar, that you have to be involved in the world . . . in fact, there is no way you can be just a scholar, Genovese proved it, he wasn't just a scholar, because he participated, and in a negative way, during the Vietnam War by opposing the attempt to have the American Historical Association go on record against the war.

"So, as you can see," concluded Zinn, "I take sides in that, and Staughton and I are very much in agreement."[2]

The specific occasion for Genovese's criticism of Lynd was his review of Lynd's book *Intellectual Origins of American Radicalism* in the *New York Review of Books* in 1968. Genovese had been troubled that Lynd's book was "plainly meant to serve political ends." Specifically, Genovese did not like the way Lynd used the ideas of the Declaration of Independence as a kind of "moral absolutism" transcending time, connecting eighteenth-century radicals with twentieth-century radicals, while failing to discuss "the role of class or the historical setting of the debates among radicals." Genovese went so far as to claim that all this made Lynd's book "a travesty of history." Zinn, of course, differed. For one thing, he has made essentially the same kind of use of the Declaration of Independence and its ideals in his own work. More specifically, he considered Lynd's book "useful history," dealing with it in his *The Politics of History* as an example of one of the five criteria for radical history ("*We can recapture those few moments in the past which show the possibility of a better way of life than that which has dominated the earth thus far.*") Thus, said Zinn, "I believe Genovese is wrong." He felt compelled to remind "even Marxist historians" that insufficient attention had been paid to Marx's admonition: "The dispute over the reality or nonreality of thinking which is isolated from practice is a purely scholastic question." Thus, said Zinn, any dispute over a "true" history could not be resolved in theory; rather, "the real question is, which of the several possible 'true' histories (on that elementary level of factual truth) is *true* not to some dogmatic notion about what a radical interpretation should contain, but to the practical needs for social change in our day?" Finally: "If the 'political ends' Genovese warns against and Lynd espouses are not the narrow interests of a nation or party or ideology, but those humanistic values we have not yet attained, it is desirable that history should serve political ends."[3]

The tension between Zinn and Genovese, or at least between their approaches to history, did not end in 1968. Genovese is now the president of a new organization called simply the Historical Society. Despite that organization's claims—for example, that it is "open to all who want to do serious history, whatever part of the political and ideological spectrum they come from," that it seeks "neither a restoration of the Good Old Days, which never existed, nor the perpetuation of the irrationalities of recent years," and that it intends to "reintegrate the profession—to provide economic, political, intellectual, social, and other historians with a place to exchange ideas, contribute to each other's work, and learn from each other"—despite all that, Zinn sees it as "a conservative group suspicious of 'revisionism' and therefore hostile to the kind of history I do."[4]

Staughton Lynd provides a helpful perspective on all this. He considers Zinn not only a friend, but also one of his two greatest influences (the other being E. P. Thompson). "I identify 'New Left' as 'from the bottom up,'" he writes; he sees himself, Zinn, Jesse Lemisch (who is usually credited with coining the phrase, though there is some doubt about that), Alfred Young, and Vincent Harding as prominent among the many practitioners of the approach. Williams and Genovese, he feels, come from "an entirely different tradition." Their approach also had value, he felt—but he was clearly bothered when he learned that Williams was "very hostile to the abolitionists (as propagandists for Northern capitalism)," and that Genovese "idealized . . . Southern plantation owners."[5]

Radical History Review published a special thirtieth-anniversary issue in 2001. Zinn did not contribute, but was mentioned several times, including in Lynd's essay, and as cofounder (with Lynd) in 1969 of a "radical history caucus" within the New University Conference, which was an attempt to set up a national organization of radical scholars to work in tandem with "the movement." And surely every contributor would agree that Zinn's work, especially his *People's History*, is an integral part of what Ellen Carol DuBois writes about (and celebrates). "The substance of and approach to American history is so dramatically different from the unreflective, top-down, soporific national history that people my age were raised on that almost nothing of the old ways is left," she says—an exaggeration? "In this one area, understanding history, perhaps the sixties has really triumphed: radical history rules! Long live radical history!"[6]

So there is no doubt that the radical historians of the 1960s had an impact. Textbooks do indeed now commonly take a less celebratory approach to American history, and show more of a concern with social history, that is, with the lives of common people. This latter, "from the bottom up" kind of approach seems even to have established itself as a legitimate approach among those who do not think of themselves as on the left in any sense. Also, there is little doubt that the radical movements of the 1960s, of which Howard Zinn was also an important part, had an impact. The civil rights movement led to powerful civil rights and voting rights legislation, and the anti–Vietnam War movement helped lead to the end of the war. (Zinn by his own admission was less involved in the women's movement and the environmental movement, though those of course also had a profound impact.)

Attempting to assess Zinn's impact individually is a more difficult endeavor, and must of necessity be a preliminary one. Asked to do so, he has speculated some about his own importance. He feels sure that *A People's History of the United States* has had the greatest impact of his books. It is hard to argue with that considering its sales, the bulging folders related to it among his papers, and the continuing large number of speaking invitations he receives related to it. He believes, again correctly, that *The Politics of History* had the greatest effect on other history teachers. In a different vein, he feels that his 1967 *Vietnam: The Logic of Withdrawal*, as the first book to make the case for complete withdrawal, "served a need," and says that he has "run into people from time to time who tell me how important that book was to them." Considering that it went through eight printings in a very short time, he is surely justified in feeling that the book helped stimulate the movement that helped to end the war. More generally, and with typical modesty, Zinn says, "I feel good that I've stimulated, I feel I've always played some part in stimulating the production of new kinds of history."[7]

Assessing Zinn's impact is somewhat difficult for another reason. He clearly has not been a traditional historian, so that his contribution cannot be assessed in traditional ways. Staughton Lynd's essay in *Radical History Review* is again helpful here. "I believe that those who consider themselves radical historians need to grapple with the fact that Howard Zinn's *People's History of the United States* has probably done more good, and influenced more people (especially young people), than everything the rest of us have written put together." Excessive praise from a friend? Perhaps not. Lynd is even more helpful when he focuses on the nontraditional nature of Zinn's work. Why has Zinn's impact been so great, he wonders? His answer: Zinn's "indifference to the usual rewards and punishments of academia." Lynd remembers when he was a new faculty member in Zinn's department at Spelman asking Zinn "what scholarly papers he was writing and what academic conferences he planned to attend in the near future." Zinn "looked at me as if I were speaking a foreign language," Lynd recalls. What Lynd learned from that encounter, he says, is that "although Howard Zinn was *making a living* as a college professor," what "absorbed his intellectual attention" was how to relate the work he was doing in academia to broader social and political concerns, especially at that point the civil rights movement.[8]

Lynd is not the first to notice Zinn's "magical ability to make emotional contact with an audience." But he carries the point further: "Self-evidently, this gift stays by him when he writes. . . . Throughout, he has steadily directed what he had to say to an audience off campus, and thereby taught us all."[9]

Elsewhere, Lynd has said that he believes Zinn's importance is primarily as a popularizer. His original scholarly contributions are "not much cited, to my knowledge." His most important book, Lynd agrees with everyone, is the *People's History*, with *Vietnam: The Logic of Withdrawal* holding a solid second place. Neither of these, of course, constitutes a traditional scholarly work. "It seems to me your challenge is to rescue the notion of 'popularizer' from the adjective 'second-class,' not quite a real historian." But clearly, "You will do Howard Zinn a disservice if you try to present him as a pathbreaking original scholar. That has not been his importance."[10]

Another prominent figure on the left—and friend of Zinn—has evaluated Zinn's work quite similarly. Noam Chomsky has been a linguist at MIT, but for many years has been best known for his critique of U.S. foreign policy. Robert F. Barsky's biography, *Noam Chomsky: A Life of Dissent*, mentions Zinn several times. Interestingly, he reveals information about Chomsky that helps us observe both similarities and differences between the two friends. Chomsky is of Jewish immigrant parents, an optimist who has faith in the common people, has continued active in his radical causes over the course of a long life. He and Zinn have usually found themselves in agreement on important issues and have occupied the same stage many times, especially during the anti–Vietnam War movement. Barsky even suggests they are both "marginalized thinkers," though that seems a bit dubious, especially for Zinn. Differences include the fact that Zinn has not responded to his critics as often as Chomsky, and, perhaps most dramatic, the fact that Chomsky claims to be "superscrupulous at keeping my politics out of the classroom."[11]

There is no ambiguity when it comes to Chomsky's evaluation of Zinn's life and writings. Speaking specifically of Zinn's books, Chomsky agrees that *A People's History of the United States* is the most important;

further, he considers it "one of the most important and influential books of the past generation," for it "really changed the climate of opinion and opened the eyes of a whole generation." His praise is almost as strong for Zinn's 1967 Vietnam book. "Within a few years," claims Chomsky, "his arguments had sunk in and inspired a good part of the popular movement against the war." He makes the same case for Zinn's work on civil disobedience, 1968's *Disobedience and Democracy*. Chomsky's own importance—and his passion and eloquence in speaking of Zinn—make his overall assessment of Zinn worthy of quoting in full; he was asked "What do you think his contribution has been? To historical writing? To 'the movement'? Etc."

> His contributions have been in many dimensions. He was a pioneering figure in the study of the history of people, not just dominant elites and power systems: their lives and struggles, their aspirations and concerns, their victories and defeats. From that point of view, the whole of history looks quite different. In the case of the United States, in considerable measure thanks to his work, its history, domestically and in the international arena, is understood very differently from the doctrinal framework that prevailed 30 to 40 years ago; more realistically, in greater depth, and from a perspective that responds to elementary moral values. But that's only a fraction of his achievement. His scholarship is engaged, part of his daily life of engagement in struggles for justice, peace, and a more decent world in general. "Inspiring" is not a word I would use very freely, but he has really been an inspiring figure, in his work and in his life.[12]

Most historians, obviously, even those considered very important, never become widely known outside relatively narrow academic circles. Zinn's *People's History of the United States*, on the other hand, has sold well, been read by many nonacademics, and been adapted for high school use (the "Teaching Edition," with typically Zinnian questions, though he had nothing to do with them, at the end of each chapter, such as "What were the methods of control used by the Revolutionary elite to control disobedient and rebellious colonists?"). Wall charts have been designed to accompany it, it has been translated into several languages (including Spanish, Chinese, Japanese, and Hindi), a second edition has been published, the twentieth-century portions have been lifted out and printed as a separate volume, and, perhaps most surprising of all, it has been mentioned positively in an Academy Award–winning 1997 movie, *Good Will Hunting*.[13]

In the movie, Matt Damon as Will Hunting tells Robin Williams as his psychiatrist that unlike most history books Howard Zinn's *A People's History of the United States* "will knock you on your ass." The story behind the movie reference is an interesting one. Damon, costar and cowriter of the movie, set in working-class South Boston, was a neighbor of Howard Zinn and his family. Let Zinn tell the story. "We've known Matt since he was about five years old, when his mother, a divorced woman with two boys, was our next-door neighbor." The mother Zinn portrays as "a very politically savvy person who raised her boys with a deep social consciousness." Zinn thinks that social consciousness "shows best in the movie where Will Hunting (Matt) is being offered a job with the National Security Agency, and he goes into a fast-talking monologue about what would be the consequences for poor people in the Third World if he worked for them." Zinn concludes, tongue somewhat in cheek, that Damon recommends the *People's History* in his movie for two reasons: "that he is a politically aware young man; and that he is repaying me for the cookies I gave him when he came around to our place at the age of five." Damon invited the Zinns to the Boston premiere of the movie.[14]

The Zinn-Damon connection may well have another result that will spread Zinn's influence even further, onto television. According to *TV Guide*, Zinn, Damon, and others entered into negotiations with the Fox network to turn the *People's History* into a TV miniseries. The idea, stated one source, was "to take the book's irreverent take on American history and do a multipart dramatization of it."[15] According to Zinn, "There's not much to say beyond the *TV Guide* article. Negotiations are going on for Fox to take an option on the book for a miniseries. Anything can happen. Maybe [Rupert] Murdock, who owns Fox, will read my book and that will be the end!"[16] And maybe he did. For the latest word from Zinn, in the fall of 2002, is that "the TV series, with HBO [not Fox], is still alive, though moving very slowly. Two scripts are being written (on Columbus–Las Casas and on the American Revolution) and if HBO approves them they will be made into films, and then more episodes will follow."[17]

One traditional way of assessing the influence of a scholar is to look at other scholars he or she trained. Boston University did have a Ph.D. program in political science during Zinn's years there, and he did, according to his own report, direct a number of dissertations. Is it any surprise that Zinn's view of all this, however, is not the standard one? "I confess," he says, "I never liked dealing with doctoral dissertations because I've always considered the dissertation process an enormous waste of time. Years spent researching and writing, usually on an obscure topic, with the result seen only by a handful of people." He remembered two names, David Meyer, who did a dissertation on the nuclear freeze movement and "is teaching somewhere now," and John Tirman, who wrote on the ecology movement and became executive director of the Winston Foundation for World Peace in Boston,[18] and more recently program director for the Social Science Research Council.[19] Tirman edited the volume *Empty Promise: The Growing Case against Star Wars* for the Union of Concerned Scientists in 1986.[20]

Asked about students of his who became prominent in their respective fields, Zinn is more likely to emphasize Spelman College students such as Alice Walker, Marian Wright Edelman, and Herschelle Sullivan (who went on to receive a doctorate from Columbia University and to work for the United Nations in Africa), and Boston University students "who went on to take unorthodox jobs doing good things" such as setting up a center in Washington, D.C., that "file[s] lawsuits on behalf of whistle-blowers who have been fired from their jobs for blowing the whistle on corporate misdeeds and government misdeeds."[21]

It has been noted that an employee of the company that published *A People's History of the United States* has already referred to it as a modern classic. Perhaps it is too soon to say that of a book published only in 1980. But others have begun to use the "classic" label as well. Something called the *Independent Reader* on the Internet recently referred to it as "an acknowledged classic."[22] So what is a classic? "Of the highest rank or class. . . . Having lasting significance or recognized worth. . . . Of lasting historical or literary significance. . . . An artist, author, or work generally considered to be of the highest rank or excellence."[23] Maybe, after all, *A People's History of the United States* does already qualify.

Philadelphia's *City Paper* makes the case somewhat differently: "In less than two decades this radical revisionist tome has become an accepted part of the historical canon."[24] The *Utne Reader* has sometimes been called a left-wing *Reader's Digest*; its own subtitle carried on each issue is "The Best of the Alternative Media." It, too, has suggested that Zinn's *People's History* belongs in a new canon. Specifically, Jay Walljasper and Jon Spayde, in the May–June 1998 issue, present "The Loose Canon: 150 Great Works to Set Your Imagination on Fire." Included are books, movies, plays, television shows, and works of music "that broaden, deepen, or define the experience of being alive." *A People's History of the United States* is one of the books. Say Walljasper and Spayde: "From Columbus to corporate power, here's what your high school history teacher glossed over: bare-knuckled injustice and ruthless class bias that has sparked an impassioned tradition of resistance." A closer look at the criteria and motivation for this new canon suggests that Zinn's work certainly belongs. The goal was described by the editor, Hugh Delehanty, as "creating a new canon for the 21st century, a list of thought-provoking books, films, and works of music that, as one editor wryly put it, 'goes beyond the valley of the dead white males.'" And coauthor Jay Walljasper explains that "this is a post-angst list. It's about finding a third way." The first way, he says, is "thinking the status quo makes sense." The second way is "thinking 'No, things are terrible.'" The third way is "'Yes, you're right, the world doesn't make sense, but what are we going to do about it?'"[25] Certainly Zinn's philosophy of history is consistent with the third way.

One historian has suggested that Zinn's little book responding to Justice Abe Fortas, *Disobedience and Democracy: Nine Fallacies on Law and Order*, is also a classic, though not exactly using that word. It is, he says, "the greatest political tract of the twentieth century, rivaling Tom Paine's 'Common Sense' but lacking the historical framework for Paine's fame." This same historian is eloquent and passionate in his praise of Zinn's work overall. Zinn, he says, is "one of the most important American historians of the twentieth century. His writings, his modeling, his spirit, his courage—who else has done as much? His modesty and humility and his refusal to write pop crap like 1,000 (or is it 100?) Things You Should Know About American History . . . has not made him a 'popular' well-known historian among lay folks. And, of course, 'real' historians, in most instances, see him as an ideologue and miss the import of his life and analysis of things American."[26]

That is strong praise indeed, though not at all out of line. Perhaps we should take issue with the idea that mainstream historians dismiss Zinn as an ideologue and fail to see the import of his work; that is clearly true of some historians, but not all, as evidenced by some of the reviews of Zinn's books, and even more by the sales of such a volume as the *People's History*, sales which are so high in part because of classroom adoptions. Perhaps we should also take issue somewhat with the suggestion that Zinn is not well known among "lay folks," for recent events, including the reference to the *People's History* in the movie *Good Will Hunting* and the *TV Guide* coverage of negotiations hopefully leading toward a television miniseries, have probably made Zinn's name better known than most academic historians.

What other historian has been profiled in *Rolling Stone*? "Howard Zinn's Rage Against the Machine," it was called, in reference to both his radical stance and a popular rock and roll band called Rage Against the Machine who are "overtly revolutionary and . . . big on arming the peasants and storming the citadels of power." The feature includes a pretty good interview with Zinn, but covers topics basically covered everywhere else. Most interesting is *Rolling Stone*'s claim (the article was written by Charles M. Young) that for four decades Zinn has been "changing the way we think about our past." Specifically, his *Vietnam: The Logic of Withdrawal* had been "influential," along with his "twin bill" appearances with Noam Chomsky. Zinn would "soften up the crowds, making an unthinkable war discussable with his perfectly timed sense of humor," then Chomsky would "flatten them with his devastating critiques of American foreign policy." Zinn's *People's History* was considered by *Rolling Stone* a "monumental contribution to the teaching and perception of our history. . . . For anyone who suspects but doesn't quite have proof of the vast and savage lies that infect our national self-image, the relief of reading *A People's History* is almost physical." Zinn and his *People's History* "launched a whole new industry of teaching history 'from the bottom up.'" Finally, *Rolling Stone* even claimed that "when the right gets jazzed about 'political correctness' among history teachers, they are referring in large measure to the influence of Zinn."

Zinn said more in that interview about the political correctness phenomenon, the question of the impact of the 1960s and its various movements (and by implication his own influence), and hope for the future. "You can tell the 1960s are still reverberating on campus because the extreme right is hysterical about what it calls political correctness and multicultural education," he says. "It's quite justified in getting hysterical. And that should make the rest of us happy." Political correctness, Zinn says further, is "one of those propaganda terms like 'welfare.' It has no content." What is important, he thinks, "is that now thousands of history teachers around the country are teaching their lessons in a different way than they did in decades past." He supposes "that's why the right is in such a furor, which you could say is depressing. But you might also say, 'Isn't it encouraging that something is getting their goat?'" Apparently referring to the U.S. Senate's vote to condemn the proposed national history standards, Zinn says, "The Senate recently passed a resolution 99–1 saying that as a nation we must in our history teaching extol the virtues of Western civilization. That must mean there are a lot of people not extolling the virtues of Western civilization. Now *that's* cause for optimism."[27]

Appearance in *Rolling Stone* is surely a rarity for an academic historian; similarly, few academic historians would be chosen as subjects for interview by rock stars. But when Eddie Vedder, lead singer/songwriter of the popular rock-'n'-roll band Pearl Jam, was given the opportunity to interview someone for (Andy Warhol's) *Interview* magazine in 1999, he chose Howard Zinn. Zinn was impressed with Vedder as a "really nice guy," noted that they shared a "working-class background," and even tentatively recruited him to write a song and/or perform for the *People's History* TV series.[28] As for the interview itself, Zinn, interestingly, actually asks most of the questions. Little new emerges, not surprisingly, but it is a fun read, and it is somewhat interesting that Vedder read *A People's History*—and Zinn attended a Pearl Jam concert. The editors are not really wrong in saying that while rocker Vedder and historian Zinn lead very different lives, "their conversation here shows there's no greater bridge than a desire to shake up the status quo."[29]

Zinn was an interesting choice, in 1997, to represent the academic discipline of history in a volume entitled *The Cold War and the University: Toward an Intellectual History of the Postwar Years*, a collection of essays examining the effects of the Cold War on various university departments. But while one might be tempted to conclude that he was chosen because of his prestige in the field, one should also take note of the volume's nature, published as it was by the New Press, a not-for-profit alternative to the large commercial publishers established in 1990. The New Press compares itself to the Public Broadcasting System and National Public Radio "as they were originally conceived," and lists as one of its aims "to bring out the work of traditionally underrepresented voices."[30] Noam Chomsky is also included among the authors in the volume.

In any case, Zinn's contribution, entitled (revealingly), "The Politics of History in the Era of the Cold War: Repression and Resistance," is direct, and deeply personal. He recounts the story of a 1949 automobile trip with his wife, six months pregnant, and their two-year-year-old daughter to an outdoor Paul Robeson and Pete Seeger concert near Peekskill, New York; on the way out, hostile crowds threw rocks, breaking all the windows in their car. And he tells the story of his and his wife's painful and later regretted decision to burn all their letters to each other from the war years because they had mentioned friends involved in the Communist movement. He relates, again, his travels to North Vietnam, including with Fr. Daniel Berrigan in 1968 to receive three American pilots being freed by the Vietnamese. And he writes again of the FBI's interest in his activities.

Zinn even remembers, from his childhood, Charles Dickens's *Hard Times*, specifically the character Mr. Gradgrind admonishing a young teacher to "teach these boys and girls nothing but facts." This latter is in connection with an excellent brief overview Zinn gives of the historio-graphical background for radical or revisionist history. He acknowledges, for example, Charles Beard as a forerunner and the "seminal work" of William Appleman Williams in breaking from the benign interpretation of American foreign policy. Zinn concluded his chapter by referring, with apparent pride, to the existence of what conservatives have labeled with apprehension a "permanent adversarial culture." Said Zinn: "In that adversarial culture, the new history had come to play an important part."[31] As, of course, Zinn had played an important part in the new history—and the broader adversarial culture.

When the New Press began publication not long ago of a People's History Series, the logical choice for a series editor was Howard Zinn. (So far there is only one volume in the series, Ray Raphael's *A People's History of the American Revolution*.) And when South End Press began a Radical '60s Series, reprinting works they considered seminal and still worthy of attention, the first seven (yes, seven) volumes announced in the series were by Howard Zinn: *SNCC: The New Abolitionists*, *The Southern Mystique*, *Vietnam: The Logic of Withdrawal*, *Disobedience and Democracy*, *Postwar America*, *Justice in Everyday Life*, and *Failure to Quit*.

If it is true, as Zinn has suggested, that you cannot be neutral on a moving train, it is also true that people seem unable to be neutral about Howard Zinn and his approach to history. Among those who do know his name, mention of it provokes strong response, whether positive or negative. After hearing a lecture that merely presented Zinn's views on American history, one historian responded that Zinn seemed "so angry." When Zinn himself goes into a town to lecture, he has an impact; people talk for years about it. "Did you hear Howard Zinn when he was here?" "I thought he was really extreme on freedom of speech." "I thought everything he said was true."[32] But anger is hardly the dominant tone of Zinn's work. And his intent, after all, a part of it anyway, is to provoke not just discussion, but also action.

"Who controls the past controls the future. Who controls the present controls the past." That is from George Orwell, of course. Zinn and other radicals control neither the past nor the present. But the sales of Zinn's books, especially the *People's History*, the thousands of people who have heard him lecture, both in and out of the classroom, and the testimonials that fill those folders among his papers, all suggest that he has had an important, for many people a profound, impact. Is it too much to suggest that this will lead to even more influence in/on the future? Bill Harvey, reviewing Zinn's *Failure to Quit: Reflections of an Optimistic Historian* in 1993, said that Zinn "has spent nearly 40 years working to help wrest control of the present and future, by way of an examination of the past, from the rich and powerful who dominate our society." Harvey considers Zinn "one of the most cutting and affable thinkers of our time," and says that "what he does best" is "to puncture the myths of ideological power and to try to bring our understanding of the past (and present) more into line with the lived experience of the majority of the people."[33]

Zinn, in the introduction to his 1997 collection, *The Zinn Reader*, looking back specifically on the essay comparing the abolitionists with 1960s activists that he had written for Martin Duberman's *The Anti-Slavery Vanguard*, said this was "an approach I was going to use again and again—to find wisdom and inspiration from the past for movements seeking social justice in our time."[34] Zinn has found wisdom and inspiration enough to keep him going his entire adult life; more, he has shared it with, provided it to, many others. Explaining better than anywhere else the title for his 1994 memoir, he wrote in that same introduction: "As I told my students at the start of my courses, 'You can't be neutral on a moving train.' That is, the world is already moving in certain directions—many of them horrifying. Children are going hungry, people are dying in wars. To be neutral in such a situation is to collaborate with what is going on. The word 'collaborator' had a deadly meaning in the Nazi era. It should have that meaning still."[35] Zinn has not been a collaborator.

"No other radical historian has reached so many hearts and minds as Howard Zinn," claimed the Boston University Bookstore trying to sell copies of the *Reader*, a claim also made on the back of the book itself. Hyperbole? Perhaps in part; at least not something that can be readily verified at this point in time. But surely the statement contains an element of truth.

Still another reviewer, this time of *You Can't Be Neutral on a Moving Train*, went beyond the book itself to comment on Zinn's career and contribution. Zel Levin, writing in the *Cape Codder Summery*, said *You Can't Be Neutral* was "a must-read book," then: "In an ideal world, war would be obsolete, the equality of 'all men' would be unquestioned and a program of jobs, health care, housing, and education would be implemented without political maneuvering." Noting that that day obviously has not arrived, Levin concluded, "but don't blame Mr. Zinn. No one has tried harder, and this book may serve as a catalyst in speeding change for the better."[36] Probably no one has tried harder, and perhaps Zinn's entire life and body of work can serve as such a catalyst.

In *You Can't Be Neutral*, Zinn remembers the "joy and pride" he felt when he was a teenager reading books and writing reviews of them for himself on the rebuilt typewriter his parents bought him.[37] Pride and joy in reading and learning. Those who teach today wish they saw more of that in their students. Howard Zinn has not only felt it himself, throughout his life, he has also helped to foster it in many others, no small contribution.

We have mentioned sales of Zinn's *People's History* several times. To be specific, it has now sold over 1,000,000 copies! Few historians accomplish that. And the pattern of sales is incredible if not unique—since publication in 1980, it has sold more copies each year than the year before. James Green, reporting on the recent celebration of Zinn's milestone at the Ninety-second Street YMCA in New York, emphasized that the book's appeal went well beyond academic circles. It was, he suggested, "probably the only book by a radical historian that you can buy in an airport." Specifically, its treatment of Columbus is "so famous that it found its way into a script of *The Sopranos* last fall." Finally, Green notes that Zinn, ever-willing to criticize himself and to change with the times, has expressed some regret that the *People's History* was not multicultural enough because it slights the struggles of Latinos for justice in the West and of gays and lesbians for equal rights.[38]

Shawn Setaro, in something called *Instant* on the Internet, recently became another to make a sweeping claim for Zinn and his *People's History*; it was, he said, "a book that almost single-handedly reshaped the way American history is thought of and taught." Typically, Zinn, in the interview Setaro conducted with him, was more modest about his contributions. Setaro quoted Zinn: "As one of the many whose contribution to society is so indirect, so uncertain, I thought of those who give immediate help. I thought of the Chilean poet Pablo Neruda, who wrote a poem about his life-long wish that he could do something useful with his hands—that he could make a broom, just a broom." Then Setaro said to Zinn that this was "a real surprising sentiment for a person who is as tirelessly [committed] to social change as yourself," and asked, "Had you ever considering [*sic*] becoming, or have you become, one of those people who give immediate help?" Zinn's answer:

No, I wish I could say that I did. Only in small ways; that is, I communicate with people in prison, and I try to help them. For instance, there are people in prison who write, and they have a hard time getting their writings out. I try to be helpful to them. Of course, just communicating with people in prison, you are being helpful in the sense that they need contact with the outside world. So I suppose in small ways I've tried to be of immediate help to people.

However, it's still true that most of my work consists of what I describe as you throw ideas and information out in the world and you hope that it will have an effect. I suppose when you get active politically in a movement, you are doing something more immediate than when you are writing something, and you hope that the writing will help. I recently was involved a little bit in the movement to defeat the restoration of capital punishment in Massachusetts. I participated—I spoke at meetings, appeared at a press conference, and added my voice to the voice of others. We did defeat, by one vote, the bill to restore capital punishment in Massachusetts. So how direct a help is that? It's halfway between the indirect help of writing and the direct help of going into prison and helping somebody escape [laughs]. And if I speak and somebody writes to me later and says, you've inspired me to become politically active and to join organizations, well then, I suppose that's indirect activity, except you might consider it direct activity in the sense that you maybe changed the direction of somebody's life, and given them something immediate if they should now look upon the world differently that [sic] they did before.[39]

That answer has a poignant quality about it, as well as a modesty (and, of course, humor) that is remarkable coming from one who surely has been as important in as many different movements for social change as almost anyone still around in the United States at the end of the century.

Setaro asked two other questions of Zinn to which Zinn's answers are helpful in any effort at an assessment of Zinn's life and work. First, Setaro asked Zinn what had happened to the "fresh generation of radicals" he had written about in the 1970s. Mentioning teachers "who are teaching differently than the schoolteachers of thirty years ago," "progressive lawyers" who are "following in the footsteps of William Kunstler and the handful of radical lawyers we had available in the early 1960s," and physicians who are now active in such organizations as Physicians for Social Responsibility and International Physicians Against Nuclear War, Zinn concluded that "many of the people who were activists in the 1960s and early 70s are still activists today, but less visible because they're not part of a national movement. Yet they are still doing good work in many, many different ways." And second, reminding Zinn of his claim that many people when asked what changed their lives would give a one-word answer, Setaro said, "I was just wondering what yours was." Said Zinn:

Well, that's a tough question. I said for a lot of people there was one word. I'm not sure if there's one word for me. Maybe "fascism." I was growing up in a world in which fascism was encroaching, and I was finding fascism not just in the Axis powers of World War II, but finding elements of fascism in what is called democratic government or in the marketplace or in prisons or in racist institutions, and becoming aware of it. I always think of fascism as bullying, and I was finding that as a constant antagonist in my life—the bully, whether on a national scale or a local scale, in the workplace or in an educational institution, or in the form of police. That's as close as I can come to a sort of central thread, and that, I think, accounts for my ways of thinking and being.[40]

In another place Zinn had said, not inconsistently, that *The Zinn Reader* carried the subtitle *Writings on Disobedience and Democracy* because that "comes close to summing up many of my ideas."[41]

One does not have to look too closely at Howard Zinn's body of work to see that optimism is a recurrent theme also; perhaps his unique concept of optimism also helps to sum up his ideas. It comes up repeatedly in his writing, his speaking, in these pages. He has said it so many times in so many ways in so many places. And people have repeatedly reminded him of it, asked him about it (sometimes in a very skeptical manner, as in "How can you possibly still be optimistic?"), thanked him for it.

Ron Kovic wrote in 1994 to tell Zinn how "important and inspirational you have been to me. You are a wonderful person," he continued. "How can words even begin to express what you have meant to our country and to the millions of people who have been touched by your teachings and your work. Your students, your colleagues and friends, both here in the United States and around the world," Kovic effervesced, "will never forget you. You have truly made your life stand for something important. Your service to others has been nothing less than inspirational. You have given us hope and strength, provided us with the faith to go on, instilled in us a spirit and confidence which are essential to the eventual victory of all people who fight against injustice and strive to make this world a better place."[42]

Fellow historian Richard Drinnon, after reading *You Can't Be Neutral on a Moving Train*, wrote in a similar vein, "You're the only revolutionary I know who can propose turning the world topsy-turvy without raising his voice." And: "You know that I have not been able to be as hopeful as you in these bad times. But your exemplary career and enduring courage give me hope. Thank you for that."[43]

Still another correspondent wrote, this time responding specifically to

Failure to Quit, to say, "I love your humor. To be reading about the horrors of our history and our times, our world, and still be able to laugh—that makes it possible, I think, to take in what you have to say because it becomes human, not something we turn away from because it is too terribly heavy to bear." But also: "And you have hope, and give me hope, which is the greatest thing of all."[44]

As usual, Zinn's own words are the best way to deal with this optimism factor. It shows up at numerous points in his writings, and, especially since 1993, when he chose to entitle a book *Failure to Quit: Reflections of an Optimistic Historian*, he seems to expect to have to deal with it in every question-and-answer session following a lecture (whatever the topic of the lecture might be) and in every interview. Two essays in *Failure to Quit* raise the issue of optimism, the title essay and one called, significantly, "The Optimism of Uncertainty," dated 1988, the year of Zinn's retirement from teaching, and appearing originally in *Z* magazine. Zinn introduced the latter essay by saying, "The word 'optimism,' used here, and in the subtitle of my book, makes me a little uneasy, because it suggests a blithe, slightly sappy whistler in the dark of our time. But I use it anyway, not because I am totally confident that the world will get better, but because I am certain that *only* such confidence can prevent people from giving up the game before all the cards have been played." What an interesting metaphor; but it is deliberate, Zinn continued, for "it is a gamble. Not to play is to foreclose any chance of winning. To play, to *act*, is to create at least a possibility of changing the world. I wrote this essay to show that there is some evidence in support of that possibility."

In the essay itself, Zinn presents his usual litany of historical examples of people organizing and accomplishing great things, despite the odds, except that this time they are not limited to the United States. All this "evidence of unpredictably in human affairs," he says, leads to two important conclusions. "The first is that the struggle for justice should never be abandoned because of the apparent overwhelming power of those who have the guns and the money and who seem invincible in their determination to hold on to it." That apparent power, over and over, has "proved vulnerable to human qualities less measurable than bombs and dollars: moral fervor, determination, unity, organization, sacrifice, wit, ingenuity, courage, patience." So, "No cold calculation of the balance of power need deter people who are persuaded that their cause is just." The second conclusion is that, "in the face of the manifest unpredictability of social phenomena, all of history's excuses for war and preparation for war—self-defense, national security, freedom, justice, stopping aggression—can no longer be accepted." This includes civil war. In short, massive violence "cannot be justified by any end, however noble, *because no outcome is sure.*"[45] The optimism of uncertainty.

The title essay in *Failure to Quit* approaches optimism somewhat differently. "I can understand pessimism, but I don't believe in it," Zinn begins. To take that interesting stance, he insists, is "not simply a matter of faith, but of historical evidence. Not overwhelming evidence, just enough to give hope, because for hope we don't need certainty, only possibility." This essay grew specifically out of dealing with his students at Boston University during the 1980s and failing to find "the apathy, the conservatism, the disregard for the plight of others, that everybody (right and left) was reporting about 'the me generation.'" Zinn's conclusion seems rather cautiously—dare we say realistically?—optimistic. "Surely history does not start anew with each decade. The roots of one era branch and flower in subsequent eras. Human beings, writings, invisible transmitters of all kinds, carry messages across the generations." Harking back to his opening sentence, Zinn says, "I try to be pessimistic, to keep up with some of my friends. But I think back over the decades, and look around. And then it seems to me that the future is not certain, but it is possible."[46]

In one of the profiles of Zinn done by a BU student in 1987, just before he retired, the student asked him, "How do you remain optimistic rather than cynical?" Zinn smiled and answered with a question, "How do you know I'm optimistic?" The student suggested, "You must be if you're doing all you do." Said Zinn: "What makes me optimistic is, well, I guess two things, maybe several things, I'll just mention a few. One is I've gone through the experience, twice, of seeing a movement build up from what seemed to be nothing, into a movement that was very big, important, and shook the nation and changed things." He went on to talk at some length about the civil rights movement and the anti–Vietnam War movement.[47]

In a more recent interview, almost a decade into his retirement, Zinn held on to those views, and elaborated upon them. Reminded of the title of his 1993 book, *Failure to Quit: Reflections of an Optimistic Historian*, and asked, "What does that mean to you, and are you still optimistic?" he responded at some length, in a rather run-on fashion, but in a manner that provides great insight into what he means by optimism:

> Well, optimistic not in the sense that I am certain that everything will turn out okay. But optimistic only in the sense that I think there is a good chance that things will turn out to be okay. As I said, I don't predict for

the future, whether things will be good or bad, because I think that things are so uncertain, that I have—here, I think, history is instructive. So many things have happened which we could never have predicted, bad things and good things, and so, who would have predicted in Germany in the 1920s that Hitler would rise to power? And who would have predicted that in South Africa that Mandela would become president? So, I believe in the volatility of events and that people, to move things one way or the other, very often, not deliberately but by actions, each action may be deliberate, but the totality of the actions don't have any guiding, and somebody once talked about the natural selection of accidents, and so I believe that we have enough examples of history and good surprises taking place to suggest that we can have more of them, but it depends on what we do. And it depends on doing things, no matter how small our actions are, having the kind of faith that if enough people take enough small actions that at some point they may come together in some great change which is desirable. I guess basically I believe that there is no reason to be optimistic if we just stand by and do nothing, and if we do something, there is some possibility.[48]

That hardly seems like blind optimism, but rather a realistic optimism grounded in historical facts. People have made good things happen, and therefore might be able to make more good things happen. It is all based on hope (and action); it looks to possibilities but not to certainties.

Zinn evinces that brand of optimism not just in general but in specific situations. One of the many speeches he gave in 1998 was at the University of Georgia in Athens, where, he said, "a large crowd responded enthusiastically to what I had to say about war and other matters. It was refreshing to think back to what Athens, Georgia, was like twenty-five years ago. We have made progress!"[49] He even finds hope in the attacks by the right on the kind of history he does. "If history weren't so important," he says, "people wouldn't get so upset by it." Zack Stenz, who quotes Zinn on this matter, says correctly that Zinn "has dedicated his life to the notion that the knowledge of history is important to people's everyday lives, and can be a powerful force for social change." Zinn admits, notes Stenz, that "the current American landscape of temporary workers, multinational corporations, and citizens' increasing isolation from one another hinders the formation of his cherished mass movements." Again he quotes Zinn: "Building a movement is difficult, given the fragmentation and isolation of people today and just the very diverse nature of the United States. But when people's outrage is felt strongly enough, a new social movement will be born." Notice: "will be born." Stenz concludes his piece with one more quote from Zinn: "I *am* hopeful. But hope rests on doing something. If you're not doing anything to change things, you have no right to be hopeful."[50] The right to be hopeful. Now there is an interesting idea.

Writing a biography of someone, an author is likely to become obsessed (biographer's disease, some call it), and, among other things, to see connections where others might not see them—but hopefully not where they do not exist. Reading Andrew Burstein's *The Inner Jefferson: Portrait of a Grieving Optimist* while working on this biography of Zinn was reve- latory. Burstein quotes Jefferson (from a letter to John Adams, late in both their lives): "It is a good world on the whole . . . framed on a principle of benevolence, and more pleasure than pain dealt out to us. I steer my bark with Hope in the head, leaving Fear astern. My hopes indeed sometimes fail; but not oftener than the forebodings of the gloomy."[51] Howard Zinn chooses to live in hope rather than fear as well. Writes Burstein: "Jef- ferson's optimism urged the removal of strict social distinctions, extolled government by consent, the broadening of citizens' rights, and the careful scrutiny of public officials on the basis of their disinterestedness and benev- olence: the values of 1776."[52] Zinn's vision is clearly grounded in the ideals of 1776 also. The final sentence of Burstein's book suggests that "Jef- ferson's optimism endures in the minds of Americans and others who con- tinue to search for happiness."[53]

Howard Zinn is one of those Americans. For Howard Zinn has evinced throughout his life and writings a radical American vision.

It is radical because it seeks to bring about fundamental change in the political, social, economic order, to get to the roots.

It is American because it is firmly grounded in the ideals on which the United States of America was founded, the ideals of the Declaration of Independence, such ideals as life and liberty and the pursuit of happiness and equality and self-determination that are so self-evident and inherent that no government has the right to take them away; much of Zinn's ver- sion of American history is the story of a continuing effort, still by no means complete, to live up to those ideals in reality. When David Barsamian asked Zinn a question about "left values," the first thing he thought of was socialism. Left values, he insisted, were egalitarian values. "If I had to say what is at the center of left values, it's the idea that everyone has a fundamental right to the necessary things of life and the good things of life, that there should be no disproportions in the world." But Zinn also thought of the Declaration of Independence. "The principles of the Decla- ration of Independence—even though it was not written by a leftist—

Thomas Jefferson, a leftist?—the idea that everybody has an equal right to life, liberty, and the pursuit of happiness, to me is a remarkable statement of left values."[54]

Finally, it is a vision because indeed it is not yet a reality but a hope. But visions do not become reality through mere hope. Much work is required. Howard Zinn has done his share.

A single sheet of paper was found among the papers in Zinn's office, unattached to anything else. On it were very few words. At the top, like an intended title for something: "The Biggest Secret." Only one line followed: "That we have power."[55] That seems to be related to a passage from his book, *Declarations of Independence*, in which Zinn says that "a fundamental principle of democracy" is that "it is the citizenry, rather than the government, that is the ultimate source of power and the locomotive that pulls the train of government in the direction of equality and justice."[56] And that seems to be a concept close to the heart of Zinn's life and work.

At the end of a 1991 essay, "Law, Justice, and Disobedience," Zinn asked a series of questions. "What kind of person can we admire, can we ask young people of the next generation to emulate—the strict follower of law, or the dissident who struggles, sometimes within, sometimes outside, sometimes against the law, but always for justice? What life is best worth living, the life of the proper, obedient, dutiful follower of law and order, or the life of the independent thinker, the rebel?" By now, his answer should be obvious. But he answered here in an interesting and effective manner— by quoting Tolstoy. In his story, "The Death of Ivan Ilyich," Tolstoy told of a proper, successful magistrate, who on his deathbed wondered why he suddenly felt that his life had been horrible and senseless. "Maybe I did not live as I ought to have done. . . . But how could that be, when I did everything properly?" he wondered. And, concluded Tolstoy, he then "remembered all the legality, correctitude, and propriety of his life."[57] Zinn should not have that particular problem on his deathbed.

Much earlier in his career, in 1969, Zinn had speculated about the role of the "Historian as Citizen." "In a world hungry for solutions, we ought to welcome the emergence of the historian—if this is really what we are seeing—as an activist-scholar, who thrusts himself and his works into the crazy mechanism of history, on behalf of values in which he deeply believes. This makes of him more than a scholar; it makes him a citizen in the ancient Athenian sense of the word."[58]

Zinn himself has been a citizen in that broader sense for eighty years. He has played, for virtually his entire adult life, the role that radicals have always played historically. They are always out there—outside the mainstream, redefining the mainstream—raising the hard questions, pulling the rest of society along, sometimes kicking and screaming. The abolitionists of the 1830s and the women's rights advocates of the 1840s are just the two most obvious examples from American history. Even those who do not define themselves as radical, by very definition the majority of any given group of people, can usually be brought to acknowledge the important role radicals play, the changes they help bring about from which all people eventually benefit. It can even be argued, without doing violence to the definition of any of the terms, that Zinn is a radical/patriot/historian. For radical suggests getting to the root of something; and patriot means of our fathers, thus suggesting getting back to the basic principles, for example, the Declaration of Independence, upon which this country was founded; and history has as one of its root words, *historia*, to inquire—no limits, to inquire! Zinn's inquiry has left us a legacy that respects all people, that insists all people are a part of history, not just the presidents and kings and queens and generals and the rich. If his focus has often been on the common people, and even more on those who have worked to bring about fundamental change, that is simply because those people were for so long excluded from history (or ridiculed when included).

David Barsamian brought Zinn out well—not that it is particularly difficult to bring Zinn out—on many subjects in the excellent series of interviews entitled *The Future of History*. "Clearly it's too soon to talk about a Zinn legacy," said Barsamian (in 1998), "but I was wondering if you could speculate on that." Zinn's response, a typical blend of humor and seriousness, the personal and the philosophical, deserves quoting in full—and provides a fitting conclusion:

> I don't think it's too soon to talk about a legacy. I think we should have started talking about it a long time ago, maybe when I was ten years old. A Zinn legacy. What do I leave? I think the best legacy one can leave is people. I can say, I would like to leave a legacy of books, and yes, there are writings that have an effect on people and it's good to think that you've written something that has made people think, and think about their lives. When I say legacy is people, I guess I mean people have been affected by reading, by your life, or people you've encountered. The best kind of legacy you can leave is a kind of example of how one should live one's life, not that I've lived my life in an exemplary way, but let's put it this way, people should be very selective about what they look at in my life. If I were to single out, as I would be prone to do, only the good

things, I would think of the necessity to work at changing the world and at the same time maintain a kind of decency towards all the people around you. So that what you are striving for in the future is acted out in the present in your human relations.[59]

NOTES

1. This author, among others, did so in Michael Kraus and Davis D. Joyce, *The Writing of American History* (Norman: University of Oklahoma Press, 1985).

2. Howard Zinn, interview, Boston, Mass., March 14, 1997.

3. Howard Zinn, *The Politics of History* (Boston: Beacon Press, 1970), pp. 47–51.

4. Material on the Internet from The Historical Society, P.O. Box 382602, Cambridge, MA 02238-2602; Howard Zinn, e-mail message to the author, June 21, 1998.

5. Staughton Lynd, e-mail message to the author, August 6, 2000.

6. Staughton Lynd, "Reflections on Radical History," pp. 104–107; NUC reference, p. 56; Du Bois reference, p. 92—all in *Radical History Review* 79 (winter 2001).

7. Zinn, interview, March 14, 1997.

8. Lynd, "Reflections on Radical History," pp. 105–106.

9. Ibid.

10. Staughton Lynd, e-mail message to the author, August 6, 2000.

11. Robert F. Barsky, *Noam Chomsky: A Life of Dissent* (Cambridge, Mass.: MIT Press, 1998), pp. 224, 199, and 121.

12. Noam Chomsky, e-mail message to the author, July 29, 2000.

13. Howard Zinn, *A People's History of the United States*, teaching ed. (New York: New Press, 1997), p. 78; Howard Zinn and George Kirschner, *A People's History of the United States: The Wall Charts* (New York: New Press, 1995); Howard Zinn, *The Twentieth Century: A People's History* (New York: Harper and Row, 1984).

14. Howard Zinn, e-mail message to the author, February 17, 1998.

15. J. Max Robins, "The Robins Report: Damon and Affleck to Make *History?*" *TV Guide*, June 20–26, 1998, p. 37.

16. Howard Zinn, e-mail message to the author, June 21, 1998.

17. Howard Zinn, e-mail message to the author, October 7, 2002.

18. Howard Zinn, e-mail message to the author, July 20, 1998.

19. John Tirman, e-mail message to the author, December 9, 2001.

20. John Tirman, ed., *Empty Promise: The Growing Case against Star Wars* (Boston: Beacon Press, 1986).

21. Zinn, interview, March 14, 1997.

22. *Independent Reader*, May 1998, http://www.indpendentreader.com/books/bp098.html.

23. *American Heritage Dictionary*, 2d college ed.

24. "Howard Zinn: Interview by Sam Adams," *Philadelphia City Paper Interactive*, May 5, 1998, http://www.citypaper.net/articles/012298/20Q.Zinn.shtml.

25. Jay Walljasper and Jon Spayde, "The Loose Canon: 150 Great Works to Set Your Imagination on Fire," *Utne Reader* (May–June 1998): 56; and Hugh Delehanty, "The Cosmic Jaywalker," ibid., p. 5.

26. Charles Angeletti, e-mail messages to the author, February 26 and August 6, 1998.

27. Charles M. Young, "Howard Zinn's Rage Against the Machine," *Rolling Stone*, October 17, 1996, pp. 93–94, 98, 100–101.

28. Howard Zinn, e-mail message to the author, February 25, 1999.

29. "This Month's Jam Session: The Rocker and the Teacher," *Interview*, March 1999, pp. 48, 50, 174.

30. Information on the New Press is from their Web site, http://www.thenewpress.com/.

31. Howard Zinn, "The Politics of History in the Era of the Cold War: Repression and Resistance," in *The Cold War and the University: Toward an Intellectual History of the Postwar Years*, ed. Noam Chomsky et al. (New York: New Press, 1997), pp. 35–72.

32. These comments are based on a lecture the author gave, actually in England, just after Zinn's *People's History* appeared, and Zinn's visit to the author's home town at the time, Ada, Oklahoma.

33. Bill Harvey, review of *Failure to Quit* by Howard Zinn, *Baltimore Chronicle* (October 1993): 3–4.

34. Howard Zinn, *The Zinn Reader: Writings on Disobedience and Democracy* (New York: Seven Stories Press, 1997), p. 16.

35. Ibid., p. 17.

36. Zel Levin, review of *You Can't Be Neutral on a Moving Train* by Howard Zinn, *Cape Codder Summery*, August 9, 1994, pp. 4, 16.

37. Howard Zinn, *You Can't Be Neutral on a Moving Train: A Personal History of Our Times* (Boston: Beacon Press, 1994), p. 170.

38. James Green, "Howard Zinn's History," *Chronicle of Higher Education* (May 23, 2003): B13–B14.

39. Shawn Setaro, "A People's View of Howard Zinn," *Instant* May 5, 1998, http://www.instantmag.com/articles/zinn.htm.

40. Ibid.

41. Howard Zinn, e-mail message to the author, March 19, 1998.

42. Letter to Howard Zinn from Ron Kovic, October 28, 1994, Howard Zinn Papers.

43. Letter to Howard Zinn from Richard Drinnon, October 19, 1994, Howard Zinn Papers.

44. Letter to Howard Zinn from "Ruth," September 5, 1993.

45. Howard Zinn, *Failure to Quit: Reflections of an Optimistic Historian* (Monroe, Maine: Common Courage Press, 1993), pp. 23, 26–27.

46. Ibid., pp. 157, 164.

47. Wendy Gillespie, "Howard Zinn: A Profile," November 23, 1987, Howard Zinn Papers.

48. Zinn, interview, March 14, 1997.

49. Howard Zinn, e-mail message to the author, February 24, 1998.

50. Zack Stenz, "Mighty Zinn: Howard Zinn brings his passion for history to Sonoma County," *Sonoma Independent*, April 18–24, 1996, http://www.metro active.com/papers/sonoma/04.18.96/books-9616.html.

51. Andrew Burstein, *The Inner Jefferson: Portrait of a Grieving Optimist* (Charlottesville: University Press of Virginia, 1995), p. 257.

52. Ibid., p. 278.

53. Ibid., p. 291.

54. Howard Zinn, *The Future of History: Interviews with David Barsamian* (Monroe, Maine: Common Courage Press, 1999), p. 55.

55. Howard Zinn Papers.

56. Howard Zinn, *Declarations of Independence: Cross-Examining American Ideology* (New York: HarperCollins, 1990), p. 62.

57. Howard Zinn, "Law, Justice and Disobedience," *Notre Dame Journal of Law, Ethics and Public Policy* 5 (1991): 920.

58. Howard Zinn, "Historian as Citizen," *Page 2: The Best of "Speaking of Books" from The New York Times Book Review* (New York: Holt, Rinehart and Winston, 1969), p. 77.

59. Zinn, *The Future of History*, p. 146.

INDEX

Abernathy, Ralph, 104
abolitionists
    new abolitionists, 59–60, 66–67, 70,
        206
    Reconstruction era, 67, 70, 162
"Abolitionists, Freedom Riders, and
    the Tactics of Agitation," in *The
    Anti-Slavery Vanguard*, 206
Active Service in War and Peace, On
    (Lemisch), 213
Ad Hoc Committee for a True Univer-
    sity, 87
aggressive unilateralism, 10
Air Force. *See* Zinn, Howard, Air
    Force years
Alinsky, Saul, 150
al Qaeda, 10
    See also terrorism
America (review), 123–24

American Association of University
    Professors, 73, 86
American Book Award, 178
American Dream, Global Nightmare
    (Vogelgesang), 175
American Heritage Series, 74, 77
American Historical Association,
    54–55, 118
    Beveridge Award, 48
American Historical Review (reviews),
    54, 55
American ideology. *See Declarations
    of Independence: Cross-Exam-
    ining American Ideology*
American Indians. *See* Native Americans
American Journal of Orthopsychiatry,
    "Non-violent Direct Action," 209
American Political Science Associa-
    tion, 9

American Political Science Review
　(review), 54, 122
American Political Tradition, The
　(Hofstadter), 41–42, 63–64, 114,
　167–68
　consensus approach, 122, 213, 231
American Revolution, 159–60
American Scholar
　reviews, 154
　"Southern Mystique," 57
America Revised (FitzGerald), 175
Anarchy and Order (Read), Zinn intro-
　duction to, 208–209
Angeletti, Charles E., 109, 225
Angelou, Maya, 141
Annals of the American Academy
　(review), 122–23
Anti-Slavery Vanguard, The
　(Duberman), 206, 244
antiwar beliefs, 12, 101, 193, 217–18,
　224–25, 227
　evolution of Zinn's beliefs, 37, 39–40
　recommended authors and titles,
　153, 164, 213
Aptheker, Bettina, 98
"Archivist and the New Left, The," at
　Society of American Archivists
　meeting, 210
Armstrong, David, 175
Arnold, Thurman, 76
Arnove, Anthony, 223–27
arson, accusation of Zinn, 87
Attica prison, 145
authors and titles recommended by
　Zinn, 43, 239, 243
　antiwar beliefs, 153, 164, 213
　for courses, 83, 179–80
　in *Declarations of Independence*,
　179–80
　in *A People's History of the United
　States*, 160–61, 162, 163, 164
　on philosophy of history, 114, 118,
　121

on race relations, 59–60, 64, 67, 212
　in *The Zinn Reader*, 212–13

Baker, Ella, 66
Baker, Etta, 198
Baldwin, James, 198
Baltimore Chronicle (review), 197
Barbusse, Henry, 213
Barksy, Robert F., 236
Barsamian, David, 25, 27, 195–96,
　219–20, 251, 253–54
　Progressive interview of Zinn, 91
Barzun, Jacques, 41
Beard, Charles, 114, 160, 212, 243
Beatty, Warren, 209
Berle, Adolf, 76
Berrigan, Daniel, 101
Beveridge Award, 48, 55
Bill of Rights, 69, 94, 186
Black Reconstruction (Du Bois), 114
Bloomsbury Review (review), 197
Bond, Julian, 198
Booklist (review), 198–99
Bookmark (review), 54
Book Week (reviews), 64–65, 70
Boorstin, Daniel J., 42
Born on the Fourth of July (Kovic),
　201
Boston (Sinclair), Zinn introduction to,
　208
Boston City Hospital, 148
Boston Globe, 88, 151
Boston Phoenix
　interview of Zinn, 202–203
　"Silber, the University, and the
　Marines," 221
Boston University, 77, 81–92
　salary, 86, 89
　tenure, 88–89
Brandeis University, 100
Brooke, Edward W., 99
Brooklyn College, 32
Brown, John, 104, 161

Buhle, Paul, 199
Bulletin of the Atomic Scientists
    (review), 188–89
Bush, George H. W., 12, 120, 168
Bush, George W., 10, 223–24, 226

Cape Codder Summery (review), 244
capitalism, history of, 163, 170
Capital Times
    review, 204
    review by Zinn, 207
Carmichael, Stokely, 198
Carr, E. H., 120
Carter, Jimmy, 168
causation in history, 120
Chang, Nancy, 222–23
Choice (reviews), 77, 144, 201
Chomsky, Noam, 213, 241, 242
    Pentagon Papers, 24, 127
    on Zinn, 27–28, 236–37
Christchurch Press (review), 173
Christian Science Monitor (reviews),
    99, 108, 123
Chronicle of Higher Education
    "Compassion, Not Vengeance," 220
    review, 150
City Paper (Philadelphia) (review),
    239
civil disobedience, 102–108, 125–26,
    143, 185–86
    and the justice system, 149
Civil Liberties (course at Boston Uni-
    versity), 82
civil rights movement, 47–48, 68–69,
    166–67
    in New Deal era, 76–77
    See also race relations; segregation
    issues
Civil War, 161–62
class in America, 38, 193
    and capitalism, 169–70
    conflict, 120–21, 158–59, 163
    middle class, 75, 158

Clinton, Bill, 171
cold war, 166
*Cold War and the University: Toward
    an Intellectual History of the
    Postwar Years, The* (Chomsky),
    242
Colorado coal strike (1913–1914), 42,
    220
Color Purple, The (Walker), 81–82
Columbia University, 41, 48
Columbus, Christopher, 156, 214
Commager, Henry Steele, 41, 49
Commentary, "Radical Historians,"
    175
Commonweal
    "Negroes and Vietnam," 92
    review, 174
Communism, 193, 227
    and Vietnam War, 95–96
Communist Manifesto, The (Marx and
    Engels), 34
"Compassion, Not Vengeance," in
    Chronicle of Higher Education, 220
*Concerning Dissent and Civil Disobe-
    dience* (Fortas), 102–109
Congressional Record (February 3,
    1967), 99
consensus interpretation of history, 42,
    122, 137, 213, 231
Cook, Fred J., 55
*Counting Our Blessings: Reflections
    on the Future of America*
    (Moynihan), 175
*Courage of Their Convictions: Sixteen
    Americans Who Fought Their Way
    to the Supreme Court, The* (Irons),
    150
Crime of Imprisonment, The (Shaw),
    147

Daily Free Press (review), 178
Damon, Matt, 237–38
Daughter of Venus (play), 214

Davis, Saville R., 99, 108
death penalty, 142
Debs, Eugene V., 164
Declaration of Independence, 94, 107,
    138, 143, 251–52
*Declarations of Independence: Cross-
    Examining American Ideology*, 24,
    69, 190–91, 196, 221, 252
  basis for book, 179, 186
  reviews, 186–90
Degler, Carl, 171–72
Dellinger, Dave, 135
democracy, participatory, 192
democratic socialist, 35
Depression, 165
Dewey, John, 76
Dickens, Charles, 31, 242
"Discovering John Reed," in *Boston
    Globe*, 209
Disinherited, The (Van Every), 160–61
*Disobedience and Democracy: Nine
    Fallacies on Law and Order*, 24,
    102–108, 108–109, 237, 240, 243
domino theory and Vietnam War, 96
Donald, David, 41, 42, 82
Douglass, Frederick, 162, 212
Dow Chemical Company, 207
"Dow Shalt Not Kill," in *The New
    South Student*, 207
Drinnon, Richard, 151, 213, 247
Duberman, Martin, 206, 244
Du Bois, W. E. B., 76, 114, 212, 216
Duncan, Donald, 94–95

*Economic Interpretation of the Consti-
    tution, An* (Beard), 114, 160
economics, impact on society, 139–40
Edelman, Marian Wright, 71, 82, 199,
    239
Eisenhower, Dwight D., 96
Ellison, Ralph, 64–65
Ellsberg, Daniel, 126–28
Emma (play), 151, 179, 214

*Empty Promise: The Growing Case
    against Star Wars* (Tirman), 239
English Journal (review), 175

Facing West (Drinnon), 213
Factbook on John Silber, 87
*Failure to Quit: Reflections of an Opti-
    mistic Historian*, 24, 177, 195–96,
    221, 243, 249
  reviews, 197–98, 244, 248
Fall, Bernard, 11
fascism, 247
"Finishing School for Pickets," in
    Nation, 71
First Amendment rights, 69
FitzGerald, Frances, 175
Foner, Eric, 155–56, 173, 177
Ford Foundation grant, 48
Foreign Affairs, 9, 10
Foreman, Jim, 198
Fortas, Abe, 102–109, 150, 240
Forten, Charlotte, 65
*Foundations of Historical Knowledge,
    The* (White), 119–20
Frank, Dana, 25, 220
Franklin, H. Bruce, 188–89
Franklin, John Hope, 212
freedom of information, 128, 195
freedom of speech, 69, 103, 106, 190,
    194–95, 199
  in universities, 83, 85, 212
freedom versus determinism, 117
free enterprise, 120
Friedenberg, Daniel M., 222
Fulbright Distinguished Professor at
    University of Bologna (Italy), 186
*Future of History: Interviews with
    David Barsamian, The*, 25,
    219–20, 252–53

Gandhi, Mahatma, 105
Gannett Center Journal, "How Free Is
    Higher Education?" 210

Gannon, Francis X., 98
Generalization in the Writing of History (Gottschalk), 119
Genovese, Eugene, 162, 232–34
Gilbert, Felix, 118
Gold, Mike, 35
Goldman, Emma, 151, 164, 208
Good Will Hunting (movie), 237–38, 240
Gottschalk, Louis, 119
government deceptions, 227
Gramsci, Antonio, 13
Grapes of Wrath, The (Steinbeck), 212
Green Berets, 95
Greene, Jack P., 135, 136, 144
Gregory, Dick, 198
Gross, Daniel, 89
Gruening, Ernest, 99
Guardian (London) (review), 214
Gulf War. *See* Iraq

Hamer, Fannie Lou, 58
Handlin, Oscar, 154–55, 156, 160, 162, 171–72, 173
Harding, Vincent, 234
Hard Times (Dickens), 31, 242
Harvey Wasserman's History of the United States, Zinn introduction to, 204
Haywood, "Big Bill," 49
HBO, 238
Heller, Joseph, 213
Hicks, John D., 55
Higginson, Thomas Wentworth, 65
Higham, John, 118
Hiroshima, 39, 137, 138–39
historians, role of. *See* philosophy of history
Historical Society, 234
history, philosophy of. *See* philosophy of history
history, radical, 115–16
history, usefulness of. *See* philosophy of history, value of teaching history

History of American Society series, 135
History of the American People, A (Johnson), reviewed by Zinn, 214–15
History: The Development of Historical Studies in the United States (Higham, Krieger & Gilbert), 118
Ho Chi Minh, 97
Hofstadter, Richard, 50, 158
American Political Tradition, The, 41–42, 63–64, 114, 167–68
on consensus, 122, 213, 231
Hopkins, Harry, 76
Howard Zinn on History, 25, 220–21
Howard Zinn on War, 25, 220, 221
"Howard Zinn's Rage Against the Machine," in *Rolling Stone*, 240–41
"How Free Is Higher Education?" in *Gannett Center Journal*, 210
Huntington, Samuel, 9
Hurston, Zora Neale, 212
Hurwitz, Morton, 213
Hussein, Saddam, 101
See also Iraq

Ickes, Harold, 76
ideology, American, 190–91
See also Declarations of Independence: Cross-Examining American Ideology
Ikenberry, John, 10
imperialism
in Soviet Union, 172
in United States, 164
Independent Reader (Internet site), 239
Indians. *See* Native Americans
Instant (Internet site) interview of Zinn, 245–47
integration versus desegregation, 59, 60, 69
Intellectual Origins of American Radicalism (Lynd), 122, 233
International Physicians against Nuclear War, 246

International Workers of the World, 49

Interstate Commerce Act of 1887, impact of, 163

Interview, interview with Zinn, 242

Introduction to Political Theory (course at Boston University), 82, 179, 186

   recommended authors and titles, 83, 179–80

Invisible Man (Ellison), 64

Iraq

   Gulf War, 101, 168, 187

   2003 war, 227

Iron Heel, The (London), Zinn introduction to, 208

Irons, Peter, 150–51

Jackson, Andrew, 177

Janer, Christ, 87

Japanese Americans in World War II, 166

Jervis, Robert, 9

Jews without Money (Gold), 35

Johnny Got His Gun (Trumbo), 164

Johnson, Lyndon, speech written for, 97–98

Johnson, Paul, 214–15

Josephson, Matthew, 114, 213

Journal of American History (reviews), 144, 189–90, 200–201

Journal of Education (review), 173–74

Jungle, The (Sinclair), 212

Justice in Everyday Life: The Way It Really Works, 24, 142, 145–50, 194, 243

   reviews, 150–51

justice system, 141–43

Kelley, Robin D. G., 25, 220

Kennedy, Edward M., 99

Kennedy, John F., 11

Kennedy, Robert F. assassination, 100–101

Kerner Commission, 105

Keynes, John Maynard, 76

Kimball, Roger, 212

King, Martin Luther, Jr., 60

Kirkus Reviews, 203

Kissinger, Henry, 157

Kliatt Young Adult Paperback Book Guide (review), 174

Knowledge for What? (Lynd), 213

Kovic, Ron, 201–202, 247

Kozol, Jonathan, 148

Krieger, Leonard, 118

Kunstler, William, 246

La Follette, Robert, 51

LaGuardia, Fiorello, 42, 48–54, 165

LaGuardia: A Fighter against His Times, 1882–1933 (Mann), 55

LaGuardia in Congress, 23, 43, 49–54

   reviews, 54–55

Lasch, Christopher, 121–22

Last Reflections on a War (Fall), 11

Law and Justice in America (course at Boston University), 82–83, 145, 179, 186

   recommended authors and titles, 83, 179–80

"Law, Justice, and Disobedience," in *Notre Dame Journal of Law, Ethics, and Public Policy*, 252

Leftist beliefs of historians. *See* New Left historians

legal history, recommended authors and titles, 213

Lemisch, Jesse, 123, 213

   leftist historians, 234

Leuchtenburg, William, 41, 48–49, 50

Levin, Murray, 84, 89–90

Levy, Leonard, 75

Lewis, John, 69, 198

Library Journal (reviews), 64, 99, 123, 150, 174

Lichtheim, George, 120

lies in government, 227
Lilienthal, David, 76
Lincoln, Abraham, 162
Lingua Franca, "Under the Volcano:
    Boston University in the Silber
    Age," 89
Lippmann, Walter, 76
Little Flower. *See* LaGuardia, Fiorello
Living My Life (Goldman), 151
Locke, John, 107
Logan, Rayford, 216
London, Jack, 208
Long, Priscilla, 221
"Loose Canon: 150 Great Works to Set
    Your Imagination on Fire, The," in
    Utne Reader, 239–40
Luce, Henry, 139
Ludlow Massacre, 42
Lynd, Alice, 213
Lynd, Robert, 213
Lynd, Staughton, 93, 213, 232–33
    leftist historians, 122, 234
    at Spelman College, 48, 49, 73
    on Zinn, 235–36

Making of the English Working Class,
    The (Thompson), 213
Malcolm X, 212
manifest destiny, 161
Manifest Destiny (Weinberg), 114
Manley, Albert, 71–73
Mann, Arthur, 55
Marcuse, Herbert, 151
Marx, Karl, 196, 213, 233
"Marxism and the New Left," in *The*
    New Left, 221
Marxism and Zinn, 33–34
McCarthyism, 48
McGill, Ralph, 64, 70–71
McNamara, Robert, 101
McWilliams, Carey, 76
Meier, August, 33
Mexican War, 161

Meyer, David, 239
Millis, Walter, 213
Miner, Barbara, 18
Moley, Raymond, 76
Monthly Review (review), 176–77
Morgenthau, Hans, 97
Morris, Richard B., 41
Moynihan, Daniel Patrick, 175
Mumford, Lewis, 76
Murdock, Rupert, 238
Muste, A. J., 166

Nash, Gary, 213
Nation, 197
    "Finishing School for Pickets," 71
    reviews, 54, 55, 77, 109, 174, 199–200
    "Vietnam: Means and Ends," 92
    "Vietnam: The Logic of With-
        drawal," 92
    "Violence: The Moral Equation," 95
National Advisory Commission on
    Civil Disorders, 105
National Aeronautics and Space
    Administration (NASA), 141
National Student Strike for Peace, 98
Native Americans in history, 160–61,
    167, 177
NBC News (TV) (review), 99
"Negroes and Vietnam," in *Common-
    weal*, 92
neo-Progressive historians, 231–32
Nevins, Allan, 17
new abolitionists. *See* abolitionists
New Deal era, 75–76, 165
New Deal Thought, 24, 74–77
    reviews, 77
New Left, The (Long), 221
New Left historians, 121, 175, 225,
    227, 231–32, 234
Newman, Edwin, 99
New Republic (reviews), 108, 144–45
New South Student, The, "Dow Shalt
    Not Kill," 207

New Statesman (review), 175
Newton Teachers Quarterly (review), 175
New University Conference, 234
New York Newsday, 202
New York Times, 12, 104, 126–28
   review, 98
   "Speech for LBJ," 97–98
New York Times Book Review
   (reviews), 123, 155–56, 177, 201
Nichols, John, 204
9/11 terrorist attack. *See* terrorism,
   attack on 9/11
Nixon, Richard, 207–208
Noam Chomsky: A Life of Dissent
   (Barsky), 236
No More Vietnams (Nixon), 207–208
nonviolence, 104–105
Non-Violence in America (Lynd and
   Lynd), 213
"Non-Violent Direct Action," in *Amer-
   ican Journal of Orthopsychiatry*,
   209
non-Western studies at Atlanta Univer-
   sity, 82
Norris, George, 51, 52
"Nothing Human Is Alien to Me," in *Z*
   magazine, 196
*Notre Dame Journal of Law, Ethics,
   and Public Policy,* "Law, Justice,
   and Disobedience," 252
Novick, Peter, 33, 121, 213
No Vietnamese Ever Called Me Nigger
   (movie), 94
Nuechterlein, James, 175–76

objectivity in history. *See* philosophy
   of history, objectivity of historians
oil and politics, 224
optimism, 248, 249–50
   *See also Failure to Quit: Reflections
   of an Optimistic Historian*
"Optimism of Uncertainty," in *Z* magazine, 248

Organization of American Historians,
   144, 189

Paine, Thomas, 152–53
Parenti, Michael, 123
participatory democracy, 192
peace activists, 217–18
Pearl Jam (music group), 241–42
Peck, John, 68
Pentagon and 9/11. *See* terrorism,
   attack on 9/11
Pentagon Papers, 126–28
*Pentagon Papers: Critical Essays,
   The,* 24
*People's History of the American Rev-
   olution, A* (Raphael), 243
*People's History of the United States,
   A,* 17, 24, 94, 154–71, 234
   popularity of, 186, 218, 235, 241
   recommended authors and titles,
      160–61, 162, 163, 164
   reviews, 154–56, 162–63, 171–72,
      173–78
   sales of, 237, 240, 243, 245
   scholarly importance of, 92–93, 110,
      187–88, 200, 236, 239
   as television mini-series, 238, 240
Perkins, Frances, 76
philosophy of history, 90, 136, 252
   neutrality of historians, 113, 135
   objectivity of historians, 18, 112–13,
      121, 190–91, 211
   radical history, 115–16
   recommended authors and titles,
      114, 118, 121
   role of historian, 110–20
   use for political purposes, 126
   value of teaching history, 115, 116,
      250–51
philosophy of teaching, 81–85, 90–92,
   210–12
philosophy of writing, 173
Physicians for Social Responsibility, 246

Plain Dealer (Cleveland) (editorial), 98

Podhoretz, Norman, 12

political correctness, 216–17, 241

Political Science Quarterly (reviews), 54, 55, 189

Politics and History (course at Boston University), 82

politics and oil, 224

politics and use of history, 126

politics and wealth, 222

Politics of History, The, 24, 74–75, 109–21, 221, 233, 235

    reviews, 16–17, 121–24

"Politics of History in the Era of the Cold War: Repression and Resistance, The," in *The Cold War and the University*, 242

Politics of Non-Violent Direct Action, The (Sharp), 213

Polk, James K., 161

Populist movement, 163

Postwar America, 24, 135–43, 243

    reviews, 138, 144–45

preemptive war, 10

prison system, 142, 145, 146–48

Progressive, 101

    interview of Zinn, 91

    reviews, 187–88, 197, 204–205

progressives, 50, 51, 52, 53, 54, 164

Publishers Weekly (review), 150

race relations, 61–62, 140, 190, 216

    recommended authors and titles, 59–60, 64, 65, 67, 212

    See also civil rights movement

racial prejudice, 38, 58–59, 152, 157–58, 165

"Radical Historians," in *Commentary*, 175

radical history, 115–16

Radical History Review, 234

    Lynd on Zinn, 235

    review, 176

Radical '60s Series, 243

Raines, Charles A., 64

Raphael, Ray, 243

Read, Herbert, 208–209

Reagan, Ronald, 10, 12, 168

Rebel in Paradise (Drinnon), 151, 213

Reconstruction era, 62, 162–63

    See also abolitionists

Reds (movie), 209

reform versus revolution, 149–50

Rehearsal for Reconstruction: The Port Royal Experiment (Rose), 70

Remarque, Erich Maria, 213

Rethinking Schools: An Urban Educational Journal, interview with Zinn, 18

Road to War, The (Millis), 213

Robber Barons, The (Josephson), 114

Roll, Jordan, Roll: The World the Slaves Made (Genovese), 162, 232–33

Rolling Stone, interview of Zinn, 240–41

Roosevelt, Eleanor, 76

Roosevelt, Franklin Delano, 75, 76

Roosevelt, Theodore, 163–64

Rose, Willie Lee, 70

Royan (France), bombing of, 39–40

Rudwick, Elliott, 33

Russo, Anthony, 127–28

Saturday Review (reviews), 54, 64, 70–71

Saving Private Ryan (movie), 221

Sayre, Wallace S., 55

Second Reconstruction, 59

Second Treatise on Government (Locke), 107

"Secrecy, Archives, and the Public Interest," in *Midwest Archivist*, 210

"Secret Word, The," in *Boston Globe*, 152–53

segregation issues, 56–57, 58–59

    See also civil rights movement

Shaping of America: A People's History of the Young Republic, The (Smith), 174

Sharp, Gene, 213

Shaw, George Bernard, 147

Shechter, Roslyn. *See* Zinn, Roslyn Shechter

Sherman Anti-Trust Act of 1890, impact of, 163

"Showcase of Repression, A," in *Progressive*, 221

Silber, John, 85–89, 148, 174, 189, 200, 221

"Silber, the University, and the Marines," in *Boston Phoenix*, 221

Silencing Political Dissent (Chang), Zinn forward to, 222–23

Sinclair, Upton, 114, 208, 212

slavery, 161–62

Smith, Page, 174

SNCC, 74, 167

SNCC: The New Abolitionists, 24, 57, 66–70, 74, 199–200, 243
  reviews, 70–71

socialism, 35, 152–53, 164

social role of the historian, recommended authors and titles, 213

Society of American Archivists, 210

Sold to the Highest Bidder (Friedenberg), Zinn forward to, 222

Sopranos, The (TV series), 245

Southern Mystique, The, 24, 57–64, 69, 74, 151, 243
  reviews, 64–65

"Southern Mystique, The," in *American Scholar*, 57

space program, 141

Spanish-American War, 163–64

speech, freedom of. *See* freedom of speech

Spelman College (Atlanta), 10, 43–44, 55–57, 71–73

Steinbeck, John, 114, 212

Stone, I. F., 227

Straight Shooting: What's Wrong with America and How to Fix It (Silber), 86

Strange Career of Jim Crow, The (Woodward), 59–60, 114

struggle for democracy. *See People's History of the United States, A*

Student Nonviolent Coordinating Committee. *See* SNCC

subjectivity in history. *See* philosophy of history, objectivity of historians

Sullivan, Herschelle, 239

Supreme Court, 106–107, 194

Takaki, Ronald, 212

"Tale of Two Cities, A," on Tripod (Internet site), 215–16

teaching philosophy. *See* philosophy of teaching

television mini-series, 238, 240

Tennessee Valley Authority, 52

Tenured Radicals (Kimball), 212

terrorism, 10, 220, 221–22
  attack on 9/11, 220, 223–27

Terrorism and War, 25, 223–27

Tet offensive, 11

That Noble Dream: The "Objectivity Question" and the American Historical Profession (Novick), 121, 213

Thernstrom, Stephan, 123

Thomas, Norman, 76

Thomas Jefferson High School (Brooklyn), 32

Thompson, E. P., 213

Thoreau, Henry David, 104

Three Strikes: Miners, Musicians, Salesgirls, and the Fighting Spirit of Labor's Last Century, 25, 220

Times Literary Supplement (review), 98–99

Tirman, John, 239

Tripod (Internet site), Zinn writings, 215–18
Trumbo, Dalton, 164, 213
Trumpet to Arms: Alternative Media in America, A (Armstrong), 175
Tugwell, Rexford, 76
TV Guide, 238, 240
Twain, Mark, 106

"Under the Volcano: Boston University in the Silber Age," in *Lingua Franca*, 89
United States as a superpower, 9, 224
United States history
  Revolutionary War, 159–60
  manifest destiny, 161
  Mexican War, 161
  Civil War, 161–62
  Reconstruction era, 62, 162–63
  Spanish-American War, 163–64
  World War I, 164–65
  Depression, 165
  New Deal era, 74–77, 165
  World War II, 39–40, 165–66
  post–World War II, 136–43, 166
  Vietnam war, 167
United States v. *"The Spirit of '76,"* 62–63, 165
University of Bologna (Italy), 186
University of Paris, 151
Unsafe Distances (play), 214
Upsala College (East Orange, NJ), 42
USA PATRIOT Act, 222–23
"Uses of Scholarship, The," in *Saturday Review*, 204
Utne Reader, "The Loose Canon: 150 Great Works to Set Your Imagination on Fire," 239

Van Every, Dale, 160–61
Vedder, Eddie, interview of Zinn, 241–42
Vietcong, 96

"Vietnam: Means and Ends," in *Nation*, 92
Vietnam: The Logic of Withdrawal, 24, 92–98, 221, 243
  impact on public opinion, 16, 235, 241
  reviews, 98–101
Vietnam War, 11, 167
  and black Americans, 94
  domino theory, 96
  Japanese views, 93–94
"Violence: The Moral Equation," in *Nation*, 95–96
Vogelgesang, Sandy, 175
Vonnegut, Kurt, 213

Walker, Alice, 81–82, 212, 239
Wallace, Henry, 76
Wallace, Mike, 176–77
war, preemptive aggressive, 10
war on terrorism. *See* terrorism
war protests. *See* antiwar beliefs
Wasserman, Harvey, 204–205
wealth and politics, 222
Weaver, Robert C., 76
Weinberg, Arthur, 114
Weld, William, 87, 88
West, Cornel, 212
What Is History? (Carr), 120
"When Will the Long Feud End?" in *Boston Globe*, 151–52
White, Morton, 119–20
Whitehead, Alfred North, 118
"Whom Will We Honor Memorial Day?" in *Boston Globe*, 153
"Who Rules B. U.?" (pamphlet), 88
Wilkerson v. *Utah*, 146–47
Williams, William Appleman, 163, 171–72, 213, 232, 243
WIN, 175
Wobblies, 49
women in history, 160, 167, 217
"Women's History Month," on Tripod (Internet site), 217

Woodward, C. Vann, 59–60, 114
World Social Forum, 13
World Trade Center and 9/11. *See* ter-
    rorism, attack on 9/11
World War I, 164–65
World War II, 39–40, 165–66
Wright, Marian. *See* Edelman, Marian
    Wright
Wright, Richard, 212
writing methods of Zinn, 173

*You Can't Be Neutral on a Moving
    Train: A Personal History of Our
    Times,* 17, 24, 29, 195, 245
    interest in Marxism, 33–34
    reviews, 81–82, 198–203, 244
    source of title, 91–92, 115–16, 198
    on Spelman College, 71–73
Young, Alfred, 74, 75, 234
Young, Marilyn, 213

Zinn, Bernie, 31
Zinn, Eddie, 28, 29–30, 43
Zinn, Howard
    Air Force years, 36–37, 38–40
    arrests, 60–61, 125–26, 185
    arson charge, 87
    birth, 28
    books. *See* individual titles
    at Boston University, 81–92
    college years, 41–42

dissertations, 42, 48–49
early education, 31–32
marriage and children, 37–38,
    40–41, 124–25, 154, 180
poverty during childhood, 29–31,
    32, 35–36
radicalization, 32–33
recommended authors and titles. *See*
    authors and titles recommended
    by Zinn
retirement, 180–81, 186, 203, 219
at Spelman College, 43–44, 55–57,
    71–73
writing methods, 173
Zinn, Jeff, 41, 151
Zinn, Jenny Rabinowitz, 28, 30
Zinn, Jerry, 31
Zinn, Myla, 41
Zinn, Roslyn Shechter, 37–38, 40–41,
    154
Zinn, Shelly, 31
*Zinn Reader: Writings on Disobedi-
    ence and Democracy, The,* 24,
    151, 203, 205–206, 244, 247
recommended authors and titles,
    212–13
reviews, 203–205
Z magazine, 195, 196, 225
    "Nothing Human Is Alien to Me,"
    34
    "Optimism of Uncertainty," 248